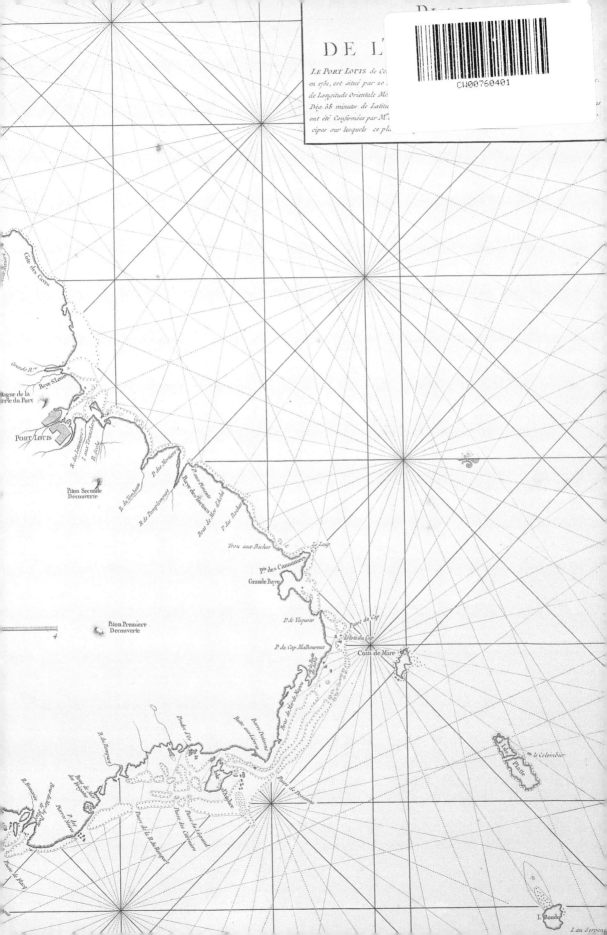

DE L'

LE PORT LOUIS de Ce...
en 1761, est situé par 20 ...
de Longitude Orientale Me...
Dég. 58 minutes de Lattit...
ont été Conformées par M'...
cipes sur lesquels ce pla...

Côte des Cavs

Grande R.te

Baye St Louis

agne de la
erie du Port

PORT LOUIS

R. des Latanier

I. aux Tonneliers

R. Sèche

R. des Moriens

P. des Moriens

R. de Tortoue

Piton Seconde
Decouverte

R. de Pamplemous

Pr. aux Arnaud

Baye des Tortues

Bras de Mer d'Ambli

P. des Roches

Trou aux Roches

Le Loup

Pte des Canonniers

Grande Baye

Piton Première
Decouverte

P. de Vaquoas

Port du Cap

P. du Cap Malheureux

Islottds

Coin de Mire

Poude d'Or

Bras de Mer de Merse

Port Naturel

R. de Rempart

Baye de
des Petites

Poude ...

Isle Plate

le Colombier

R. Françoise

P. des
Petites Naves

Isle Ambre

Port du Passage

I. au Serpent

I. Ronde

MAURITIUS
On the Spice Route
1598–1810

Acknowledgement/Photo credits
The author thanks the following, who have been kind enough to
permit their engravings to be reproduced in this book:
Mrs Maryse Piat (pages 62–63 and 102); Private collection (page
84); Mrs Hélène Vernazobres (page 96);
Dr. Jean-Claude Rey (page 146); the late Dr. France Staub (page
151, top); Collection of the Mauritius Commercial Bank (page 243).

Pages 23, 24, 59, 111, 114, 143, 144, 153, 156, 160, 167, 188, 195,
206, 224 and 238 have been enhanced in watercolour by Marie-
Ange Piat; pages 46–47, 67 (top), 70 and 182 by Denis Piat; pages
152 and 218 by Camille Monnier.

Photos by Pierre Argo:
pages 46–47, 70, 180–181, 220–221 and endpapers.

Documents and photos from the Bibliothèque Nationale, Paris:
pages 55, 90–91 and 99.

Published in 2010 by
Editions Didier Millet Pte Ltd
121 Telok Ayer Street, #03-01
Singapore 068590
www.edmbooks.com

Originally published as *Sur la Route des Épices, L'île Maurice*
© Les Éditions du Pacifique, 1994, 2004, 2010

Translated from French by Monica Maurel

MAURITIUS
On the Spice Route
1598–1810

DENIS PIAT

PREFACE BY PATRICK POIVRE D'ARVOR

edm EDITIONS DIDIER MILLET

FOREWORD

When a passion catches hold of you, it invades you, carries you away and ends up taking such a place in your life that you become addicted to it, in spite of yourself. Thus, my passion for antiquarian books and lithographs, which I fostered for a great many years, gave me the idea of writing this book.

To begin with, I had become interested in antiques, with a special partiality for naval instruments and maps. I took delight in going round the island in my quest for such objects. I remember that, before each purchase, I would spend a long time contemplating the coveted object and could not stop myself from imagining its place of origin. This interest for objects from the past soon led me to study the genealogy of my ancestors, who had settled at Isle de France since 1768, and whose way of life I wished to discover and understand. Intrigued by the world which I was entering, I let my imagination wander to other horizons: the voyage, the seafarers, the discovery of the Indian Ocean, the spice trade, the French East India Company, the first French trading posts... My imagination led, quite naturally, to the discovery of Mauritius and the life of its first inhabitants. In order to explore these vast topics further, I began to search for rare and antiquarian books which described European settlement in this area of the world and, particularly, in Isle de France. I experienced real pleasure at finding myself immersed in the 18th century among those who had laboured to establish a community on this uninhabited desert island in the Indian Ocean. When I thought of the meagre means they had then, I marvelled at the courage and perseverance they needed in order to succeed in their mission.

Thanks to all this reading, through which I deepened my knowledge of the subject, I entered a world which gradually became peopled with characters as fascinating as they were admirable. I discovered the great figures of our island's history: Mahé de La Bourdonnais, Pierre Poivre,

Robert Surcouf and so many others. Bernardin de Saint-Pierre transported me into an exotic dream. Schall's superb etchings, engraved by Augustin Legrand to illustrate scenes from his famous novel introduced me to a fresh approach to the past, which sent me in search of prints and old engravings. I thus built up a collection of documents which gave me more information about daily life at Isle de France.

To round off my overview of this period, I needed the portraits of those who had gone before us on this island. However vividly one tries to imagine a character, there is nothing like an artist's skilful brushstroke to bring his features to life. Having filled this gap, I came closer to reality and slowly gained a deeper understanding of the life of these key figures to whom we owe so much. It then became clear to me that the rich fund of information my two collections had brought together could throw new light on this period of our history and on the men who, two centuries ago, laid the foundations of contemporary Mauritian society. Moreover, it seemed to me that the least I could do for such exceptional figures as Captain L'Hermitte, Bouvet de Maisonneuve, naval Lieutenant Roussin and Moulac, was to rescue them from an unfair oblivion.

I would like to warmly thank my wife, Marie-Ange, for her precious collaboration in preparing and writing the numerous texts of the first edition, for taking pains to type them, and for her patience.

Finally, I hope that the special care I have taken with this book, in close collaboration with Les Éditions du Pacifique, may encourage many to read it and meditate for a while on the rich experience of those whose constant preoccupation was to make this small island the "Star and the Key of the Indian Ocean".

PREFACE

In the early 1970s, my feet began to itch. Stopping in my tracks, I suspended my studies and sent in an entry for a competition organised by the radio station France Inter. The idea was to choose a destination, visit it for 15 days, and return with television footage which would be shown for an hour a day, over a whole week. Competition was tough. I was lucky to be selected and to leave for the island of my choice: Mauritius. My luck held to the end. After the broadcast of this television feature and those of all my fellow competitors, who had been selected by the Envoyé Spécial team over one year, I was proclaimed the winner by a jury. This allowed me to join a profession which I had never practised before.

I have always been very grateful to Mauritius for this and that is one of the reasons why I agreed without any hesitation to write this preface to Denis Piat's book. There are many other reasons. Starting, of course, with Pierre Poivre. My childhood had fed on his adventures in Cochin China, the story of the cannonball which had blasted his hand away and led to the amputation of his right arm, his capture by the English, and his stays in the Moluccas Islands of the Celebes Sea, his interest in nutmeg and cloves, his passion for Pamplemousses Gardens, the attraction of Bernardin de Saint-Pierre to his wife... All this would be enough to fire more than one romantic soul. When I was at last able to leave with my brother to follow the footsteps of the Intendant of Isle de France, we discovered an unknown Poivre, resurrected an apocryphal exchange of letters between his wife and the author of *Paul et Virginie*, and came up with a book, written jointly: *Le Roman de Virginie*. We followed the tracks of our improbable ancestor as far as the Château du

Réduit, which was for a long time the home of French and British governors before it become the residence of the President of the Republic of Mauritius. We asked for his portrait to be produced and posed proudly before the picture of our namesake. Alas, at the end of this quest and of the book, disappointment was to dampen our enthusiasm: we were not descended directly from Pierre Poivre himself, but from his brother, Jacques.

Nevertheless, this dive into the bailiff's world revived my desire to find out more about the island of my dreams. *Mauritius: On the Spice Route* has helped me and will help many others learn more about the amazing history of this jewel, which was discovered at the beginning of the 16th century by the Portuguese, but happened upon long before by other seafarers.

You will thus discover the dodo, the extinct mythical bird, victim of its cumbersome wings and of human stupidity; the premonitory role of the Compagnie des Indes, the figure of the great Mahé de La Bourdonnais, that of famous visitors, Dupleix, Bougainville, Lapérouse, Suffren, Surcouf and so many others. You will find out how, surrendering to the English a few years before the Emperor himself, Isle de France became British. And you will certainly ask yourself, as I did, why, after more than two centuries, this island, which remained British until its independence in 1968, continues to cherish the French language.

I wish to thank those who contribute to the passing on of this beacon of heritage. Denis Piat and his wife have done so, on behalf of us all.

Patrick Poivre d'Arvor

CONTENTS

RAVÉNALA.

INTRODUCTION

When Mauritius is mentioned today, the idyllic image of a tropical paradise immediately springs to mind. This image, forged by tourism professionals by dint of advertising spreads in tourist brochures, has become a cliché aimed at dazzling the eventual traveller by attracting his custom with a whole range of exotic pleasures whose "ingredients" remain unchanging, namely: endless white sandy beaches, majestic coconut trees with glistening fronds, transparent turquoise lagoons with multi-coloured fish, sweet fruits and spicy cuisine. All these are certainly major attractions of this jewel of an island, which does not lack admirers. But very few would probably be able to trace the stages of the historical evolution which lies behind this shimmering façade. A few vague literary memories may surface here and there to evoke *Paul et Virginie*, or perhaps Baudelaire and his *Dame Créole*; but the island's historical development remains almost totally unknown, even to those whose own ancestors contributed to its fame.

It is true that it is only a very small island, similar to hundreds of others around the world. However, it is finally recovering the aura which had formerly made it the "Star and Key of the Indian Ocean". It is therefore worth returning to the period of the earliest discoveries of the first sea routes towards the faraway East, whose riches had attracted merchants from all over the world since antiquity. The merchants were responsible for the first trading exchanges between people of various lands. Driven as much by the spirit of adventure as by the lure of wealth, they were tireless travellers, ready to face all sorts of challenges and dangers in order to get rich.

During Antiquity, these commercial exchanges focused mainly on the Mediterranean, but traders gradually began to venture further. During the 2nd century BCE, a network was created between East and West through the caravan route, that very route which Marco Polo, the famous Venetian merchant, followed when he went to China, and

PREVIOUS PAGE: Red-tailed tropicbird (*Phaethon rubricauda*), the other iconic bird of Mauritius.
Print, 18th century.

OPPOSITE: The Madagascar ravenala, also called "traveller's palm" because the sheaths of its leaves fit together to form a sort of reservoir of fresh and clear water, which brought great relief to travellers.
Drawing by P. Sonnerat, engraving by Poisson, from Voyages aux Indes Orientales et a la Chine, 1774–1781.

which subsequently became the celebrated "Silk Road". Whole convoys, coming from the farthest East, faced the perils of the deserts, steppes and mountains of Central Asia in order to spread their fabulous treasures as far as the shores of the Black Sea, the Mediterranean and the Red Sea: silks and brocades, spices and perfumes, ivory and ceramics, gold, silver and precious stones, flowed abundantly through Aleppo, Damascus and Alexandria before being transported to the West, via Venice and Genoa. However, these caravan journeys had many disadvantages. The tolls exacted along the way by local governments were very exorbitant. Moreover, the cargo were exposed to the many plunderers who coveted these treasures. This led to the gradual abandonment of the land route so that, as navigation techniques improved, attempts were made to reach the East by sea.

From then on, the first sea routes were attempted. Around the 1st century BCE, Greek pilot Hippalus opened the way, thanks to a precious discovery: the system of monsoons in the Indian Ocean. Instead of carrying out the usual coastal navigation from the mouth of the Red Sea to India, this skilful sailor had the nerve to strike out across the ocean to make straight for the coast of Malabar. He was thus the first seafarer to take advantage of the southwest wind, which allowed ships from the region to sail to the Indian continent between April and October. This wind, which the Arabs were later to call the "monsoon"(from the Arab "mausim", meaning season) was, at the time, called "hippalus".

Thanks to this crucial information, a new opening towards the East became available, but this sea route would be used regularly by the Arabs only from the 8th century. The "Spice Route" then took over from the Silk Road, turning the Indian Ocean over the years into a profitable trading ground for merchants of all countries: enormous cargoes of precious goods and spices, pepper, cinnamon, ginger, turmeric, and especially, cloves and nutmeg, would be sent along this route, which very soon became dotted with trading posts from the east coast of Africa to the gates of China.

These spices, which seem common to us today, were in those days as precious as gold, not only because of their scarcity, but also on account of how they were used. They were not only intended to improve the taste of dishes for privileged society, but they were indispensable for the preservation of meats, as well as for the preparation of certain remedies. Thus they took on untold worth, and for centuries aroused the greed of the great naval powers, which constantly clashed in attempts to control the sources of their production.

From the 8th century, the Arabs established their supremacy over the Indian Ocean and were the first to reach China. The Chinese, for their part, were remarkably well-equipped for sailing, and more interested in forging diplomatic links with other nations than in accumulating wealth through trade. The dawn of the Renaissance saw the grand naval epic of the Europeans[1]. Egged on as much by the fever of discovery as by the prospect of a profitable trade with the East, they would eventually overcome their fear of the unknown to brave the vast ocean, which ancient tales had filled with sea monsters and other imaginary beings.

The Portuguese were the first Europeans to reach India by sailing round the Cape of Good Hope, thanks to the feat of Vasco da Gama. After sailing along the east coast of Africa, he discovered the trading post of Calicut on the coast of Malabar in 1497. This first base was the start of a trade domination which would spread to all the ports of the Indian Ocean up to the Moluccas Islands, where the rarest spices, cloves and nutmeg, were concentrated.

Although situated at the heart of the "Spice Route", Mauritius did not interest the Arabs, who were content to call it "Dina Robin" and occasionally call there to pick up fresh supplies. Later, the island provided a port of call to the Portuguese, who first landed there in the early 16th century and named it "Cirné". It had appeared on maps under that name when the Dutch happened to land there in 1598 in order to shelter during a cyclone. They later tried to establish a colony, but it was in vain. Discouraged by the cyclones which regularly destroyed their installations and crops, and by the threat of pirates on

the island, they abandoned it for good in 1710 to concentrate on their Cape colony.

This unexpected withdrawal proved a boon to France, which wished to consolidate its presence in this part of the world. As the French had already established trading posts at Pondicherry since 1674 and in Chandernagor since 1690, the island would provide them with an ideal base from which to strengthen their influence. So, France took possession of Mauritius in the name of Louis XIV in 1715. Mauritius was then renamed "Isle de France". The first inhabitants arrived from Lorient in 1722 to launch a colonisation effort, which at first, proved difficult.

It was only in 1735 that the colony really took off, thanks to the genius of a governor, Mahé de La Bourdonnais, who strove to ensure that it became not only a naval base for France, but also a warehouse for its trade with India. He also distinguished himself by the conquest of Madras in 1746, which led to his unfortunately notorious conflict with Dupleix, the Governor of Pondicherry. Other governors and administrators of Isle de France also became renowned, each playing his part in building up the colony: they included Pierre Poivre, the Viscount of Souillac, the Chevalier d'Entrecasteaux, a famous seafarer who was commissioned by the Convention to go in search of what might have happened to Lapérouse.

It was during the second half of the 18th century that Isle de France reached its peak, thanks to its strategic situation. Frequent conflicts pitted European nations against each other: the Austrian War of Succession (1744–1748), the Seven Years' War (1756–1763), the American War of Independence (1775–1783), then that of the Revolution and Empire wars (1792–1815). These conflicts had repercussions for the Indian Ocean, where the English and the French fought relentlessly for control of Indian trading posts. Isle de France then became an indispensable port of call, and most importantly, a military base from which all reinforcements were to be drawn. Consequently, it was visited by the squadron of the glorious Suffren on its way to his Indian campaign during the American War of Independence.

Naval base and warehouse, but also host country for passing visitors and favourite stopping place for scientific expeditions, Isle de France was the scene of the love story between Paul and Virginie, the heroes of the famous novel written by a royal engineer-turned-writer in the tropics, Bernardin de Saint-Pierre. Bougainville stopped there on his return from Tahiti, and Lapérouse stayed there for nearly six years before his great expedition across the Pacific, from which he was never to return.

At the beginning of the 19th century, however, Isle de France was somewhat neglected by the "Mother Country", which was involved in the Napoléonic wars. The island survived only thanks to the French corsairs. They never stopped harassing the English in the Indian Ocean and, in spite of the systematic blockade which the latter tried to maintain, managed to supply the settlers with rich cargoes of foodstuffs. Among the corsairs, the formidable Surcouf, nicknamed "the King of corsairs", chose Port-Louis as his home port and helped to boost the settlers' morale with the bountiful spoils he captured. England was not slow to work out that "as long as the French have Isle de France, the English will not be the masters of India", as the famous British politician Lord Chatham rightly asserted. That was why "Perfidious Albion" very gradually tightened the screws around the island and, on a morning in November 1810, landed a stream of troops there, taking the French by surprise. Faced with such a show of force, the latter could only surrender their beautiful island to the English, in spite of some stiff resistance.

On 3 December 1810, Isle de France became a territory of His British Majesty. However, a major restriction was included among the surrender clauses: the victors were bound to allow the continued use of the French language, as well as the preservation of the customs and laws of the inhabitants. Isle de France reverted to the name of Mauritius, at least officially. As for the inhabitants, who remained deeply attached to France, they preferred to call it "l'île Maurice".

Today, French is still spoken on the island. Most newspapers are still published in French and some articles of the Code Napoléon remain in force.

INDIAN OCEAN EXPLORATION

Map on which the cartographer, lacking information, haphazardly sprinkled a handful of islands to the east of Madagascar.
Early 17th century.

FIRST EXPLORERS:
THE ARABS

Arab navigators were the first to establish a sea route to India and China through the Indian Ocean. During the 9th century, the vast and powerful Arab-Islamic empire, spreading at that time from Spain to the Indus, was founded essentially on trade. Mindful of the empire's prosperity, the first caliphs of the Abbassid dynasty focused mainly on seaborne trading, which in turn brought new impetus to trade with the East by greatly increasing communication opportunities. Many dhows sailed from the ports of Siraf and Suhar in the Persian Gulf towards the coasts of Malabar and Canton, where small Muslim communities had already settled under the leadership of a *cadi*. However, these Indian Ocean peregrinations were made possible only thanks to the Arabs' technical knowledge of navigation, and especially their experience with the monsoon cycle, a climatic phenomenon specific to this region of the globe, which had to be taken into account by every sailor hoping to return safely to his home port.

The Arabs used not only the mariner's compass, a Chinese discovery, but also the astrolabe, which is the ancestor of the sextant, itself an Arab invention. The astrolabe, by indicating latitude, enabled the seafarers to find their position on the globe. Although such information was incomplete – as longitude was missing, a gap which was not filled until the 18th century with the development of nautical clocks – they overcame this difficulty by steering according to the stars, a skill at which they were real experts. The extreme lightness of their boats, made of caulked planks tied together with coconut-fibre ropes, and the use of the lateen sail, gave them the ability to sail against the wind with great ease.

The Arabs very soon learnt to take advantage of the monsoon system by adapting their sea travel in this region to the rhythm and movements of the wind, which, as is well known, has the characteristic of changing its direction when the seasons change. The southwest monsoon facilitated navigation towards India or China between April and mid-October, while the northwest monsoon pushed ships towards the African continent between mid-October and mid-March. Navigation in these waters would have been hazardous were it not for the knowledge these masterly sailors had of this key fact.

Thus, since the beginning of the 8th century, well before the Europeans had discovered a sea route between East and West, the Arabs had reached not only India, but had also explored the African coast as far as Sofala, as well as the northwest coast of Madagascar, where they had a settlement in

OPPOSITE: Native to South America, the pineapple was taken to Europe by Christopher Columbus. At that time, the fruit was closely associated with the discovery of the New World , in 1492, and was considered the noblest of all fruits. *Drawing by Turpin, engraving by Lambert, 1845.*

the 9th century. During this period, the first Arab expeditions began to reach the shores of the Malay peninsula and China. Expeditions became more and more frequent as commercial links began to be established with the Chinese, who had by then become masters in manufacturing porcelain, which, together with silk and tea, made up the bulk of Chinese exports via the land route.

IN PURSUIT OF PRESTIGE: THE CHINESE

The Chinese embarked on their great seafaring adventure from the 10th century, during the Sung dynasty (960–1279). Their know-how in navigation was far from negligible as they not only invented the compass and the rudder, but even designed an extremely sophisticated ship, the high-sea junk, which was a monumental vessel. Some of these junks had up to seven masts and were no less than 130 metres long by 50 metres wide. In comparison, Christopher Columbus's caravel seems a very frail barque, at a mere 30 metres in length. Thanks not only to these giants of the seas, but also to their increasingly accurate knowledge of cartography, Chinese seafarers were able to venture out of the China Sea and into the Indian Ocean with huge cargoes of precious porcelain, which they transported to the shores of India as well as to the ports of the Arab-Islamic empire in the Strait of Ormuz.

These naval expeditions reached their height in the early 15th century, during the reign of Emperor Yongle (1402–1424) of the Ming dynasty, under Admiral Cheng Ho, who made the Chinese navy the most powerful of the time. Between 1405 to 1433, this brilliant admiral organised a total of seven expeditions, all headed west. These huge expeditions, some of which had a crew of over 20,000 men distributed among several fleets, were not focused on trade, but bore witness, above all, to the desire of the Chinese to show off the splendour and might of their civilisation. Convinced that it indeed was superior to other nations, China considered that it had nothing to learn from them: the "Middle Kingdom", as it called itself, owed it to itself to become renowned for its power. As such, these magnificent voyages were conceived to demonstrate this indisputable fact. The fabulous Chinese cargoes, given away and not open to negotiation, were meant to demonstrate "the wealth and generosity of the Middle Kingdom" to the subordinate states it visited. These states were, for their part, expected to pay tribute in recognition of this "supreme truth". China thus established diplomatic relations with all the kingdoms and sultanates of the Indian Ocean, along the coasts of the Asian continent, from Borneo to Mecca, then along the African coast as far as Malindi and Zanzibar.

But whereas Emperor Yongle favoured these epic voyages across the Indian Ocean and transformed the nation's sailing skills into a showcase for China's prestige, he was the only sovereign of the Ming dynasty to show such open-mindedness. His successors, in contrast, proved so profoundly nationalistic that they implemented a policy of outright xenophobia from 1433. Henceforth, all navigation outside Chinese territorial waters was forbidden and whoever disobeyed this decree was liable to severe punishment. China isolated itself for several centuries. The accession of the Qing dynasty in 1644 did not lead to a reversal of this policy, until the reign of the last emperor, Xuantong (Puyi), which ended in 1911. If China had not withdrawn from the rest of the world, it is likely that the Chinese would have reached the Mascarene Islands, and might have even ventured beyond the Cape of Good Hope.

On the other hand, the Arabs, with their enterprising and adventurous spirit, never ceased sailing across the Indian Ocean since the 9th century. It is presumed that they must have drawn alongside Mauritius around that time and may have possibly come ashore to repair their ships or look for supplies. The island could even have been used as a refuge by Arab pirates who hid their loot there, so it was said. Unmistakenly, the island is featured on many Arab maps, though wrongly positioned in most cases, with various names being given to it: it was sometimes known as Dina Robin, sometimes Dina Arobi or Dina Novare[2]. As early as 1489, the merchant and traveller Sulhiman-al-Madri mentioned the Mascarene archipelago by the name Tirrakha.

These names were used later on early European marine maps, as can be seen on the famous Portuguese "Cantino" planisphere, established around 1502. It is presumed that the Portuguese may have obtained this information following the capture of Arab dhows they would have met at sea during their very earliest explorations in these waters. It is obvious that they must have been in possession of this precious information when they drew alongside the island.

FIRST EUROPEANS IN THE INDIAN OCEAN: THE PORTUGUESE

The Portuguese adventure in this region of the world started at the end of the 15th century, soon after Manuel I's accession to the throne. The Portugal of Manuel I was given the nickname "the Fortunate" because he inherited the bold naval exploration projects conceived long before his time by a ruler passionate about map-making and discoveries. The ruler, Infant Henry, also known as "the Navigator", was the prime architect of this conquest of the seas.

The latter had set up a proper research centre at Sagres, in a fortress which overlooked Cape Saint-Vincent on the extreme southern tip of Portugal, and in which he established his headquarters. There, he received pilots, cartographers and astronomers from all over the world and continuously organised ever bolder expeditions towards the south. From 1424, many seafarers, driven by his constant encouragement, braved the unknown in attempts to go as far south as possible by following the western coast of Africa. This gradual descent along the African continent took place over many long years before culminating, in 1487, with the discovery of the Cape of Storms by Bartolomeu Dias. This was renamed the Cape of Good Hope by the king of Portugal, John II.

The achievement of Vasco da Gama

Encouraged by this bold exploration and driven by the desire to open up the much coveted spice route for Portugal, King Manuel I entrusted to Dom Vasco da Gama the mission of finding a route to the Indian sub-continent.

Leading a fleet of four caravels, da Gama left Lisbon on 10 July 1497, commanding the vessel *Sao Gabriel*. After having cleared the Cape of Good Hope quite easily, the four ships ran into a violent storm and were forced to sail along the coastline of the African continent. On Christmas Day, the expedition sailed along an empty coast, which they named "Natal" for the occasion. Setting course towards the north after that, they stopped at Mozambique, then at Mombasa, and finally at Melinde (now Malindi, in Kenya). Vasco da Gama had the good fortune to meet the best Muslim pilot of the time, the mu'allim Ibn Madjid, who was also the author of a guide on the nautical expertise of the Arab navigators [*Kitab al-Fawa'id fi Usul 'Ilm al-Bahr wa 'l-Qawa'id (Book of Useful Information on the Principles and Rules of Navigation)*] in the Red Sea and Indian Ocean. With the latter having agreed to show him the way, da Gama handed over the wheel of the *Sao Gabriel* to him. It was under the expert hands of this famous pilot that the Portuguese expedition reached the south coast of Malabar.

When he reached Calicut on 23 May 1498, da Gama was amazed to discover hundreds of ships in the harbour. He then realised that Calicut was an enormous port, a proper trading post through which all the riches of the Orient passed through – not only fabrics, exotic woods, gold and precious stones, but also the coveted spices so sought after in Europe:

OPPOSITE: After a first trial by Bartolomeu Dias, Vasco da Gama was the first European to discover the sea route to the Indian Sub-continent via the Cape of Good Hope. He later became Viceroy of the Portuguese colony in India. *Engraving by Gabriel.*

VASCO DE GAMA.

cinnamon, pepper, cloves, ginger, nutmeg. Although he was suspicious at first, the Zamorin of Calicut finally agreed to receive da Gama, and the Portuguese thus obtained the right to trade in this port. A sea link between Europe and India was henceforth established, opening up the spice route to Portuguese seafarers. Vasco da Gama was back in Portugal on 10 July 1499, the holds of his ships laden with precious goods. Among the treasures he laid at the feet of the king and queen were the famous "blue-and-white" porcelain from China. There was no question that the Portuguese would be content with getting mere crumbs in this lucrative trade with the East. They established their supremacy by force, and secured their rule in this region by the might of the cannon. Trading posts transformed into real fortresses were set up in the main ports of the spice route, first at Quiloa (Kilwa) and Sofala on the Mozambican coast, then at Malindi and Zanzibar. Then came the first trading posts on the Asian continent: Cochin and Goa in India, then Malacca and Amboine, the main island of the Moluccas. Later, settlements at Macau and Canton, in China, gave the Portuguese the possibility of developing the trade in fine porcelain, the acme of the luxury goods intended for the Portuguese aristocracy. Through this relay system, enormous cargoes of Oriental goods were henceforth sent to Lisbon. In addition to spices, there were also Chinese "blue-and-white" porcelain decorated with Portuguese heraldry and designs, as well as sculpted ivory objects and furniture from China. Since that period, the word "spices" was used not only to name these valuable foodstuffs, but also applied to any luxury merchandise coming from afar. During the entire 16th century, the Portuguese quickly put an end to Arab supremacy in the sea trade with the East and held the monopoly of that trade instead. The "Spice Route" would henceforth replace the Silk Road, thereby bringing financial ruin to Venice and Genoa which had up to that time, through the Silk Road, dominated the spice trade with the West.

The discovery of the Mascarene Islands

The discovery of the Mascarene archipelago, which includes Mauritius, by the Portuguese, can probably be dated around the beginning of the 16th century. Several hypotheses have been proposed concerning the exact circumstances of this discovery, only to be frequently queried thereafter by many historians.

Several historians maintained that Dom Pedro Mascarenhas was the first Portuguese to have reached this group of islands. Some declare the date of the discovery to have been 1505, 1507 or between 1511 and 1512;

OPPOSITE: A Portuguese delegation welcomed by the Zamorin of Calicut, end of the 15th century. The ruler of Calicut bore the name "Zamorin" which meant "King of Kings".
Drawing from Cochin, engraving by Chedel.

others 1528 and even 1545. What we know for certain, at any rate, from the works of J Codine[3] and Albert Pitot[4], as well as from a remarkable study by Georges de Visdelou Guimbeau[5], is that Dom Pedro Mascarenhas appeared in the Indian Ocean only in 1512. As captain of the *Santa-Eufemia*, he was part of the expedition of Dom Garcia Noronha, which left Lisbon on 25 March 1511. This expedition had been ordered by King Manuel to try out a new route to India, by sailing along the east coast of Madagascar, in order to avoid the fearsome storms of the Mozambique Channel that caused many shipwrecks. The fleet only reached its destination one year later, on 11 March 1512.

On the other hand, Codine, a learned researcher from Réunion Island, proposed an interesting hypothesis which is worthy of attention. He dated the discovery of the Mascarenes to the beginning of February 1507, and attributed its discovery to the famous Portuguese Captain Diego Fernandez Pereira. Basing his opinion on the work of João de Barros, *Decade II*, published in 1777, he reported that, in December 1506, Tristão da Cunha and Admiral Afonso de Albuquerque were despatched to Mozambique by order of Francisco de Almeida, then king of Portugal and first viceroy of India, at the head of an expedition consisting of 14 ships, including the *Cirné*, *Santa-Maria*, *San-Iago*, *San-Antonio* and *Santa-Maria das Virtudes*. Quoting Barros, Codine informs us that, after having been through a storm at the Cape, Cunha decided to put his enforced stay in Mozambique to good use. He decided to explore the coasts of Madagascar on board a smaller ship, the *Santa-Maria*, leaving his flag captain, Diego Fernandez Pereira, in command of the *Cirné*. While Cunha discovered the island of Sainte Marie, which he named after his ship, Diego Fernandez Pereira is said to have discovered Réunion Island on 9 February 1507, on the feast-day of Saint Appollonia, and therefore named it "Santa-Apollonia". While later pursuing his exploration, Diego Fernandez Pereira is thought to have landed in Mauritius, which he called "Cirné" after his caravel, and finally in Rodrigues, to which he gave his own name, Diego Fernandez.

However logical, this hypothesis cannot, unfortunately, be checked and confirmed, for want of firsthand accounts. It cannot be denied that these islands were known by these names for a long period. Nevertheless, when one thinks of the inaccuracies of naval navigation, which had no option but to rely on luck to a large extent, it hardly seems likely that these three islands could have been discovered simultaneously during a single short expedition in 1507.

Another version worthy of more attention is that of Guimbeau's, whose thorough research, based on original 16th-century maps profiled by the

OPPOSITE: In 1642, Richelieu ordered the Compagnie de l'Orient to establish a trading post in Madagascar. The company entrusted this mission to Jacques de Pronis. He built a fort in the southeast of Madagascar and named it Fort Dauphin, in honour of the future King of France, Louis XIV.
Map drawn in 1747 by Nicolas Bellin, a French naval engineer.

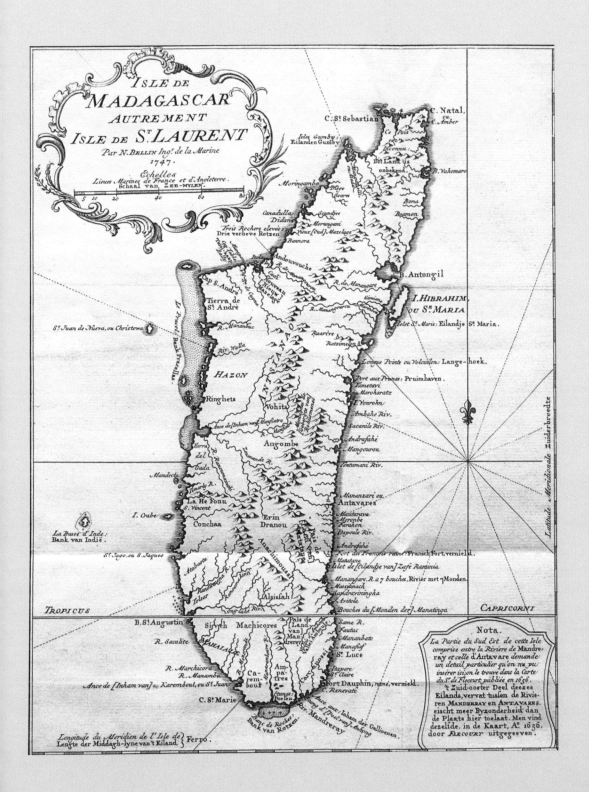

Portuguese during their many passages off the coasts of these islands, led to a precise description which seems credible.

He attributes the discovery of Mauritius in 1511 to Domingos Fernandez, while the latter was on an Indian Ocean exploration mission on board the *Santa-Maria da Serra*. This pilot's discovery was noted on a naval map drawn up in 1519 by Lopo Homem, a famous cartographer at the Portuguese court. It happens to be one of the few documents which not only situates Mauritius at a geographical point very close to its real position, but also gives, as was customary, the name of the pilot who discovered it, namely, Domingos Frz. (the Portuguese abbreviation of Fernandez).

By means of a thorough study of the five maps drawn by the Portuguese at that time[6], between 1517 and 1538, Guimbeau proved that Mauritius does not appear even once under the name of Diego Fernandez Pereira, but certainly under that of Domingos Fernandez. The confusion, created by those who dated the discovery as 1507, is due, according to him, to the similarity between the two names. In 1563, the name "Sirne" appeared for the first time, instead of Domingo Fernandez, on a map drawn by Lazaro Luiz. This name, whose origin remains obscure, was definitely chosen by all the cartographers from that period on account of its short length, which fitted more conveniently on a map. It later turned into "Cirné", the island being first mentioned by that name on a Dutch map drawn in Amsterdam in 1595[7]. It was known by that name when the Dutch took possession of it in 1598.

Dom Pedro Mascarenhas probably approached the islands only in 1528, long after they had been discovered in 1511 by Domingos Fernandez. But, in contrast to what is generally thought, he may have anchored only at Réunion Island, then named "Santa-Apollonia". The island was later to be named "Mascarin" on maps, this most probably being the French equivalent of Mascarenhas at the time. It would suggest that the islands were named after him. We could then draw the conclusion that the dates of these discoveries fell between 1507 and 1511, according to whichever hypothesis one chooses to adopt. As for the name "Mascarene Islands" which refers to the archipelago, it must be pointed out that it did not appear on maps before 1825[8] and was therefore not in use during the 16th century. The name was, in any case, certainly selected to commemorate the passage of the great navigator in the region. Such confusion and lack of precision as to the exact position of the islands, and the frequent changes to their names were quite characteristic of the time. We must bear in mind that, at the speed of naval navigation, news concerning Indian Ocean discoveries sometimes took up to a year before becoming known to cartographers in

Europe. Even more long months would pass before they could be found on the official maps, which were still mostly in manuscript form. This explains why other explorers, being unaware of these discoveries, would rename the islands, thinking that they were the first to discover previously unknown lands.

Moreover, seafarers often made up their own maps according to their own parameters and would sometimes position the same island under a slightly different latitude. The result: when final maps were made, these mistakes were systematically duplicated by cartographers who were accustomed to trusting the data completely. Thus, it was possible that an island be mentioned twice, or even bear two or three different names. False maps were also common. These were mostly intended to mislead the enemy in the event of war, or to lead pilots from another nation off course, with the aim of preserving trade interests. While on this topic, it is useful to remember that the Portuguese court favoured a policy of secrecy in order to preserve its monopoly of the Spice Route: whoever delivered a map to a foreigner, whoever he might be, risked the death penalty. As for the pirates, they would readily use this trick to divert suspicion from an island they might be using as a lair.

As far as errors go, we can mention here the famous example of the island of João de Lisboa, which the cartographer Jorge Reinel had placed on the manuscript map he drew in 1520. He had listed it based on the journal of a pilot called João de Lisboa, who was a member of da Gama's expedition to India. De Lisboa declared that he had seen the island from afar, during his many voyages in the Indian Ocean, and was one of the islands discovered by the Arabs to the east of Madagascar, to which he gave his own name. In the absence of any other information, Reinel merely wrote down the name of this island on his map and, probably trusting Cantino's 1502 map, on which the three Mascarene islands appeared under Arabic names, he gave it an approximate position without defining its outline. Other cartographers subsequently thought it was a good idea to define its position, and thus the mistake spread from map to map, through the 16th, 17th and 18th centuries. Naval expeditions searched in vain for this imaginary island, which gave rise to many legends throughout the 18th century. It was not until the 19th century that it was proven that the island never existed. There are numerous such examples to caution us against trusting maps from that period. This is why historical research, however thorough and detailed it may have been, has only been able to come up with conjectures, so that no final version can be conclusively established.

It seems obvious that the Portuguese, like their predecessors, had no desire to use the islands of the Mascarene archipelago for any other purpose than that of collecting supplies in the course of their voyages towards India. Apart from some domestic animals they are thought to have released on the islands, the Portuguese apparently left no trace of their passage. No evidence has been found, other than the wreckage of a caravel, said by some to have been discovered on the shore by the Dutch during their first visit to the island of Cirné in 1598.

These bold Portuguese navigators, who had become the masters of the route to India by seizing the monopoly of the trade in Oriental products, would, nevertheless, be ousted by the arrival of the Dutch.

ENTER THE DUTCH

This new turn of events was, above all, due to a change of the political situation in Spain. In 1580, King Philip II annexed the kingdom of Portugal to the Crown of Spain. In retaliation against the Dutch provinces for breaking free from Spanish rule in 1576, he unexpectedly decided, in 1594, to ban Dutch vessels from entering Spanish ports. By suddenly depriving Dutch merchants from calling at the ports to replenish Oriental goods consisting of spices and porcelain, the ban forced them to go to the countries of origin to get their supplies.

Taking the geographical position of Holland into account, Dutch merchants believed it would be much more advantageous for them to reach the China Sea by choosing a northern route, which would enable them to avoid the Cape of Good Hope route. They felt that, apart from being too dangerous, it was also too popular with their enemies, the Portuguese. However, as they had not sufficiently assessed the risks of navigation through the polar regions, they were compelled, after several attempts, to give up this far too perilous undertaking.

It was then that a Dutch navigator, Cornelisz Houtman, having obtained valuable information on the route to India from some Portuguese sailors, made haste to share this with the Amsterdam merchants. These merchants then got together to launch the "Distant Lands' Company", which lost no time in organising its first expedition to the Indian Ocean. This expedition, under the command of Cornelisz Houtman, left Amsterdam in 1595. The expedition returned without any trouble two years later with its precious cargo of pepper. As the route to India was now open to the Dutch, new opportunities became available to them, bringing with it the promise of a prosperous future.

LEFT: A Dutch vessel similar to those which entered the Bay of Mahébourg on 17 September 1598. *Engraving, 17th century.*

Mauritius, a Port of Call on the "Spice Route"

A second expedition, with eight ships, left Texel on 1 May 1598. Admiral Cornelisz van Neck was in command. Vice-Admiral Wybrandt van Warwyck was also a member of the expedition and in command of one of the ships, the *Amsterdam*. While rounding the Cape of Good Hope, the fleet ran into a violent storm, which scattered it. At the head of five ships which managed to stay together, the *Amsterdam, Zeeland, Gelderland, Utrecht* and *Vriesland*, Vice-Admiral van Warwyck caught sight of the island of Cirné on 17 September 1598 and, sailing along the coast, discovered on the southeast of the island, a harbour large enough to shelter the ships while repairs were carried out. Thus, through an opportune stop in bad weather, the Dutch discovered an ideal harbour – presently the port of Mahébourg – which would henceforth allow them to not only replenish their supplies of water and fresh food, but also for repairing their ships. The island was then named "Mauritius" in honour of Prince Mauritius van Nassau, the second son of the Prince of Orange, William of Nassau, founder of the Dutch Republic.

News spread as soon as the fleet returned, and since then many Dutch vessels stopped at the island of Mauritius on their way to India and the

MAVRITIVS D. G. WILHELMI ARAVSIONVM PRINCIPIS FIL. COMES
Naſſaviæ, Cattimeliboci, Viandæ, Dieſly, Murſæ, &c. MARCHIO Veræ, Fleſſingæ, &c.
DOMINVS Polanæ, Leckæ, Graviæ, Cuycky, S. Viti, Daeſburgi, &c. GVBERNATOR
Præfectusᖩ Generalis Gelriæ, Hollandiæ, Zelandiæ, Weſt-Friſiæ, Traiecᖰ ad Rhenum, Trans-
Iſalaniæ, &c. ſummus earumdem Provinciarum nomine terra mariᖩ militiæ IMPERATOR.

Moluccas islands. In 1601, Matelief de Jong planted fruit trees and cotton, and introduced domestic animals, including goats, oxen and pigs.

However, the enthusiasm of the first expeditions soon gave way to a certain distrust of the island. The tragic shipwreck of a Dutch squadron near the coast of Mauritius in 1615 left such a deep mark on people's minds that for many years, Dutch expeditions avoided the now accursed port of call.

The ill-fated fleet, under the command of Admiral Pieter Both, was returning from the East Indies (present-day Indonesia) laden with a huge cargo of precious goods. After five years in charge of the administration of Batavia as governor-general, Admiral Both had decided to call at Mauritius before returning to Amsterdam for good. After dropping anchor at Port-Nord-Ouest, his fleet was suddenly overtaken by a cyclone of such rare violence that, along with their anchors, the four vessels were blown along the west coast of the island until they crashed on the reef off the region now known as Médine, sending the unfortunate governor and his crew to their deaths.

It is said that the name Pieter Both was given to the mountain which overlooks Port-Louis and whose remarkable shape still surprises visitors. At the narrow peak of the mountain sits a huge boulder that appears to have been placed there as a warning by some wicked spirit, giving this curious mountain an ominous air.

Twenty years went by before the Vereenigde Oost-Indische Compagnie (VOC or Dutch East India Company)[9], having considered the benefits it could eventually gain from the island's resources, decided to construct the

OPPOSITE: Portrait of Mauritius van Nassau. The island of Cirné was named "Mauritius" by Vice-Admiral van Warwick in honour of his monarch Mauritius van Nassau. *Engraving, 17th century.*

BELOW: First known engravings showing the visitors and their activities on the island of Mauritius. The engravings show the landing of the Dutch in 1598, taken from a description of this voyage published by de Bry in 1601. *Translations on page 249.*

beginnings of a colony at Port-Sud-Est, under the command of Captain Cornelisz Simonsz Gooyer. The captain's main assignment was to build up a permanent stock of ebony, which grew abundantly on the island. He was also directed to search for ambergris[10], a substance which at that time was worth a fortune in Europe, and which could formerly be found on the shores of these islands. On 7 May 1638, Captain Gooyer raised the Dutch flag at Port-Sud-Est, which was given the name "Warwyck Haben"(Port Warwyck). By this symbolic gesture, he took possession of the island on behalf of the VOC.

The first concern of the small party of men was to build a basic fort from fencing and latanier-palm leaves, in order to provide rudimentary lodgings for themselves. The fort was named "Fort Frederick-Hendrick", this time in honour of Maurice of Nassau's brother.

The Dutch had not been the only ones to covet the island. The English and the French, knowing that the island held ebony in abundance, and, furthermore of much better quality than those found elsewhere, had been accustomed to calling there frequently to collect cargoes of the wood. Thus, very soon after they had settled on the island, the newcomers were disturbed by unwelcomed visitors. We learn from a letter written by Captain Gooyer to the directors of the company that, in this respect, a French ship, the *Saint-Alexis* was twice sighted near the coast on 6 June 1638. This ship, indeed, had been seen for the first time at Port Warwyck, then at "Ebony Bay"[11], where its crew was found loading a cargo of the precious wood.

After being allowed to stay for a while on the island, the captain of the *Saint-Alexis*, Alonz Goubert, from Dieppe, was soon ordered by Captain Gooyer to set sail. The latter's distrust was certainly not unfounded, as the French captain had been given the mission to take possession of the island in the name of the French Crown, no less.

Being fully aware of the advantages of this new port of call en route to India, and with no inclination to face such a threat again, the Dutch quickly took the initiative of establishing look-out posts at strategic points on the island: at "Noortwyk Vlakte" (Flacq), "Noordwester Haben" (Port-Nord-Ouest), and at "Zwarte River" (Black River). It was out of the question for another nation to attempt to seize the island! In fact, the Dutch occupied the island between 1638 and 1710, although they abandoned it between 1658 and 1664. Apart from sugar cane, they introduced the Indonesian deer in 1639, as well as many other animals, including boar, hare, the domestic rabbit and goat. During Dutch rule, there were never more than 300 inhabitants on the island at any given

OPPOSITE: Map from the early 18th century showing the old Dutch names formerly given to parts of the island.

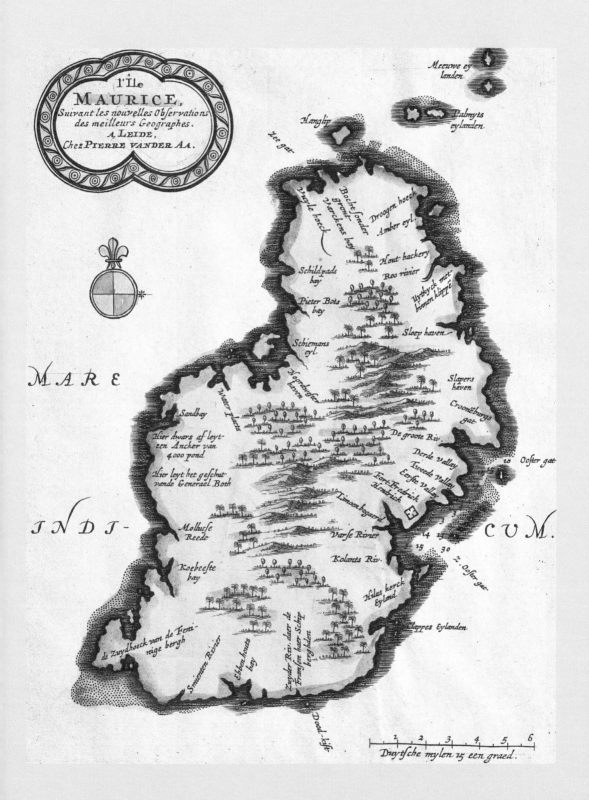

l'Île
MAURICE,
Suivant les nouvelles Observations
des meilleurs Geographes.
A LEIDE,
Chez PIERRE VANDER AA.

Meeuwe ey
landen

Palmyts
eylanden

Hanglip

Zee gat

Bocht sonder
gront
Varckens bay
Dragle hoeck

Droogen hoeck

Amber eyl.

Hout hackery

Roo rivier

Schildpads
bay

Uytleyck met
binnen klippe

Pieter Bots
bay

Sloep haven

Schiemans
eyl.

MARE

Noordhoeck
haven

Slapers
haven

Water Lacs

Crooneburgs
gat

Sandbay

De groote Riv

Hier dwars af leyt
een Ancker van
4000 pond

Derde Valley
Tweede Valley
Eerste Valley
Fort Frederick
Hendrick

10 Ooster gat

Hier leyt het geschut
vande Generael Both

INDI-

Molucse
Reede

Limoenbogaard

Varse Rivier

Koebeeste
bay

Kolonts Riv.

CUM.

Z. Ooster gat

Hilas kerck
Eylandt

Clappes Eylanden

de Zuydhoeck van de Feni
rige bergh

Smienten Rivier

Ebben houts
bay

Zuyder Riv. daer de
Fransen haer Schip
berghden

Dood Isse

2   3   4   5   6
Duytsche mylen 15 een graed.

35

time. The governors who administered the colony never succeeded in developing it properly, due to a lack of perseverance and sometimes, it would seem, incompetence. In their defence, it must be acknowledged that they had cause to be discouraged by the many scourges which constantly hit their crops, such as cyclones, invasions by rats and locusts, as well as damage caused by monkeys. The frequent presence of pirates on the island was also an important factor. The settlers themselves, mostly adventurers and convicts, were not cooperative at all. We may conclude that the main advantage of the occupation of Mauritius for the VOC, therefore, was derived from the collection of ebony, from which it gained some profit.

As the colony's progress was stagnant, and given that the Dutch were very firmly established at the Cape of Good Hope, where they greatly benefited from the many advantages of this trading post, the VOC finally decided to evacuate the island of Mauritius. The last settlers left Moluccas Harbour (Port-Louis) on 17 February 1710 on board the *Beverwaart*, leaving the island to its fate.

A Remarkable Traveller, François Leguat

It was during the Dutch presence in Mauritius, under the governorship of Deodati, that a French Huguenot, François Leguat de la Fougère, landed on the island in 1693, after an amazing adventure on Rodrigues island, which was then called Diego Ruiz. The tale of his extraordinary adventures, published in 1708, aroused the scepticism of his contemporaries, who, for a long time, doubted that it was true.

The saga of this 52-year-old man, born in the region of Bresse, in the Vosges, began in fact in Amsterdam, where he had fled on 6 August 1689 after the revocation of the Edict of Nantes. Wishing to go into exile far from Europe and having heard that the Marquis Duquesne had a plan to establish a Huguenot colony at Mascarin island (Bourbon), which had been given the alluring name, Island of Eden, for the purpose, François Leguat applied. However, after hearing that a fleet of seven ships armed for war had been sent by Louis XIV to the very island on which he had intended to settle, Duquesne was compelled to give up the idea for the time being. Duquesne left the two big ships intended for the exodus in their harbour and bought a small frigate, which he fitted out with six cannons. He decided to dispatch it to the island of Rodrigues, in order to find out if conditions there might prove suitable for the future establishment of a colony. That was how François Leguat came to set sail on the *Hirondelle*, under the command of Captain Antoine Valleau. He was accom-

Table of the Dutch Commanders/Governors of the island of Mauritius

1638	Cornelius Simonz Gooyer
1639	Adriaan van der Stel
1645	Jacob van der Meersh
1648	Reynier Por
1653	Joost Van der Woutbeek
1654	Maximiliaan de Jongh
1656	Abraham Evertsz
1658	*The Dutch abandoned the island*
1664	Jacobus van Nieuwlandt
1665	Georg Frederick Wreeden
1667	Ian van Jaar
1668	Dirk Janz Smient
1669	Georg Frederick Wreeden
1672	Swen Felleson
1672	Philip Col
1673	Hubert Hugo
1677	Isaac Johannes Lamotius
1692	Roelof Deodati
1703	Abraham Momber van de Velde *(up to 1710)*
1710	*The Dutch abandoned the island*

panied by some 10 friends, all exiles like himself and fully resolved to attempt the adventure.

The new arrivals were by no means disappointed when they reached Rodrigues on 1 May 1691: the island was abound with natural resources, which provided them with food aplenty. They fell in love with the beautiful environment and the mild climate, and quickly began to enjoy their new life. François Leguat took the opportunity to study the fauna and flora of the island. Indeed he left behind invaluable information in the

PIETER BOTH
Gouv.ʳ Gener. van India.

accounts of his travels. His meticulous observations provide us with a detailed description of the famous "Rodriguan Dodo" which he named the "Solitaire", a cousin of the famous "dodo of Mauritius" as well as of the "dodo of Réunion". The doubts expressed at the time about the authenticity of his description were finally dispelled during the 19th century, when some bones which were positively identified as the remains of the bird were discovered on the island.

After two years in Rodrigues, François Leguat and his companions gave up hope for the arrival of the contingent of Huguenot settlers who were supposed to have been sent by Marquis Duquesne. Tired of their solitude on the island, they decided to build a boat in order to reach Mauritius. After the failure of their first attempt, they left Rodrigues on 21 May 1693 and managed somehow to cross the 320 miles (512 kilometres) which lay between them and the Dutch colony. They finally reached Mauritius after eight days at sea, and landed in the bay of Black River, where they were warmly welcomed by some of the inhabitants.

After a few months, they made their way to Port Warwyck to meet the Dutch Governor, Roelof Deodati. On the way, one of François Leguat's companions, La Haye, who had brought with him from Rodrigues a piece of ambergris of which value he was unaware, was fooled by a crook, who bought it from him at a ridiculously low price. When he realised the next day that he had been taken in, La Haye went in search of the buyer, with whom he had a violent quarrel.

Having been informed of this incident, Deodati, driven, it is said, by greed, slyly tried to take advantage of the situation. However, his bad intentions were promptly discovered and, worried that he might be compromised by this affair in the eyes of the company[12], Deodati took a hard line against Leguat and his companions. In order to put a stop to their protests, Deodati had them arrested. They were imprisoned at Fort Frederick-Hendrick, on a small island known today as Fouquets Island, not far from the island which the French later named Ile de la Passe, off the southeast coast.

These unfortunate men were kept prisoners there, victims of the tyranny of this inhuman governor, who treated them most cruelly. They were later transferred to Batavia (present-day Jakarta) to face judgement. The men did not obtain reparation from the company but were at last freed. They returned to Europe via Flessingue in the Netherlands, on 28 June 1698. From there, Leguat travelled to Amsterdam, where he lived for several years before publishing the account of his extraordinary adventure in 1708. He later settled in England, where he died in 1735 at the age of 96.

OPPOSITE: Admiral Pieter Both, first Governor-General (or Viceroy) of the Dutch East Indies of the VOC. He took up his post in 1610. At the end of his brilliant governorship, he left Bantam on 25 December 1614 at the head of a fleet of four ships. While stopping at Noordwester Haben (now Port-Louis), onboard the *Banda*, the ship was caught in a violent cyclone and was shipwrecked off the coast of the region now called Medine on 6 March 1615. The crew, including Pieter Both, drowned. The *Geunieerde Provincien* and the *Gelderland* met with the same fate. Only the *Delf* reached Amsterdam. *Portrait reproduced in the work of François Valentijn* Oud en Nieuw Oost Indien, *Dordrecht and Amsterdam, 1724–1726.*

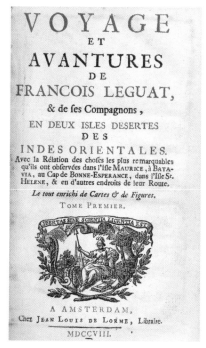

Extinction of the Dodo

We cannot end this chapter about the Dutch without mentioning the famous dodo, whose extinction dates back to about 1688, clearly during the time when the Dutch occupied the islands.

This strange bird, whose species probably appeared on the African continent about 20 million years ago, according to the experts, belonged to the bird family of the Raphidae, with the species name *Raphus cucullatus* (Linné). Dodos had existed only on the Mascarene Islands. The species included the "dodo of Réunion", as well as the "solitaire of Rodrigues". Naturalists, confused by its unusual appearance, were slow to decide which family they would assign the bird to. It was only after many hypotheses and endless controversies that they finally agreed to classify it as a pigeon. Judging from the few illustrations of this bizarre creature, as well as from the many descriptions of it, one would have some trouble, surely, in finding a likeness between a dodo and a pigeon.

We must agree that nature was not kind in bestowing such an awkward shape on the dodo and, what is more, one with so little resemblance to the characteristics of the species to which it had been classified under. The colourful description of the dodo provided by the famous Buffon in his *Histoire Naturelle* conveys the naturalist's perplexity before such a paradox of nature: "Lightness and liveliness are characteristic of birds, but the dodo cannot be said to display either of these qualities. It could indeed be mistaken for a feather-covered tortoise. Nature, decorating it with these useless ornaments, seems to have wished to add discomfort to its natural heaviness, the awkwardness of its gait to the sluggishness of its mass, and to have made its stupidity even more disgusting by forcing us to conclude that it is indeed a bird."

This species, one of the strangest among all the birds that have ever existed on our planet, became extinct more than three centuries ago. Many questions have since been asked about the true causes of this disaster. After much research, several hypotheses have emerged as to the exact period and true circumstances of its sudden extinction.

It was initially presumed that it would have been Dutch seafarers who brought about the final phase of the dodo's extinction. Indeed, even before the Dutch settled on the island, many Dutch ships had been stopping along the coasts of Mauritius since 1598. These birds, of which only a few must have been left by that time, were systematically hunted for food by the sailors. It must be said that their almost totally stunted wings, and their heavy, laboured gait made them easy prey. Although they were said to have an unpleasant taste, their flesh must have provided a substantial meal for the usually undernourished men.

It is also thought that the introduction of dogs, pigs, cats and rats on the island could, to a certain extent, have contributed to the destruction of these birds. By all accounts, the highly unusual constitution of the dodo, which made it especially vulnerable, must naturally have left it powerless against eventual predators. However, while proof does exist that man was largely responsible for the extinction of the dodo, can we nonetheless take it for granted that the dodo would still be around today if the island had remained the bird sanctuary it had been for millions of years? Nothing is less certain as, according to scientists, man is, by no means, the sole agent responsible for the extinction of many species from the face of the planet. Climate changes or natural catastrophes can, according to them, reduce the number of plant or animal species. This applies, in particular, to those species which are already scarce, and are suited to living only in certain environments, thus limiting their ability to thrive elsewhere. That is precisely the case with tropical islands. Experts have observed, for instance, that the numbers of certain species of birds diminish after violent cyclones, such as those Mauritius experienced in 1892, 1960 and 1975. We may, therefore, suppose that under such conditions, the dodos, poorly equipped to resist such violent atmospheric

OPPOSITE: Frontispiece and first page of François Leguat's original book, published in Amsterdam in 1708.

FOLLOWING PAGES (LEFT): François Leguat named this strange bird the "Solitaire", as it seemed to enjoy being alone.
Drawing by A Tissandier, engraving by Dietrich, 19th century.

FOLLOWING PAGES (RIGHT): The dodo (*Didus ineptus*). Many naturalists showed interest in this unusual bird and were able to assemble its skeleton after patient research.
Anonymous engraving made in Germany, end-18th century.

Der gemeine Dúdú.

upheavals, may gradually have fallen victim to them over the years. It is also important to emphasise that this bird, on top of all its disabilities, laid only one egg a year, a factor which obviously placed considerable limitations on its progeny.

For whatever reasons, these creatures were already on the path to extinction by the end of the 16th century, when the first Dutchmen arrived. It would probably be arbitrary to attribute the extinction of the species entirely to them. It is, nevertheless true that by hunting the dodo and introducing predators into the island, they hastened the process, so that it took barely a century for the species to finally die out. When the first French colonists settled in Mauritius in 1722, there were most certainly no dodos left, as no document, account or mentions of the strange bird exist from this period.

The last survivors were probably the twenty-odd specimens taken to Europe during the 17th century by navigators who, intrigued by their bizarre appearance, hoped to derive some benefit from them. Around 1638, a single dodo could thus be viewed in captivity in London, where it was exhibited in the street by its owner, to the great delight of passers-by. Moreover, Bontius, the naturalist, showed a drawing of the bird in one of his works and declared that he had seen a stuffed one in the study of John Tradescant, gardener to King Charles II of England. It is said that this may be the same specimen which was later transferred to Oxford's Ashmolean Museum. Only the head and right foot of this historical representative of the species remain today.

In 1830, however, thanks to the research of a Mahébourg schoolteacher, Georges Clark, who was passionate about natural history, it was nevertheless possible to piece together a whole skeleton. Indeed, Clark, having discovered many bones at Mare aux Songes, the property of Gaston de Bissy, in the southeast of the island, had them despatched to the British Museum in order to obtain an expert opinion. These bones were assembled by naturalist Sir Robert Owen, and were unanimously declared by zoologists to be well and truly those of a dodo.

Later, in 1889, new excavations were undertaken at Mare aux Songes by the government and, this time, more dodo bones were found among the many deer, parrot and tortoise bones. A second skeleton was assembled from these bones by the reputed French zoologist Milne Edwards. That skeleton is the very one which can be seen today at the Natural History Museum at Port-Louis.

As to the real appearance of the dodo, the only surviving description we have are very few sketches and drawings made by amateurs and artists who, most probably, would have seen live specimens. In this respect, there is a group of five sketches found in the manuscript of Harmans, which is kept in the La Haye archives. These sketches, dated 1601 and 1603, happen to be the most ancient representations of the dodo.

In 1606, Clusius produced a drawing of the dodo based on a sketch by a Dutch traveller, Van de Venne. The Dutch painter Roelandt Savery also made some paintings of the famous bird between 1626 and 1628. The two most well-known ones can be found in the Berlin Museum and the Belvedere Collection in Vienna. More than a century later, in 1797, George Edwards, the famous British painter and sculptor, left us a striking engraving of the dodo, which has recently been reproduced in JP Dance's book *Les Oiseaux*, published in 1990.

The dodo.
Anonymous engraving, 18th century.

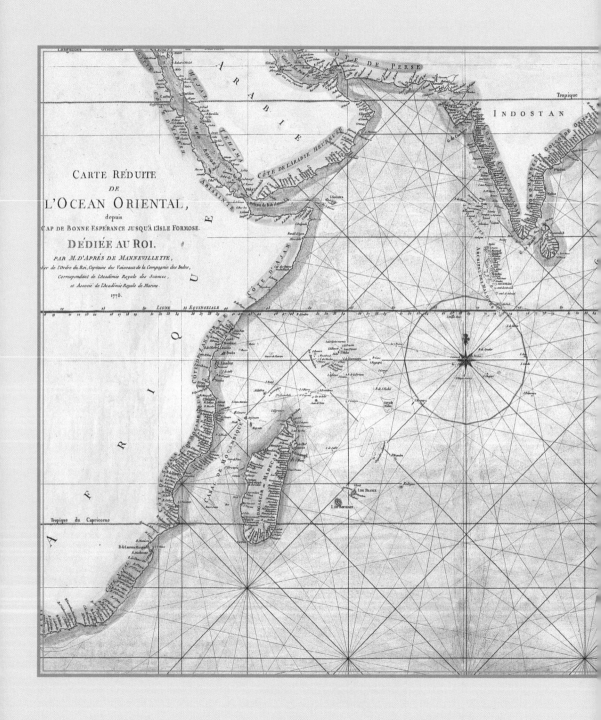

CARTE RÉDUITE
DE
L'OCEAN ORIENTAL,
depuis
CAP DE BONNE ESPÉRANCE JUSQU'À L'ISLE FORMOSE.
DÉDIÉE AU ROI.
PAR M. D'APRÉS DE MANNEVILLETTE,
Chevalier de l'Ordre du Roi, Capitaine des Vaisseaux de la Compagnie des Indes,
Correspondant de l'Académie Royale des Sciences,
et Associé de l'Académie Royale de Marine.
1775.

THE ROLE OF FRANCE IN THE INDIAN OCEAN

Summary of the History of the Compagnie des Indes

- *The Compagnie des Indes Orientales (1664–1719)*
- *Chart showing the Administrative and Territorial Organisation of the Compagnie des Indes*
- *The Compagnie des Indes or Compagnie Perpétuelle des Indes (1719–1769)*
- *The Compagnie des Indes or Compagnie de Calonne (1785–1793)*

The French Take Possession of the Island of Mauritius

- *The Beginnings of a Colony: Isle de France*

A Governor of Genius: Mahé de La Bourdonnais

- *The Conquest of Madras*
- *The Conflict between Dupleix and Mahé de La Bourdonnais*
- *Mahé de La Bourdonnais' Recall to France*

The Most Famous Governors

- *Jean-Baptiste Charles Bouvet de Lozier*
- *Table of the Governors of Isle de France*
- *The Intendant Pierre Poivre*
- *Charles d'Arzac, Chevalier de Ternay*
- *Viscount François de Souillac*
- *Antoine de Bruni, Chevalier d'Entrecasteaux*

Governors Under the Revolution and the Consulate

- *Count Thomas de Conway*
- *David Charpentier de Cossigny*
- *Hyppolite de Maurès, Count de Malartic*
- *Count François de Magallon de La Morlière*

Map drawn by ship's captain and hydrographer Jean-Baptiste d'Après de Mannevillette for the Neptune Oriental, 1775.

SUMMARY OF THE HISTORY OF THE COMPAGNIE DES INDES (1664–1793)

The Portuguese were the first Europeans to use the sea route to trade with the East, thanks to Vasco da Gama, who opened up the Spice Route in 1497. From the early 16th century, porcelain, spices, tea, silk, as well as many other products reached the banks of the Tagus in abundance, and were made available to other European nations. However, several isolated feats were already pointing to the burgeoning interest of the European trade with India and China. Soon, the Europeans were to organise themselves to create commercial firms, which gradually broke the Portuguese monopoly in that part of the world[13]. The English set up the East India Company in 1600, while the merchants of Amsterdam got together to create the Vereenigde Oost Indische Compagnie (VOC) in 1602. Although it had shown the way to these others, it was only 26 years later that Portugal deemed it useful to have its own company: the Compania de Comercio da India Oriental, launched in 1628, which closed after a mere five years' existence.

France was the last to join this international competition, although it had, very early on, a vague desire to get organised in order to exploit the riches of the East, when Francois I entrusted the Honfleur seafarer Paulmier de Gonneville with the task of seeking a sea route to India. In 1604, a company of Flemish merchants, led by Godefroy and Gerard Leroy, obtained a letter patent from King Henry IV granting them the monopoly of trade with India beyond the Cape of Good Hope for 12 years. However, this initiative failed owing to a lack of funds and poor organisation, and the company was taken over by two Rouen merchants in 1615 during the reign of Louis XIII. They renamed it the "Compagnie des Moluques" and its existence was equally brief. In 1642, at the initiative of Richelieu, the Compagnie d'Orient, or de Madagascar, was created. However, in spite of the efforts of Duke de la Meilleraye, who took charge of it in 1656, it went downhill after 14 years. It was not until the reign of Louis XIV, from 1664, that the French Compagnie des Indes (beyond the Cape of Good Hope) really took off, under the charge of Colbert. The latter took the initiative of sending François Caron to Surat, on the west coast of India, in 1667 with the intention of opening a trading post there. Caron subsequently entrusted François Martin with the mission of identifying a place on the Coromandel coast suitable for setting up a trading post. Taking advantage of the previous purchase by Bellanger de l'Espinay of a small fishing village, bought from a Moorish prince, François Martin founded Pondicherry in

A scene in the town of Pondicherry, Carnat, eastern India. *After EB de la Touane, lithography by Langlumé.*

1674 and built its first fortifications. In 1695 and the following years, he reorganised the trading posts of Chandernagor, Balassor and Cassimbazar, which had been founded by Duplessis in Bengal in 1673. A new era was beginning for the French Compagnie des Indes which was, however, to undergo some transformations before its dissolution in 1793, after nearly 130 years of existence.

OPPOSITE: Man and woman of the coast of Coromandel, India. *Drawing by JG Saint-Sauveur, engraving by Lachaussée, 1805.*

BELOW: "Procession of an Indian King". In order to impress his Indian allies, Dupleix also organised majestic processions during his official tours.

Compagnie des Indes Orientales (1664–1719)

The Compagnie des Indes Orientales enjoyed exclusive trading rights with all trading posts beyond the Cape of Good Hope for a period of 15 years. Free from any obligation to pay any tax to the State, it moreover enjoyed the support of the king's ships and army, which undertook to make good any losses during the first 10 years. In addition, it had the right to become the owner of any territories it would occupy. From the beginning, the king conceded Madagascar, Isle de France and the island of Bourbon to the company. In addition to trade, the company also had the right to practise privateering. It was allowed to fit out warships and take up arms to defend its possessions.

Of course, some obligations were attached to all these advantages. In return, the company, as a representative of His Very Catholic Majesty, had the duty of spreading the Roman Catholic religion and, as far as privateering was concerned, was bound to pay to the king one-tenth of the value of all its booty. This new organisation gave rise to the internationalisation of trade and, in some way, sowed the seeds of capitalism. However,

Chart showing the administrative and territorial organisation of the Compagnie des Indes (east of the Cape of Good Hope)

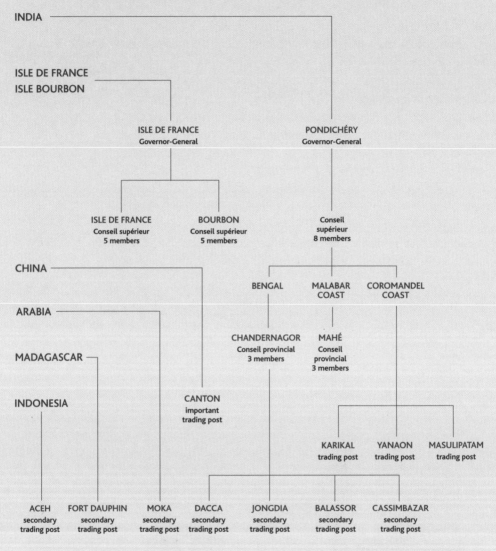

INDIA

ISLE DE FRANCE
ISLE BOURBON

ISLE DE FRANCE
Governor-General

PONDICHÉRY
Governor-General

ISLE DE FRANCE
Conseil supérieur
5 members

BOURBON
Conseil supérieur
5 members

Conseil
supérieur
8 members

CHINA

BENGAL

MALABAR
COAST

COROMANDEL
COAST

ARABIA

CHANDERNAGOR
Conseil provincial
3 members

MAHÉ
Conseil
provincial
3 members

MADAGASCAR

INDONESIA

CANTON
important
trading post

KARIKAL
trading post

YANAON
trading post

MASULIPATAM
trading post

ACEH
secondary
trading post

FORT DAUPHIN
secondary
trading post

MOKA
secondary
trading post

DACCA
secondary
trading post

JONGDIA
secondary
trading post

BALASSOR
secondary
trading post

CASSIMBAZAR
secondary
trading post

- **Defence and trade : 4 directors**
- **Cashier, accounts, purchasing : 2 directors**
- **Sales : 2 directors**
- **Administration of the port of Lorient : 1 director**
- **Archives, litigation, registers (Hôtel de Paris and presently the Bibliothèque Nationale)**
- **Control of the directors and inspection of the Departments : 6 officials**

the wars in Europe soon spread to that area of the world, and the endless naval struggles meant the ruin of the company's fortunes.

Compagnie des Indes or Compagnie perpétuelle des Indes (1719–1769)

To save the situation, economist Law engineered the merger of the three companies (Compagnie d'Occident, Compagnie des Indes Orientales and Compagnie de Chine), which became the Compagnie perpétuelle des Indes. Its influence became enormous, as it now held posts in America, Africa and China. Thus, in spite of some difficult times, the company had expanded enough to face the competition from such powerful rivals as the East India Company (English) and the VOC (Dutch).

But the Austrian Wars of Succession (1744–1748) and subsequently the Seven Years' War (1756–1763) inevitably had repercussions on the Indian Ocean and once again undermined the finances of the new company. The situation deteriorated to such an extent that, in 1769, it was decided that all its privileges would be suspended and that it would be declared bankrupt, thus allowing all to trade freely. The royal administration effectively took over the company's various facilities all over the world (including Isle de France, in 1767, by Pierre Poivre).

Compagnie des Indes or Compagnie de Calonne (1785–1793)

After the American War of Independence (1775–1783), a new company was established, but under another organisation, the Compagnie de Calonne. Unlike the previous companies, this one had no civil or military powers and was engaged purely in commercial activities. After a few years of relative

The port of Saint-Malo seen facing Saint-Servan, opposite l'Éperon.
By N Ozanne, naval engineer, 1776.

success, it suffered the repercussions of the Revolution and was stripped of its privileges on 4 August 1789. It existed briefly for a few more years before disappearing for good in 1793, when it was axed by the Convention.

THE FRENCH TAKE POSSESSION OF THE ISLAND OF MAURITIUS

Mauritius remained uninhabited for a few years after the departure of the Dutch in 1710. Having already established a colony at Bourbon island since 1654, the French became interested in this neighbouring little island[14]. In 1715, five years after the island was deserted by its first colonisers, France seized this timely godsend: the opportunity to occupy an island in a part of the world where India and its fabulous riches were at stake for the most powerful European nations. France's plan for Mauritius was indeed not merely to use it as a colony for settlers. Aware of the advantage of the island's geographical situation at the heart of the Spice Route, France thought that it would provide a good port to make its mark in the region. Just like Holland and England, France was equally anxious to strengthen its position in trade for Oriental products by exploiting the resources of India and China.

Through the powerful VOC, the Dutch were already well-established not only in the Cape, but also in Indonesia[15]. By controlling the Moluccas Islands, they had gained monopoly of the trade in cloves and nutmeg,

TOP: Portrait of Charles Alexandre de Calonne (1734–1802). As Controller-General of Finances under Louis XVI, he undertook the re-organisation of the Compagnie des Indes in 1785.

RIGHT: A French map in which Isle de France surprisingly still goes by the name "Ile du Cigne" and Rodrigues still bears the name "Diego Ruiz".

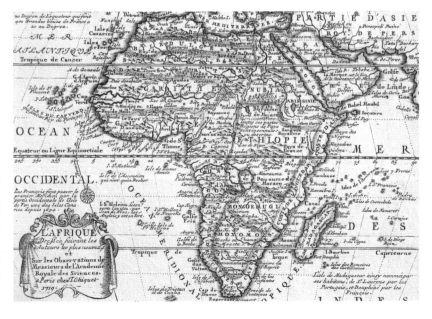

which were fetching incredible prices on the European markets. The English, for their part, having failed to compete successfully with the Dutch in the Far East, where the East India Company had tried to establish itself, quickly realised the scope of the market they could find in India, where they already had stakes at two important sites: Surat (1615) and Madras (1639).

France, on the other hand, had tried to gain a foothold on the southeast coast of Madagascar, where it had established the trading post of Fort Dauphin, but had been compelled to abandon it when the first settlers were massacred by the natives. The island of Mauritius, empty of any inhabitants, seemed an ideal place for them. Another important advantage was that it was blessed with two excellent harbours. This indeed compensated for its neighbour Bourbon's lack of any harbour. Port-Nord-Ouest, well-sheltered and comfortable as it was, could moreover provide an ideal port of call, where the crews and ships worn out by exhausting voyages from Lorient and Saint-Malo could obtain refreshment.

On 20 September 1715, on the instruction of the Minister for the Navy Monsieur de Pontchartrain, Guillaume Dufresne d'Arsel, captain of the *Chasseur*, pitched a white flag with its three fleurs de lys on the island, and, by this solemn gesture, took possession of it in the name of His Majesty King Louis XIV[16]. The island received the fine name Isle de France, according to royal orders, and was linked to its neighbour, the island of Bourbon. However, it remained uninhabited for some time before it was

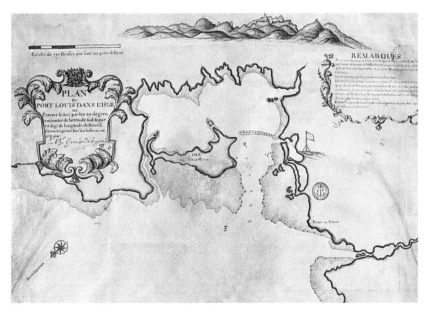

A manuscript map of Port-Louis drawn on site by Garnier de Fougerai in Chinese ink on vellum, on the occasion of the second ceremony of taking possession, in September 1721.

transferred to Compagnie des Indes Orientales in 1721. On 23 September 1721, Jean-Baptiste Garnier de Fougerai, a former officer on the *Chasseur*, conducted a second ceremony to formally mark French possession of the island, and its allegiance to France. This ceremony took place on the small island of Tonneliers, at the entrance of Port-Nord-Ouest. De Fougerai had a cross erected there. His name and that of his ship, the *Triton*, were engraved, with the royal arms, on one face. On the opposite face was an inscription celebrating the event. The name of Port-Louis was then used on a map for the first time.

The Beginnings of a Colony: Isle de France

In December of that year, Jean Durongouët Le Toullec was appointed commander of Isle de France by the governor of the island of Bourbon, Mr Beauvollier de Courchant, pending the imminent arrival of the first governor appointed by the king, the Chevalier Denis Denyon. Accompanied by a dozen settlers, a priest and a surgeon, Jean Durongouët Le Toullec sailed to Isle de France onboard a flimsy boat, the *Courrier de Bourbon*, which dropped anchor at Port-Nord-Ouest on 24 December 1721. Soon, on 5 and 6 April 1722, the *Diane* and the *Atalante* arrived, carrying the first contingent of settlers from France. Among them was Joseph-François Dupleix, who was on his way to take up his post at Pondicherry, as well as the future governor of Isle de France, Denis Denyon, to whom Le Toullec handed over the leadership of the new colony. This transfer of power marked the beginning of 45 years of administration by the Compagnie des Indes, until 1767. Soon after the arrival of Denyon, other settlers, as well as slaves, were sent from the island of Bourbon. By December 1735, the island only had about 200 inhabitants. In addition, a regiment of Swiss guards under the command of Denyon[17] was available for the island's defence. In the following years, territorial concessions began to be made, with the proviso that settlers had to farm the land granted to them and raise cattle and poultry. The company ordered that wheat, rice, vegetables, cotton and spices should be grown. However, it was no easy matter to obtain plants from which to grow spices. At that time, the Dutch were already established in Indonesia, where they enjoyed a monopoly over the trade in fine spices, especially cloves and nutmeg. These two precious ingredients, in fact, came exclusively from the Moluccas Islands, where they grew abundantly in the wild. The Dutch therefore closely defended access to these islands. Woe betide those who might venture there with the idea of collecting some plants, as they would be liable to no less than the death penalty. As a result, the wishes of the Compagnie des Indes remained mere pious hopes. However, this state of affairs was not to last forever as many years later, the monopoly was broken by the bold genius of a famous character who bore such a wonderfully predestined name: Pierre Poivre ("poivre" means pepper in French).

A GOVERNOR OF GENIUS: MAHÉ DE LA BOURDONNAIS

Fifteen years passed, during which five successive governors served their terms, before the arrival in 1735 of the man who was to be the true founder of this French colony; Bertrand-François Mahé de La Bourdonnais.

To stress the stature of this extraordinary man, we have picked this opinion of Voltaire, quoted by Pierre Crépin in his excellent book on La Bourdonnais:

"Enterprising men who might have languished unknown in their country, positioned themselves and rose on their own accord in these faraway countries, where ingenuity is rare and essential. One of these bold geniuses was Mahé de La Bourdonnais, born in Saint-Malo, the Duguay-Trouin of his time, superior to Duguay-Trouin in intelligence and his equal for courage".

The organisational genius which La Bourdonnais possessed, added to dogged perseverance and an enormous capacity for work (he frequently restricted himself to a bare three hours' sleep per night), drove him to undertake a colossal task as soon as he reached Isle de France. That is how, in five years, he succeeded in transforming the beginnings of a colony into a structured, organised and prosperous community. This was a real triumph. Few men, could have managed to achieve such a feat with such limited means and in such a short time. After his brilliant 10-year career in administration, he secured for Isle de France the reputation of being the "Star and Key of the Indian Ocean".

This fearless man from Saint-Malo had been sailing the world's oceans from the early age of 10 and had acquired, in addition to his other assets, a firm reputation for being a great sailor. In 1727, when he was an officer with the Compagnie des Indes, he resigned and engaged in trade between various regions of India on his own account. He built up a considerable fortune as well as a sound knowledge of that country. He had moreover been awarded the Cross of the Knight of Christ, an honour bestowed upon him by the Portuguese crown for numerous services rendered to the Portuguese governor of Goa. His expeditions around the world had taken him to Isle de France, where he called in 1723. He had quickly become

aware of the strategic value of this island, as well as of its natural advantages. He saw it as an undoubtedly valuable asset for the development of French commercial power in this region, superior in this respect to its neighbour, the island of Bourbon.

He was therefore thoroughly confident in what he was doing when he managed to persuade the Controller-General of Finances, Monsieur Orry, and his brother, the Cardinal de Fulvy, who was attached to the Compagnie des Indes as the king's commissioner, of the need to foster the development of Isle de France. He argued that, according to him, it could not only quickly become an important naval base for France, on account of its exceptional harbour, but that it could also be used by the company as a storehouse for its trade with India. Won over by his enthusiasm and his ideas, they obtained for him from the king the post of Governor-General of Isle de France and Bourbon, the position then most coveted by the civil servants of the Compagnie des Indes, after that of Governor of India.

Mahé de La Bourdonnais arrived at Isle de France on 5 June 1735, accompanied by his wife, Anne-Marie Lebrun de la Franquerie. He found the colony in a sad state of dereliction. At Port-Louis, facilities were precarious, and the settlers, deprived of everything, were living in a state of near-poverty. Without wasting any time, he took things in hand and bravely set to work. He demanded the support of the settlers right from the start. In view of the huge task to be tackled, it was essential, according to him, to foster team spirit. Faced with the inhabitants' indolence, the governor had to be very persevering and also display authority. He did not hesitate to join in the work himself in order to be a good example and to harness the settlers' energy. He could be seen at work from the crack of dawn, now on one site, now on another, and always with the same dynamism. In order to train the inhabitants in various trades, he brought over qualified workers and artisans from Britanny. These gradually trained a local workforce. His first concern was to provide Port-Louis with the essential infrastructure. Huge works were then undertaken, including the construction of a magnificent aqueduct of more than three quarters of a league in length, in order to supply the town with drinking water. Roads were laid out; a 500-bed hospital was built at Pointe Desforges, while stores for food, as well as barracks to house the crews and soldiers, batteries for the defence of the island, as well as offices, flour mills, power mills, brick-making factories and lime kilns were installed. At the same time, he restarted the cultivation of sugar cane, which the Dutch had introduced, and which had, up to now, been very neglected. He built the first sugar factory of the island at

OPPOSITE: Portrait of Bertrand-François Mahé de La Bourdonnais *In "Tableau du Temps", diagraph and pantograph, Gavard, 19th century.*

ABOVE: Philibert Orry, Count of Vignory, Controller-General of Finances. He placed his whole trust in La Bourdonnais and appointed him Governor of Isle de France and Bourbon.
After a painting by H Rigaud, diagraph and pantograph, Gavard.

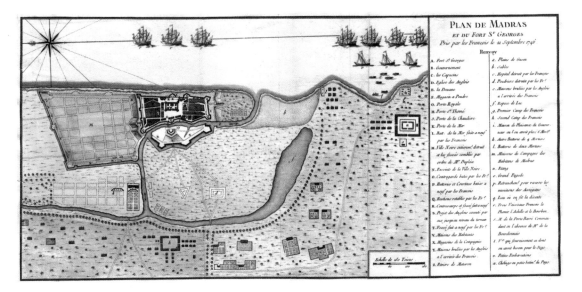

Pamplemousses, with equipment brought from France. He also started the manufacture of cotton, which he exported to Persia, Surat and Moka; and indigo, which he exported to Europe.

Thanks to these essential facilities, this enterprising and tireless administrator gave the colony its first impetus. But the most important task remained: to create a real town and, simultaneously, equip the port so that it would become an essential port of call for all vessels enroute to India and China. La Bourdonnais energetically involved himself in both projects. The plans for the future Port-Louis, up to that time called "Le Camp" were soon improved upon, based on the original plans drawn up by Jean-François Charpentier de Cossigny. La Bourdonnais also ordered that the harbour be deepened to make it accessible to ships of high tonnage, and endowed it with a dock and a magnificent shipyard so that ship repairs and shipbuilding could be carried out. Four vessels were built in this shipyard: the *Créole* and the *Nécessaire*, 150 tons each, the *Insulaire* at 350 tons, and a small vessel of 80 tons. On the Place d'Armes, facing the harbour, the Hôtel du Gouvernement, a building meant to house the administrative offices of the colony, was soon to rise[18]. The Conseil Supérieur, whose offices were formerly on the island of Bourbon, was to be transferred there to replace the Conseil Provincial, with La Bourdonnais as chairman. The Governor chose to settle at Pamplemousses, on account of its more pleasant climate. Having bought the magnificent property of Monplaisir[19], which formerly belonged to Nicolas de Maupin, he had a luxurious residence built there. Splendid receptions were often held there, to great joy of the settlers.

OPPOSITE: The first time the French took possession of Mascarin island was in 1642. By order of Flacourt, a second ceremony was held in October 1649. The island was named "Bourbon" and Possession was where the ceremony was celebrated.
Illustration from the cosmography of Manesson Malet, 1683.

ABOVE: "Plan of Madras and of Fort St George captured by the French on 21 September 1746." Mahé de la Bourdonnais' squadron with other ships, the vessels, *Pheonix, Achille* and *Bourbon* at sea.
18th-century engraving.

FOLLOWING PAGES: "Clearing out the place by fire and fast methods that art could devise." The construction of Port-Louis in 1738.
Drawing by N Ozanne, naval engineer, 1776.

In spite of its evocative name, however, this residence was not merely a place for rest and parties. As he was anxious that the colony should develop the food resources essential to its survival, La Bourdonnais encouraged the settlers to grow vegetables for their own needs. In order to show the way, as usual, he designed vegetable gardens and fruit orchards in the gardens of Monplaisir, and sent the products from these to Port-Louis as supplies for ships' crews. He conducted trials on the farming of cassava, a very resilient plant which he had imported from Brazil. He obtained such good results that he ordered the settlers to grow it too. Moreover, this plant, from which an acceptable type of flour called cassave could be extracted, also had enormous benefit: it was not vulnerable to attacks by locusts and rats, the main destroyers of all the other crops. After some misgivings, the settlers finally adopted this plant, which very quickly became the staple food of the slaves.

With all these developments, the colony henceforth had the wind in its sails. Its future seemed so promising that many colonists from respectable families, probably attracted as much by its tropical climate and driven by the spirit of adventure as much as by the hope of making their fortunes there, soon came to settle here[20]. They established themselves with their families in the shady regions of the countryside, where they built fine houses and lived peacefully from the products of their lands. A refined society, faithful to its French traditions, gradually took root.

In addition to his many activities on Isle de France, the tireless native of Saint-Malo did not stint on his efforts to administer Bourbon with the same energy. He travelled there frequently in order to make sure that it would also develop apace. He devoted much energy to supervising the construction of his brilliant "suspended bridge" at the port of Saint-Denis, built to facilitate the loading of coffee. Stores and warehouses were also built, and a new impetus was given to the cultivation of coffee.

The success and fame of Mahé de La Bourdonnais, which had earned him the Cross of Saint-Louis, were soon to provoke an atmosphere of veiled hostility among his entourage. Envious and jealous people, including the king's engineer, Mr de Cossigny, attempted to discredit him in the eyes of the company directors by complaining, among other things, about his style of administration, which was "too forceful" for their taste. In April 1740, having obtained leave after the tragic and successive deaths of his two young children and his wife, La Bourdonnais went to Paris, where he was received without any courtesy by the company directors, who then informed him about the settlers' complaints. It must be acknowledged that, owing to his military training, his "hussar" methods of administration were sometimes lacking in tact and diplomacy. After insisting that the complaints against him should be investigated, he succeeded in proving them wrong, with "cast-iron" evidence, that these accusations were purely malicious. The company then rejected his proffered resignation and he was reinstated to his post. Accompanied by a commission of frigate captains from the king's navy, and carrying instructions from the company's ministers in view of a future mission to India, he set sail on 4 April 1741, bound for Pondicherry and then Mahé on the Malabar coast, in order to restore it to the control of the company. As soon as he returned to Isle de France, he got back to work. In April 1743, the small chapel of Saint-Francois at Pamplemousses, built from the house of one Boucher, an officer of the garrison, was inaugurated. In November of that same year, La Bourdonnais organised the capture of the islands of the Seychelles by captains Lazare Picault and Jean Grossen, who gave the name, Mahé, to the archipelago's main island.

The year 1744, however, began badly: Isle de France was suffering from a terrible drought and the inhabitants were starving. To make matters worse, the *Saint-Géran*, which was carrying food supplies to the colony, as well as 54,000 pastries, sank with its crew off Ambre island, on the night of 17 August. Mills and vats which had been ordered for the sugar factory at Villebague were among the ship's cargo. It was a serious blow to the colony. With 183 persons drowned and only nine survived, the tragedy was to contribute many years later to the fame of a certain Jacques Henri Bernardin de Saint-Pierre, who was then a king's engineer at Isle de France. Inspired by the sad event of this shipwreck, Bernardin de Saint-Pierre, who was scientifically trained, was to discover in himself a late-flowering talent for writing. He wrote *Paul et Virginie*, one of the most famous novels in French literature. This work, which abundantly described the tropical flora and daily life at Isle de France, earned its author a place among the Romantics.

After this catastrophe, the settlers found themselves in a very precarious situation. La Bourdonnais coped as best he could. However, his mission to India was a greater priority: by then, France and England were at war and the English fleet was already deployed along the coasts of Coromandel. More than 10 French vessels were captured in spite of the treaties of neutrality protecting merchant ships. For many months, La Bourdonnais

OPPOSITE: The first coffee bushes were imported to Bourbon island from Moka by de La Boissière. In 1718, Mr Beauvollier de Courchant brought a new cargo of coffee plants from Arabia and developed their cultivation. Coffee became the main product of Bourbon.

Fig . 1

Sucrerie, Moulin mû p...

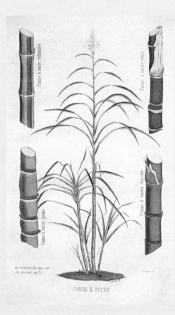

"Factory with mill driven by animals." In 1744, La Bourdonnais built the first sugar factory of the island at Pamplemousses.
Engraving, 18th century.

had been awaiting the arrival from France of a squadron of five vessels armed for war to support the forces of Dupleix in India. La Bourdonnais had to fit out ships to bolster this naval force. On top of it all, an epidemic broke out at Isle de France, and he found himself cruelly short of labour for the repair of ships, and also of supplies for their cargo. Sparing no effort, he managed to overcome all the obstacles and everything was soon ready for departure, which had been planned for 1 August 1745. On 28 July, the ship *Expédition* arrived, heralding at last the arrival of the long-awaited squadron.

The Conquest of Madras

The squadron arrived at Isle de France in February 1746, thus strengthening the fleet already assembled by La Bourdonnais. The total force then amounted to nine ships, made up of seven vessels and two frigates:

Achille (74 cannons), under Captain Lobry
Phénix (44 cannons), under Captain de la Chaise
Bourbon (42 cannons), under Captain de Selle
Saint-Louis (36 cannons), under Captain de Penlan
Duc d'Orléans (34 cannons), under Captain de Champlois
Neptune (34 cannons), under Captain de la Porte Barrée
Lys (30 cannons), under Captain Biard
Renomée (30 cannons): frigate, under Captain de La Gâtinais
Insulaire (24 cannons): frigate, under Captain de La Baume

Leaving Didier de Saint-Martin to administer the island, La Bourdonnais, acting as squadron commander on board the *Achille*, which he had chosen as his flagship, took charge of this formidable force, which sailed from Port-Louis on 24 March 1746. Equipped with 384 cannons, it had considerable fire-power at the time. The infantry corps, numbering 3,310 men, was commanded by Sicre de Fontbrune, lieutenant-colonel and Knight of Saint-Louis; Louis de Rostaing, artillery captain; Antoine Desforges-Boucher, the king's chief engineer; as well as by Mr de Passy.

After facing a terrible cyclone near the coast of Madagascar, they had to stop over at the island for longer than expected in order to repair heavy damage to the ships. It was only in May that La Bourdonnais could leave the Bay of Antongil. Bearing precise instructions concerning his mission, he made full sail towards the Coromandel Coast of India. Off the coast of Ceylon, the French engaged in their first battle against an English fleet of six vessels, commanded by Vice-Admiral Peyton. This was the famous battle of Negapatam. The battle raged for more than two hours and the cannons thundered without respite. The *Achille*, with La Bourdonnais onboard, was at the front of the fleet, firing relentlessly at the English fleet which, though equipped with more artillery, was slower to return fire. Impressed by such firepower, the English took cover in the night to disengage themselves quietly from the battle. At dawn the next morning, the French attempted a fresh attack, but the enemy squadron, with three of its ships disabled, was content to veer away and depart the scene at top speed.

The Conflict Between Dupleix and Mahé de La Bourdonnais

La Bourdonnais reached Pondicherry on 8 July 1746, at the head of his squadron. His arrival was expected by Dupleix, Governor of the French establishments in India. The two men, who had been acquainted, had not seen each other for 18 years. They did not think much of each other. The governor of the islands was not received with all the honours due to his rank, and this did not fail to irritate him. It so happened that these two governors were the most powerful and most important representatives of France in that part of the world. They were meeting on the same ground for the first time and were faced with a problem of hierarchy. It must be stressed that the limits of the powers of each of them had not been clearly laid down by the minister, and that instructions were sometimes contradictory. Moreover, there existed at the time no principle to precisely indicate which of the commanders – of the land or sea forces – should take precedence, a loophole plugged only in 1781. In the meantime, the

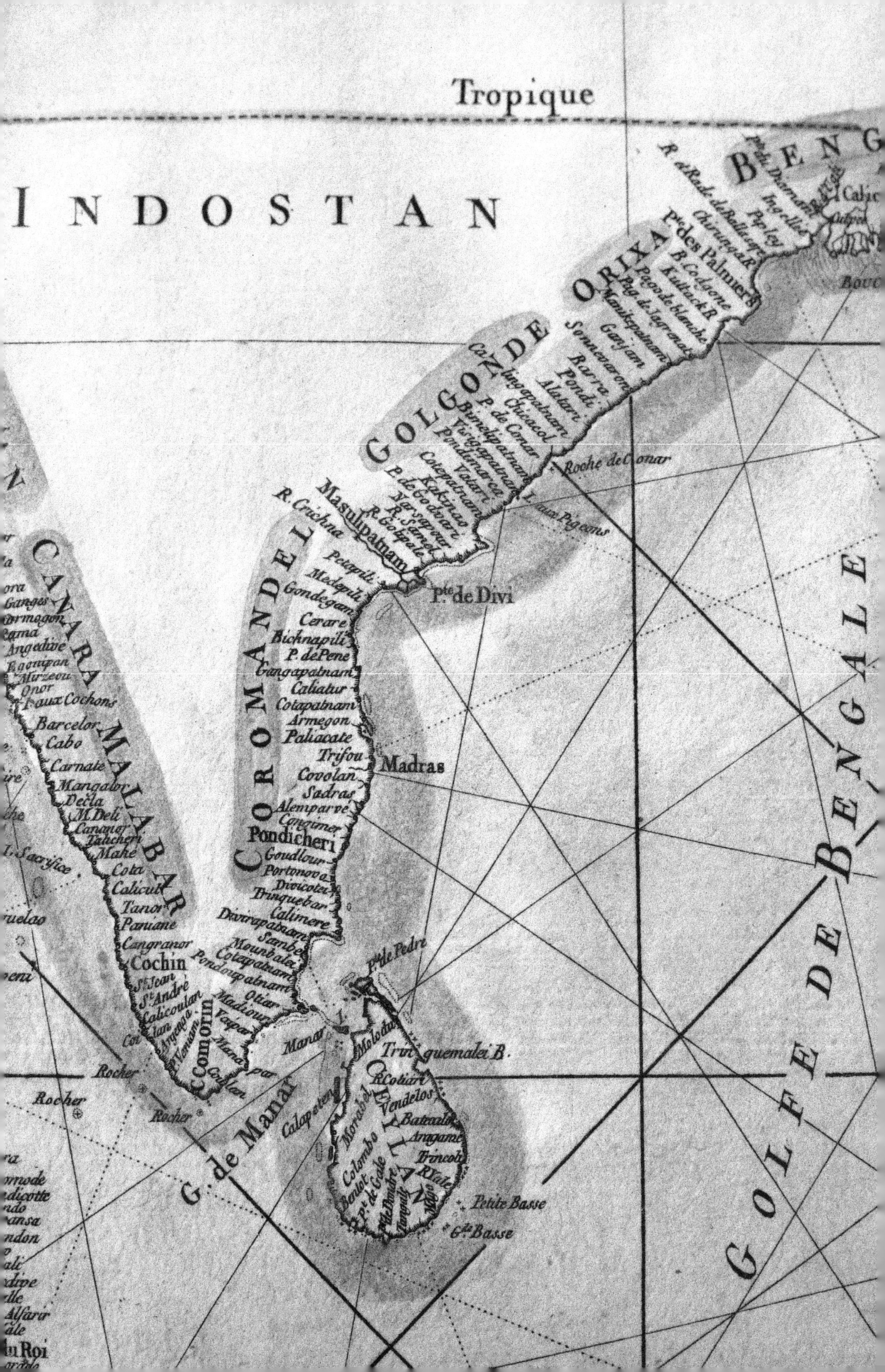

Tropique

INDOSTAN

BENG

ORIXA

GOLGONDE

CANARA

MALABAR

COROMANDEL

GOLFE DE BENGALE

G. de Manar

Madras

Pondicheri

Cochin

Comorin

Colombo

Roche de Coonar

Pte. de Divi

Pte. de Pedre

Trinquemalei B.

Petite Basse

Gde. Basse

OPPOSITE: Detail of the "Reduced map of the Oriental Ocean dedicated to the King".
by Mr d'Après de Mannevillette, Neptune Oriental, 1775.

LEFT: Mahé de La Bourdonnais's squadron in action against the powerful squadron of Vice-Admiral Peyton at the Battle of Negapatam on 6 July 1746.
Drawing by Perrot, engraving by Outhewaite.

situation was ambiguous. Dupleix, as Governor of India, held ministerial documents which made him, in many ways, the supreme master of the place. He thus refused to consider La Bourdonnais his equal or superior. The latter, confident in the orders freshly received from Minister Orry in person, was firmly convinced that he, in his capacity as squadron commander and, therefore, master of the military forces under his command, was legitimately invested with full powers with respect to any action or military decision required both at sea and on land. In fact, the letter which the Controller of Finances wrote him, dated 29 January 1745, was clear and to the point:

"Although this plan seemed good to me, the confidence that I have that you will do everything for the best, impels me to give you the authority to bring any changes to it which you will find most suitable for the general good and in the interests of the Company, and even to take an entirely different course of action, whatever it be [...]. You will inform Monsieur Dupleix of your decision. I am giving him most specific orders to assist you in every way that may be within his power."

This ambiguous situation revived old feelings of rivalry between the two men, which were not long in coming to the surface. Already in 1735, when La Bourdonnais had been appointed Governor of Isle de France and Bourbon, had it not been Dupleix who coveted the post for himself and did his utmost to oust his rival by unscrupulously discrediting him in the eyes of the directors of the company? Dupleix had written to Mr Duvelaër: "I do

Mahé de la Bourdonnais.

OPPOSITE: Bertrand François Mahé de La Bourdonnais, Knight of the Military Orders of Saint-Louis and of Christ, frigate captain in the French Navy, ship's captain in the Navy of the King of Portugal, Governor of Isle de France and Bourbon, president of the Conseils Supérieurs established in these two islands, and general commander of the ships of the Compagnie des Indes.
Drawing by V Adam and Maurin, 1845.

LEFT: Stores of the Compagnie des Indes, the Admiralty and the Governor's House at Pondicherry.
At Basset's, Saint-Jacques Street, Paris, engraving, 18th century.

BELOW: Portrait of Dupleix.
Engraving, 19th century.

not understand how the Company allowed itself to be deceived by the nonsense of this scatterbrain [...]" and to Mr d'Haudencourt: "I am amazed, you would believe that the Company wishes to lose the islands."

All this had not stopped him from playing a deceitful game by congratulating the new governor in a warm letter in which, on top of everything, he assured him of his support and total devotion. The first effects of this psychological conflict could be felt right from the time of the Madras affair, where the conquest was finally decided upon at the instigation of Dupleix. The plans by La Bourdonnais were rigorously detailed, and drawn up with such precision that, trapped under the fire of his squadron and surrounded by his troops, Madras surrendered on 21 September 1746, after a weak struggle. As a token, the English governor, Morse, handed his sword to La Bourdonnais. The victory was dazzling and the fame he rightly won would probably not fail to darken the brow of the man who was to become his worst enemy from that point on. As to the fate of Madras, it was clear to La Bourdonnais that, according to instructions, he must hold it up for ransom and, upon receipt of the ransom to be paid by Governor Morse, return it to the English. The whole transaction would, of course, be accompanied by several conditions to be contained in a detailed treaty and signed jointly by the English governor and the French squadron commander. Minister Orry's orders had been very clear on this point:

"Instructions for Monsieur La Bourdonnais, which he must follow exactly: it is expressly forbidden to Monsieur La Bourdonnais to seize any enemy establishment or trading post in order to retain it [...]".

Dupleix, for his part having great political aims for the influence of France in India, did not share that view at all. Wishing to deal a fatal blow to the empire-building impulse of the English in that part of India, he demanded that the town should be destroyed. He therefore adamantly opposed the idea of a ransom and used all his influence as Governor of the French possessions in India, to break the agreements reached. There was, from then on, an open struggle between the two giants, whose respective grievances concerning these negotiations broke out in a quarrelsome exchange of letters, in which each one strove to defend his point of view. Such a profound misunderstanding between these two men could not have arisen merely from a simple misunderstanding, but most probably from their different world views. Though each was a man of exceptional courage, they seemed fated to antagonise each other. The frank and outspoken temperament of the native of Saint-Malo, imbued as he was with a sense of duty, was incompatible with that of the ambitious Dupleix, whose concern about his personal prestige and the influence of France in India outstripped the narrow scope of his administrative duties. Each, conscious of his own status, had started a struggle for power between them right from the beginning. This, on top of the differences in their

PREVIOUS PAGES: Typical French 80-cannon ship of the period 1674–1730.
Engraving by Outhewaite, after P Perrot.

ABOVE: Madras surrendered on 21 September 1746. As a token of his defeat, the English Governor Nicholas Morse handed his sword to Mahé de La Bourdonnais.
Lithograph drawn by Desfontaines, engraving by Moret, 1789.

OPPOSITE (TOP): A court personage, Delhi.

OPPOSITE (BOTTOM): A general of the Grand Moghul's guard, Delhi.

temperaments, inevitably led to a clash of personalities, of which the Madras affair was only the culmination.

Finally, after the abrupt departure of his rival's squadron due to bad weather, Dupleix not only brought about the partial destruction of Madras, but he and his followers managed to cast a slur on the actions of La Bourdonnais by insinuating that, on top of the ransom, he had obtained personal financial gains. This slander soon reached the corridors of power at Versailles, where, since the fall from grace of Minister Orry and his brother, Cardinal de Fulvy, Dupleix enjoyed the patronage of Madame de Pompadour and her entourage.

Mahé de La Bourdonnais' Recall to France

The successive reports sent by Dupleix to Versailles with the aim of discrediting La Bourdonnais were quick to show results. When he returned to Isle de France in December 1746, La Bourdonnais not only had the surprise of finding a new governor, Barthélemy David, in his post, but he also had to bear the humiliation of learning that the latter had been commissioned by the company in his absence to conduct an enquiry into his administration. In case no charges were to be retained against him, he was ordered, as previously agreed, to go back to France with the six ships having served in the conquest of Madras. This mission, which he had accepted before his departure for India, fitted in with his deep desire to return to his motherland, as he had already mentioned on several occasions to Minister Orry.

He left Port-Louis on 5 March 1747, accompanied by his new wife, Charlotte Elisabeth de Combault d'Auteuil, and his three children, born at Isle de France: Charlotte, Louis and Pierrette. Pierre Poivre also joined the party, but left at Martinique to study its fauna and any useful plants. Off the Cape of Good Hope, they encountered a storm of such rare violence that only three of the six ships managed to reach Saint-Paul de Loango, on the Angolan coast.

After having arranged the return of his family on a Portuguese vessel bound for Lisbon, thus avoiding an encounter with the English which might have endangered their lives, La Bourdonnais sailed to France under a false identity, first via Martinique, then the island of Saint-Eustache and Flessingue, in the Netherlands. But when his ship called at Falmouth, he was spotted and arrested as a prisoner of war. However, he was granted bail and allowed to travel to France on the sole basis of his word of honour.

As soon as he reached France and without even being given a chance to explain himself, he was arrested in Paris on 2 March 1748 by two high-ranking police officers of Louis XV, in the Hôtel d'Entragues held by Mr Poupart, at rue de Condé. He was immediately transferred to the Bastille in a diligence and imprisoned there. Outraged at the injustice being done to him, La Bourdonnais bravely decided to defend himself to prove his innocence.

With the help of his wife and of Pierre de Gennes, a lawyer in the Parliament of Paris, La Bourdonnais produced a voluminous memorandum in his own defence. After an enquiry lasting three years, during which he remained at the Bastille, his innocence was at last acknowledged by the Tribunal, and he was acquitted. When he regained his freedom on 5 February 1751, he came out of prison a broken man. He returned straight to his residence at rue d'Enfer in Paris, and then to his Château du Piple in Boissy-Saint-Léger. The long period of imprisonment at the Bastille, together with the after-effects of his innumerable sea voyages in disastrous sanitary conditions, had slowly ruined his health. Worn out by scurvy and frequent bouts of dysentery, La Bourdonnais died some two years later, on 10 November 1753 at rue d'Enfer, at the age of 54.

Although after his liberation, Voltaire did write in *Le Siècle de Louis XV*: "Everybody gave La Bourdonnais a flattering compensation by calling him the avenger of France and the victim of envy", a libellous shadow remained to tarnish the reputation of this exceptional Frenchman, who had managed by his genius to transform Isle de France into "the pearl of the Indian Ocean". However, reputations at court are, alas, made and unmade according to shifts of power. Thus, the fall of Minister Philibert Orry was enough to suddenly make La Bourdonnais lose all credibility, and allow Dupleix to enjoy new powers, thanks to the support of Madame de Pompadour. It was not long before Dupleix, too, had to bear the humiliations of disgrace, and end his days deserted by all. Such is often the fate of great men, eternal pawns on the chessboard of History, who can be despatched into oblivion by mere whims.

Many successive governors came after the administration of Mahé de La Bourdonnais, all of whom contributed in one way or another to the social and economic development of the island. Thanks to their initiatives and dynamism, the foundations of the colony were strengthened, while its role as a naval base for the maintenance of the French presence in India was enhanced. A decisive step for the future of the island was taken in 1767, when the royal Government took control of the island and appointed its first representatives; Governor Jean-Daniel Dumas and Intendant Pierre Poivre. By this decision, the Government put a stop to the management of

"Everybody gave La Bourdonnais a flattering compensation by calling him the avenger of France and the victim of Envy," wrote Voltaire, after the liberation of La Bourdonnais.
Drawing and engraving by Vincent Vangelisty, 1776.

the Compagnie des Indes, which, by the same token, lost the trading privileges it had held for more than a century.

The settlers could now trade freely, and this naturally gave a boost to the island's economy and helped it to prosper. Pierre Poivre, who now had priorities other than the cultivation of spices, took the initiative to distinguish this period of his administration with extremely ambitious projects, objectives and public works. It was from that time that the immigration of younger sons of noble families to Isle de France began. This gave an extra boost to the island's development and confirmed the success of French colonisation.

Other governors also distinguished themselves. Souillac greatly contributed to the success of Suffren in India by his constant support; d'Entrecasteaux encouraged the rapid growth of industry and commerce while paying great attention to organising the island's defences. Later, during the troubled period of the Revolution, Malartic managed to adapt to the new circumstances, thanks to his moderation and diplomacy; while Decaen, after a remarkable administration, not only of the army and the judiciary but also of public education, had to deal with the landing of English troops in 1810.

THE MOST FAMOUS GOVERNORS

Jean-Baptiste Charles Bouvet de Lozier (1752–1755)

After schooling in Paris, this energetic young native of Saint-Malo, Jean-Baptiste Charles Bouvet de Lozier, began to sail the seas at the age of 16. A few years later, he was employed by the Compagnie des Indes, on whose behalf he sailed for nearly five years. In 1738, the company entrusted him with the command of an expedition with a mission to find the "Southern Land" where the Honfleur navigator Binot Paulmier de Gonneville was said to have landed in 1504. The company gave him two ships, the *Aigle* and the *Marie* to carry out his mission. They set sail on 19 July. A year later, in July 1739, in the neighbourhood of Antarctica, Bouvet, surrounded by icebergs, thought he had reached a cape of the "Southern Land", but in fact, it was really an island covered in ice and snow off the southern tip of the African continent. This island is now called Bouvet Island[21].

During the Austrian War of Succession (1744–1748), in March 1747, Bouvet commanded the frigate *Lys* in the squadron led by Grout de Saint-Georges, which was meant to support the French forces in India. After leaving Lorient, the squadron was attacked by the English off Cape Finistère. Most of the squadron was destroyed, but the *Lys* escaped and

Marquise de Pompadour (1721–1764). Mistress of King Louis XV from 1745, Jeanne-Antoinette Poisson, also known as Madame de Pompadour, secured in that same year the dismissal of Minister Philibert Orry, Controller-General of Finances and protector of Mahé de La Bourdonnais. She went along with the tales of Dupleix, the Governor of Pondicherry and was probably involved in the destitution and imprisonment of the former Governor of Isle de France. In 1751, she wrote in a letter to the Marquis de Saint-Contest concerning Dupleix: "Indeed, he cannot be blamed for living in luxury, nor for his wealth; he has well served his country, etc..." The Marquise de Pompadour regularly influenced the King of France concerning foreign affairs, war and finances. In a way, she may be considered to have ruled France with the King for more than 20 years.

19th-century engraving published by Furne, Paris, printed by F. Chardon.

Table of the Governors of Isle de France

1715 Guillaume Dufresne d'Arsel
Ship's Captain
The French take possession of the island in the
name of King Louis XIV

1721 Jean Durongouët le Toullec
Acting Major

Administration of Compagnie des Indes

1722 Chevalier Denis Denyon
Lieutenant-Colonel, Engineer

1725 Denis de Brousse
Captain

1727 Pierre Benoist Dumas
Former council member at Pondicherry

1729 Nicolas de Maupin
Agent of the Compagnie des Indes

1735 Bertrand-François Mahé de La Bourdonnais
Frigate Captain

1746 Barthélemy David
Former Governor of Sénégal

1752 Jean-Baptiste Bouvet de Lozier
Frigate Captain

1755 René Magon de la Villebague
Captain

1759 Antoine Desforges-Boucher
Sub-Lieutenant, Engineer

Administration of the Royal Government

1767 Jean-Daniel Dumas
Commander
Intendant, **Pierre Poivre**

1768 Jean Guillaume de Steinauër
Acting Military Officer
Intendant, **Pierre Poivre**

1769 François du Dresnay, Chevalier Desroches
Major-General
Intendant, **Pierre Poivre**

1772 Charles Louis d'Arzac, Chevalier de Ternay
Captain
Intendant, **Jacques Maillard-Dumesle**

1776 Antoine Guiran, Chevalier de la Brillanne
Captain
Intendant, **Denis Foucault** (1777)

1779 Viscount François de Souillac
Ship's Captain
Intendant, **Étienne Chevreau** (1781)

1787 Antoine de Bruni, Chevalier d'Entrecasteaux
Ship's Captain
Intendant, **Augustin Motais de Narbonne**
(1785)

Administration of the Convention and Directoire

1789 Count Thomas de Conway
Camp Marshal, formerly Governor of Pondicherry
Intendant, **André Dupuy**

1790 David Charpentier de Cossigny
Brigadier, former Governor of Pondicherry

1792 Hyppolite de Maurès, Count de Malartic
Camp Marshal, former Governor of Guadeloupe
Civil Commissioners, **Pierre Duboucher** and
Daniel l'Escalier

Administration of the Consulate and Empire

1800 François Magallon de la Morlière
Division General
Director-General, **Jean-Baptiste de Chauvalon**
(1798)

1803-1810 Charles Decaen
Captain-General
Colonial Prefect, **Louis Léger**

Bouvet managed to reach Isle de France in October that year. With Grout de Saint-Georges having been taken prisoner and La Bourdonnais having been recalled to France, Bouvet was made Commander of the French forces in the Indian Ocean. With the help of Governor David, who supplied him with a few ships based at Isle de France, Bouvet set sail for India in April 1748 to help defend the town of Pondicherry against the English.

On his return to France in 1750, Bouvet married Pauline David, the Governor's sister. Appointed Governor to the island of Bourbon, he stayed on Isle de France for about two months, before landing at Saint-Denis in October 1750. Two years later, he succeeded David as Governor. Struck by the enthusiasm and determination of the botanist Pierre Poivre, he was quickly convinced by the latter of the usefulness of introducing nutmeg and cloves on Isle de France. He therefore provided Poivre with a small frigate, the *Colombe*, for an expedition to the Moluccas Islands.

In 1755, Bouvet was again appointed Governor of Bourbon island. From there, he successfully engaged in several important naval missions. He administered that island very well until 1763, when he returned to France and was ennobled. During the American War of Independence, Bouvet wrote several memoranda to the Minister for the Navy, the Duke of Choiseul. These communications proved to be of some use to the French forces. Having settled at Vauréal, near Pontoise, Bouvet died there in 1787, at the age of 81.

The Intendant Pierre Poivre and Marine Commissioner (1767–1772)

This tireless "travelling philosopher" with a premonitory name truly had an extraordinary life. Pierre Poivre succeeded in stealing some plants of the most coveted spices in the world – nutmeg and cloves – from the Moluccas islands to introduce them on Isle de France. These genuine "forbidden fruits" had been under the exclusive control of the Dutch since 1621. With this bold exploit, he was to break their powerful monopoly over these products once and for all.

It is worth pointing out that Pierre Poivre had stayed at Isle de France during two quite distinct periods. After two quick passages, one lasting for four months in 1746, and the other, two months in 1750, his first extended stay lasted for three years, from 1753 to 1756, when Bouvet de Lozier was governor. Poivre was at Isle de France as a mere botanist, with the project of trying to acclimatise nutmeg and cloves on the island. It was only 11 years later, in 1767, that he returned as Intendant[22] and resided there for

Portrait of Governor Bouvet de Lozier.
Drawing by Dumontier, engraving by Hubert.

five years. Although he did not have the title of Governor, Poivre can be considered as the real administrator of the island during that period, owing to his strength of character, exceptional personality and the scope of his projects for the development of the colony.

In many ways, he carried on the work of Mahé de La Bourdonnais. Born in the area of Lyon known as "Grenette" on 23 August 1719, and coming from an influential trading family, Pierre Poivre was brought up by the missionaries of Saint-Joseph. A very gifted pupil, he was sent to Paris to study theology, but also natural history, industrial arts and drawing. At the age of 21, prior to Poivre's confirmation as a missionary, it was said that he had been imprisoned under an order by a mandarin. He is then said to have taken advantage of that stay in prison to learn the rudiments of Chinese, so as to be able to plead in his own defence. He thus managed to impress the Viceroy of Canton who, regretting the manner in which he had been victimised, had Poivre freed and did everything in his power to permit him to travel freely throughout China and Cochin China. He brought back from this exceptional exploration a valuable list of observations, not only of agriculture and commerce but also concerning aspects of the customs, mores and methods of administration of these faraway regions. On his return, while he was sailing towards France on board the *Dauphin*, the ship was attacked by the English. In his bold attempt to "take a few shots at the enemy", Poivre had his right wrist ripped off by a cannon ball: "I shall never be able to paint". It was said that this had been the only complaint voiced by this rash man who, once carried on board the English ship, had to endure his pain for a whole night before receiving any care at all. This neglect caused the loss of his whole right arm, which had to be amputated as it became gangrenous. After landing at Batavia (present-day Jakarta) to undergo treatment, he took the opportunity during his convalescence to develop a keen interest in the most flourishing activity of the Dutch in that region: the cultivation of nutmeg and cloves. These spices were highly prized in Europe at that time, not only because they were used to preserve meats, but also for their capacity to enhance the taste of the finest foods. These ingredients were therefore, goods of inestimable value.

Poivre quickly noticed that this undertaking was the real backbone of Dutch trade in that region. As long as they kept sole control over the Moluccas islands (Ambon, Banda and Geby), the only places on earth to produce these gems, the Dutch would be the only ones to benefit from a growing source of wealth. He therefore needed, at all costs, to obtain some samples. In spite of the close watch maintained over these islands and the

Pierre Poivre, the "Travelling Philosopher". Poivre's right arm was amputated in 1740, but it seems that Antoine Roussin, the lithographer of *l'Album de La Réunion* ignored this fact when he engraved this portrait.
Imp. A Roussin, 1861.

death penalty to which any "spice hunter" exposed himself to, Poivre managed to boldly steal 19 nutmeg plants as well as some nuts suitable for germination. He is said to have skilfully concealed them in the lining of his coat. On the way back, Poivre stopped at Pondicherry, where he met Joseph Dupleix, then Governor of the French establishments in India. Poivre was thus a witness to the squabbles between the latter and La Bourdonnais concerning the Madras affair. The persuasive skills of these governors, who each put his case to Poivre, helped him to arrive at the following conclusion: "When one listened to them, one could not avoid thinking each was in the right".

In October 1746, Poivre took advantage of La Bourdonnais' squadron to sail to Isle de France, with the idea of seizing from the Dutch the monopoly of the precious spices. After a stay of four months at Isle de France, Poivre took to sea again in March 1747, along with the disgraced La Bourdonnais, who was on his way to France. He became a prisoner on the island of Guernsey (in the English Channel) and reached France only in October 1748, after the signature of a peace treaty with the English, thus ending the Austrian War of Succession.

On account of his disability, Pierre Poivre had given up on taking Holy Orders, and so turned his attention to other great projects. This enthusiastic botanist thought of introducing nutmeg and cloves to Isle de France and cultivating them on a large scale, in order to present the King of France with an asset which, according to him, would not fail to bring prosperity to his country. Having convinced the Compagnie des Indes of the validity of this objective, he also obtained their agreement to establish a trading post in Cochin China, of which he laid the foundations at Faï-Foo in 1749. On his return to Isle de France in 1750, bearing many useful plants and plants of "dry rice" from Cochin China, he immediately set sail on the *Mascarin* towards Manila, with the aim of collecting a cargo of spice plants. He returned in December 1753 with five clove plants and a few nutmeg plants – a very meagre harvest with which to launch a future crop. So, his obsession now shifted to the more coveted, but also the more dangerous destinations: the Moluccas islands and the islands near the island of Celebes.

In May 1754, Bouvet de Lozier, then Governor of Isle de France, yielded to Poivre's obstinate desire to sail to these islands at all costs and gave him the use of a very fragile boat, the *Colombe*, a small frigate worn out by many ocean trips. However, in his eagerness to fulfil his dream above all else, Poivre was quite satisfied with it. Once more braving every danger, he

ABOVE: Pierre Poivre married Françoise Robin a few months before his departure to Isle de France in 1767.

OPPOSITE: An inhabitant of the island of Celebes.
Drawing by Demoraine, engraving by Taillant.

succeeded this time in obtaining 3,000 nutmegs as well as spice plants and several species of fruit, which he brought back to Isle de France in June 1755. The story goes that Mr Fusée-Aublet damaged these plants by surreptitiously dousing them with hot water at night. Poivre's enthusiasm was, however, defeated by the lack of interest in his projects shown by René Magon, the new Governor. Some facilities were granted to him, but these were absolutely insufficient for the fulfilment of his projects.

At the beginning of 1756, discouraged and disappointed, Poivre then decided to return to France. He took advantage of a long stopover at Madagascar to gather indigenous plants, which he would present to the famous botanist Bernard Jussieu. He was once again captured by the English and eventually reached France in April 1757. In 1758, his brother, Denis, found for him a pleasant little estate near Lyon. Poivre bought it and settled down at La Fréta, situated within the territory of the village of Saint-Romain-Au-Mont-d'Or, in the Saône valley. He was elected in 1759 to the membership of the Académie des Sciences, des Belles Lettres et des Arts of Lyon. His interest in botany and agriculture, as well as in the trade and resources of the Far East, had already earned him, in 1754, a nomination as correspondent of Reaumur at l'Académie des Sciences de Paris, and then as correspondent of Jussieu. He soon became such a celebrity in the field of natural sciences, and his reputation reached the higher authorities of the State. Louis XV subsquently made him a noble, granted him the sash of the Order of Saint-Michel and, in 1766, appointed him as Intendant of Isle de France and Bourbon. That is how Pierre Poivre came to be given the mission, with Jean-Daniel Dumas, of establishing the first organisational structures of the royal administration, which were henceforth to replace those of the Compagnie des Indes. He was in luck at last! He was going to, at the same time, have the opportunity to indulge his passion for exotic plants, while having the freedom to organise and develop the trade in fine spices as he wished.

Poivre left Lorient on 8 March 1767, accompanied by his 18-year-old wife, Françoise Robin. The couple's marriage was celebrated in 1766, six months before their departure. They landed at Port-Louis on 17 July 1767, at the same time as Governor Dumas. Poivre immediately assumed duty, thus launching the era of a two-headed administration: henceforth, general administration and finances were divided into two separate posts, one assigned to the Governor, who was also Commander-in-Chief of the soldiers, and the other to the Intendant. However, Jean-Daniel Dumas' personality was very different from that of Poivre. A soldier first and foremost, he used a blunt approach towards administration, and his

somewhat hasty methods were quite the opposite of those of Poivre. Poivre, therefore, used his influence to have him replaced by the Chevalier Desroches, who took up his post in June 1769. In spite of more quarrels with the new Governor, who had a difficult temperament, Poivre was able to continue the work initiated by Mahé de La Bourdonnais from 1735 to 1746. He threw himself successfully into huge public works. He redesigned the town of Port-Louis, greatly improving its appearance and amenities. Among other projects, he undertook to lay decent roads to link all the regions of the island to the capital. With valuable collaboration between Captain Boudin de Tromelin and engineer Cossigny, he drew up new plans for Port-Louis and organised the layout of the harbour which, according to the instructions given by Choiseul, the Minister for the Navy, had to become an important naval base to support the French troops in India. Works to achieve this gigantic objective, started in 1772, were only completed in 1779, seven years after the Intendant's departure. Poivre also devoted particular care to the improvement of the system of administration, in order to develop the island's economy and thus bring prosperity and well-being to its inhabitants.

However, Poivre did not give up his favourite project. During the five years he spent at Isle de France, he organised several expeditions to the Celebes Sea and the Moluccas Islands. From June 1770, Captain d'Etchéverry and Captain de Trémignon, accompanied by the botanist Provost, on board the *Étoile du Matin* and the *Vigilant*, brought back to Isle de France, after many adventures, a sizeable cargo of nutmeg and clove plants. These came mostly from the island of Geby, and had been identified and authenticated by the famous French botanist Philibert Commerson, a friend whom the Intendant had been delighted to welcome to Isle de France during the visit of the Bougainville expedition. Following this success, Pierre Poivre was confirmed by the King, in his post as Intendant on a recommendation from the Duc de Praslin. Two years later, in June 1772, the Dutch monopoly was finally broken for good when Captain Jacques Cordé and Captain Le Borgne de Coëtivy, in command of the *Nécessaire* and the *Isle de France*, accompanied by botanists Provost and Pierre Sonnerat, victoriously sailed into Port-Louis harbour, with hundreds of nutmeg and clove plants and thousands of nutmegs! In order to ensure the success of this useful crop, Poivre took the wise precaution of introducing a number of young plants to Bourbon, the Seychelles, and French Guyana, where they acclimatised perfectly. These French colonies were, henceforth, in a position to compete with the Moluccas Islands in the production of spices.

OPPOSITE: During his journey to the Moluccas islands in 1745, Pierre Poivre faced the fierce islanders of Amboine, whose ancestors were head-hunters, just like the inhabitants of the nearby island of Borneo.
18th-century document drawn and engraved by Bernard.

BELOW: Originally from Mexico, the cocoa tree was imported into Isle de France by Jean-François Charpentier de Cossigny in 1759.
Drawing by Turpin, engraving by Lambert Jr.

FOLLOWING PAGES (LEFT): The clove tree was imported into Isle de France by Pierre Poivre in 1770. Six years later, in 1776, the first cloves (unopened flowers) were gathered by his successor, botanist Nicolas Céré.

FOLLOWING PAGES (RIGHT): Nutmeg was the real gem of the Moluccas islands, the only place in the world then where the spice grew in abundance.

Lith. A Cotteret, Imp. A Roussin, 1862.

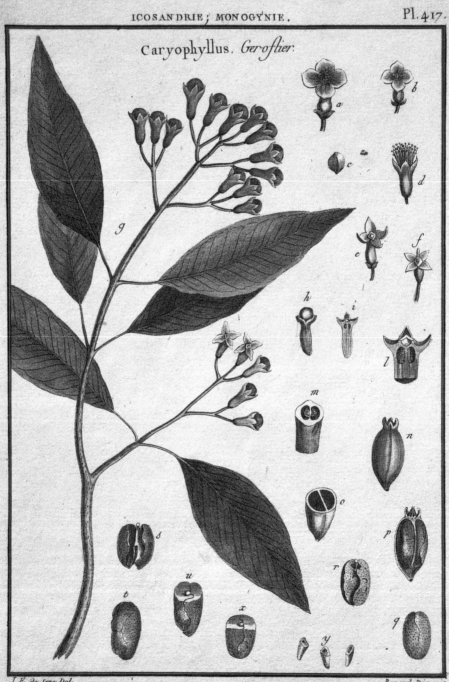

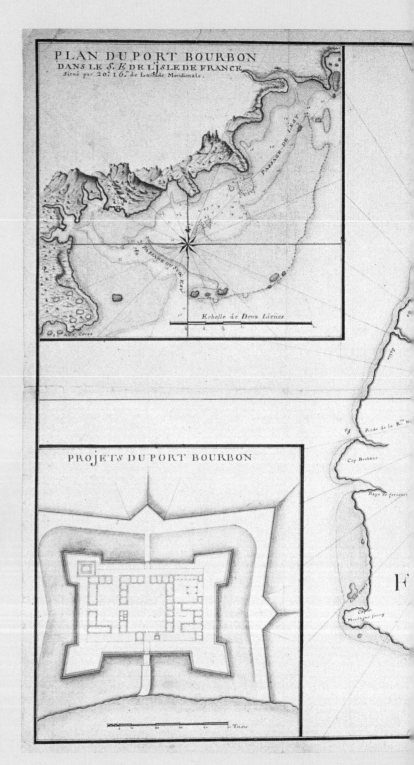

Map of Isle of France drawn on site in 1723 by the first French governor of Isle de France, the Chevalier Denis Denyon.

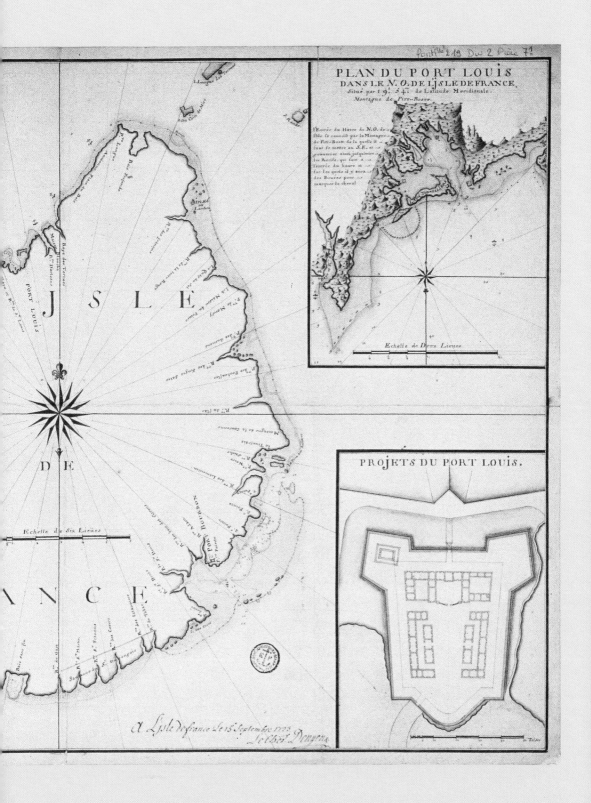

PLAN DU PORT LOUIS
DANS LE N. O. DE L'ISLE DE FRANCE,
Situé par 19°. 54′. de Latitude Meridionale.
Montagne de Pierr-Rouge.

Echelle de Deux Lieues

PROJETS DU PORT LOUIS.

A L'Isle de france le 15 Septembre 1753.

On 7 December 1778, some six years after the departure of Poivre, at an official reception at Monplaisir to which a considerable number of important people were convened, Nicolas Céré, a Créole of Isle de France, picked "the first French nutmeg" and proudly entrusted it to the Governor, the Chevalier de La Brillane, for the latter to offer to Louis XVI.

While Poivre had devoted himself primarily to the development of agriculture and to strengthening the organisation of the administration, finances and economy of Isle de France, it must be emphasised that he had also, wished to link this faraway island culturally to the major principles of the Age of Enlightenment.

In addition to starting up a printing establishment in 1768, he had also, spurred on by his friend Commerson, decided to launch a small Académie des Sciences at Isle de France to attract scientists, philosophers and men of letters. Besides the famous botanist, he had managed to retain in the colony, Véron, the astronomer of the Bougainville expedition, and had also invited the Abbot Rochon, a reputed astronomer and physicist, to stay. He also welcomed and protected other learned men, such as Cossigny de Palma, Joseph Hubert, de Lanux and Pierre Sonnerat, a cousin of his. He helped the Abbot Galloys to introduce plants and birds from China to Isle de France and supported Kerguélen and Marion-Dufresnes in the

OPPOSITE: Cycas (or false sago), introduced into Isle de France during the 18th century by Captain Charles-Henri d'Estaing, and also by the explorer Yves de Kerguelen. This plant thrived on the island.
Drawing by P Turpin, engraving by Lambert Jr.

ABOVE: "Dwelling at Pamplemousses, garden of Nicolas Céré". Céré (1737–1810) was a Créole of Isle de France and friend of Pierre Poivre. He introduced to the island fish such as gouramis and a carp, locally known as "Dame Céré".
Drawing by Milbert, engraving by Lejeune.

completion of their scientific journeys. The intellectual elite of the island could therefore enjoy the stimulation provided by the company of these exceptional travellers.

However, Pierre Poivre's most spectacular undertaking, and undoubtedly his most successful venture, remains the creation of the marvellous, exotic gardens in the grounds of his property of Monplaisir[23], in the region of Pamplemousses where he lived. More than 600 rare species, imported from the four continents and planted according to his instructions, were assembled there in a harmonious tropical wonderland. These gardens, which Poivre has left us as a legacy, and the management of which he had entrusted to Nicolas Céré on his departure, are today among the most beautiful in the world. It was later to serve as a model for many botanists.

After five active years in administration, Pierre Poivre left Isle de France in October 1772 on board the *Indien*, leaving behind a stable and prosperous colony for which he had spared no effort. On his return to France, he settled at La Fréta with his wife and his two daughters, who were born on Isle de France: Marie Antoinette Françoise, born in 1768, and Françoise Julienne Isle de France, born in 1771. A third daughter, Sarah Marie Marguerite, was born in La Fréta in 1773. His personal income provided him with the means to live comfortably. It was also augmented by a generous royal allowance, obtained thanks to the backing of Turgot, as a reward for his loyal efforts and his contribution to the rise of Isle de France and Bourbon. On his fine property, reputed to have been built by Soufflot,

PREVIOUS PAGES: Used as a means of transport on Isle de France during the 18th and 19th centuries, a palaquin was no more than an exotic version of the sedan chair.
Drawings by Chasselat after A Taunay, engraving by Choubard.

RIGHT: In 1758, thanks to his brother Denis, Pierre Poivre bought a small property near Lyon, La Fréta, and settled there. He returned there for good in 1773 with his wife Françoise and his two daughters, both born at Isle de France.

and embellished with many tropical plants, he often welcomed passing travellers who took delight in sharing ideas with this intelligent man, whose easy manner and modesty were particularly attractive. "We can learn something from everybody," he used to say. He died 14 years after his return to France, at the age of 66, and was buried in the Saint Benoît chapel of the basilica of Saint-Martin d'Ainay, in Lyon. His widow later married Pierre-Samuel Dupont de Nemours, a friend of Poivre's and comrade of La Fayette during the American War of Independence. This gentleman, who favoured a constitutional monarchy and had strongly criticised the French authorities in some virulent pamphlets during the Revolution, thought it wiser to go into exile in the United States of America with his wife. It is to him that we owe the biographical note on the life of Pierre Poivre contained in the third edition (Paris, Year II) of the *Voyages d'un philosophe*, and again in the 1797 edition.

Apart from the nutmeg and clove trees, we owe it to Poivre for the introduction to the island of many tropical plants from various parts of the world, such as the Philippines, Indonesia, Malaysia, South America and Asia, as well as from Madagascar and Mozambique, including, among others, the cinnamon tree from Indochina (present-day Vietnam), lychee from China in 1768, combava and olive tree from France, and the logwood.

Charles Louis d'Arzac, Chevalier de Ternay (1772–1776)

Born in Poitou around 1723, the Chevalier de Ternay began his career as a lieutenant in the Royal Navy in 1753. After his appointment as a ship's captain in 1761, he took part in various sea operations during the Seven Years' War, including the capture of Saint-Jean de Terre-Neuve.

Having been appointed Governor of Isle de France in 1772, Ternay reached Port-Louis on board the *Belle Poule*. He was accompanied by Jean François Galaup, Count de Lapérouse, who remained on the island during the whole of his friend and protector's term of office. Governor Ternay despatched Galaup on several occasions to the coasts of India in defence of the French flag in the area.

As he was against slavery, Ternay tried to convince Versailles to send Acadian farmers to Isle de France to reduce the need for slaves in agriculture. His suggestions were not considered, however. At the end of his mandate in 1776, he returned to France and, a few years later, was promoted to the rank of Squadron Commander. In 1780, Ternay was in command of a fleet transporting troops sent by Louis XVI to Rochambeau to support George Washington against the insurgents during the American

Pierre-Samuel Dupont de Nemours (1739–1817). A friend of Poivre and Turgot, and a disciple of Quesnay. He was in favour of a constitutional monarchy during the French Revolution. He married the widow of Pierre Poivre and settled in the United States. *Engraving by Conquy.*

War of Independence. Ternay contracted a violent illness shortly after his arrival in America and later died at Newport.

Viscount François de Souillac (1779–1787)

Viscount de Souillac was appointed Governor of Isle de France and Bourbon in 1779, after a long career in the Navy. Four years later, having become Squadron Commander, Souillac was promoted to Governor-General of French Establishments beyond the Cape of Good Hope. When Souillac went on an inspection tour of Pondicherry on board the *Subtil*, Chevalier de Parny, a famous poet from the island of Bourbon, accompanied him as aide-de-camp.

From the moment of his arrival at Isle de France, Viscount de Souillac knew how to win hearts, not only with his unassuming yet distinguished manner, but also with his kindness and constant preoccupation with improving the daily lives of the inhabitants. He often went on inspection tours around the island in the company of Nicolas Céré, to identify the needs of the settlers and to try to meet these needs. Tirelessly active and gifted with a very energetic disposition, Souillac undertook major works at Port-Louis. It is to him that we owe the completion of the works on La Chaussée, as well as the construction of the cathedral, which was completed in 1786.

Souillac was most concerned about sanitation and security of the town, and published several ordinances to that effect, including those on canteens, the police, funerals, fires, markets and the disposal of rubbish. These ordinances remained in force long after his term.

The Governor distinguished himself above all by the unfailing support he gave Bailli de Suffren when the latter stopped at Port-Louis before leaving to fight the English in India. Thanks to Souillac's vigorous intervention, Suffren's squadron obtained food supplies and was reinforced by several vessels, as well as 3,000 men. The reinforcements which he regularly sent Suffren during this campaign contributed to his success on the coast of Coromandel, especially during the famous Battle of Cuddalore in 1783.

Souillac returned to France in 1787, to the great regret of the island settlers, who thought highly of him. A few days before Souillac's departure, the inhabitants gave him such a magnificent reception at the Champ de Mars that the ambassadors of Tipu Sultan (the ruler of Mysore), who happened to be visiting Port-Louis, were absolutely dazzled by it. His name remains linked to a small village in the southwest of the island, in the district of Savanne.

Antoine Raymond Joseph de Bruni, Chevalier d'Entrecasteaux (1787–1789)

D'Entrecasteaux was born in Aix-en-Provence on 8 November 1737. A naval guardsman in 1754, he gradually climbed the promotion ladder to become a ship's lieutenant in 1770 after serving under his relative, Bailli de Suffren. Nine years later, at the age of 42, he reached the rank of ship's captain. An intelligent, energetic and brave man, he soon distinguished himself – in addition to his scientific knowledge, especially in hydrography – by his skills as a sailor, which led him to achieve a particularly brilliant seafaring career. In 1785, as head of division, he was made Commander-in-Chief of the French naval forces based at Isle de France, whose main purpose was to protect the trade of the Compagnie des Indes in these regions and to ensure respect for the French flag.

On his return from a mission in the Far East, d'Entrecasteaux was appointed governor of Isle de France and Bourbon by the Maréchal de Castries, Minister for the French Navy. D'Entrecasteaux left Pondicherry on the *Résolution*, which he commanded, and dropped anchor at Isle de France on 5 October 1787. D'Entrecasteaux was welcomed by the Governor, Viscount de Souillac, from whom he took over in November.

Being fully aware of the strategic importance of the location of Isle de France, a key stopover between Europe and Asia, d'Entrecasteaux's main objective was to turn it into a prosperous island, capable not only of meeting its own needs, but also of establishing trade relations overseas. D'Entrecasteaux therefore strove to develop the economy of the country by paying the greatest attention to agriculture, industry and commerce. In the area of agriculture, he immediately saw the need to concentrate on basic food crops, especially grains, so as to be able to feed the population at all times, as well as squadrons during wartime, and still have a surplus for export.

Moreover, he decided to launch two new industries. The first was a substantial gunpowder plant which he built in Port-Louis, an innovative venture at that time. The factory had the advantage of gathering all the workshops necessary in manufacturing the explosive mixture, which was not even the case in Europe yet. This move was essential, given the intensive military role of the harbour. The second factory was an indigo plant, which was large enough to produce sufficient goods for profitable trade.

D'Entrecasteaux also made a careful study of the defence of the island. Due to its advantageous location en route to India, the island was not safe,

The famous navigator d'Entrecasteaux was Governor for Isle de France for two years. In 1791, the Convention entrusted him with the mission to search for Lapérouse and his expedition.

he thought, from a massive attack by English troops. D'Entrecasteaux therefore advised that all the French forces based at Pondicherry should, immediately following the evacuation of that trading post, be assembled on Isle de France. The aim was twofold: to create a threat to the English possessions in the region, and to prevent the conquest of the island by the English. Meanwhile, d'Entrecasteaux restored discipline within the militia and thus provided the island with an adequate defence force. After two fruitful years in administration, d'Entrecasteaux asked for permission to step down. He left Isle de France in November 1789 and was replaced by Count Thomas de Conway.

In 1791, d'Entrecasteaux was appointed Rear-Admiral and, thanks to his reputation as a skilful navigator, was chosen by the Assembly and by Louis XVI to lead an expedition in search of any sign of the explorer Lapérouse. The disappearance of the *Boussole* and the *Astrolabe*, from which there had been no news since February 1788, had moved public opinion, and the Société d'Histoire Naturelle had taken the initiative of asking the National Assembly to order a search. The Assembly therefore decided to entrust d'Entrecasteaux with a twofold mission: first and foremost to search for Lapérouse; and second, to make every possible observation likely to be useful for navigation and geography, as well as to the arts and sciences.

Thus, d'Entrecasteaux took command of the frigates *Recherche* and *Espérance*, assisted by Huon de Kermadec. There were many reputed scientists on board, among them the hydrographic engineer Beautemps-Beaupré who was to become very famous under Napoléon, as well as the naturalist Jacques de La Billardière. While the scientific part of the operation turned out to be a success, thanks to the valuable observations that were gathered, the humanitarian one, on the other hand, drew a complete blank: in spite of a long and exhausting search throughout the Pacific Ocean, d'Entrecasteaux found no trace of Lapérouse and, at the end of the voyage, even lost his own life. Struck down by scurvy and dysentery, he died in the Java Sea on 20 July 1793, unaware that Louis XVI had promoted him to the rank of Vice-Admiral a year earlier.

Yet, the goal was almost in sight. Indeed, according to his ship's log, as the expedition was sailing towards the Santa-Cruz archipelago in May 1792, d'Entrecasteaux and his crew sighted, in the distance, a group of three islands, of which the most distant did not appear on their map. D'Entrecasteaux was content with making a note about its position and named it "Research Island". How ironic, as we know today that this little island lost in the ocean was none other than Vanikoro island, precisely where Lapérouse's *Astrolabe* and the *Boussole* were shipwrecked. Dumont d'Urville discovered their wrecks in 1828, 35 years after the tragedy.

THE GOVERNORS UNDER THE REVOLUTION AND THE CONSULATE

On 31 January 1790, a ship commanded by Lieutenant Gabriel de Coriolis reached Isle de France. The officers and crew proudly wore the tricolour cockade and, as soon as they had disembarked, rushed to announce to passers-by that there had been a revolution in France: the royal family had been transferred to the Tuileries, privileges had been abolished, and France was about to become a free republic, where all citizens would have equal rights. The cockade was the symbol of liberty and its three colours were the new colours of France!

An enthusiastic crowd immediately gathered around the newcomers, who were handing out cockades to all and sundry. Everyone wanted one. The lower classes were in a fever, amazed at this reversal of the established order. Within a few days, the citizens began to get agitated and clamoured for the creation of an assembly. It was the end of an era. A new era was beginning for the colony and the administration of the last Governors was not without some turmoil.

Count Thomas de Conway (1789–1790)

Count Thomas de Conway had just been appointed governor of the colony in November 1789 when news of the French Revolution reached Isle de France on 31 January 1790. Before assuming his new duties on Isle de France, this French soldier of Irish descent had been Governor-General of the French Establishments in Pondicherry for two years. Openly hostile to new ideas, Conway very reluctantly agreed to convene the first "Colonial Assembly", according to the instructions of the Convention. In spite of his dissent, the new measures were confirmed by the arrival of the decree from the Constituante bearing the date 8 March 1790, which vested the Colonial Assembly with additional powers. In May, the fleet of Captain Henri de Mac Nemara, newly appointed Commander-in-Chief of the French naval forces, dropped anchor at Port-Nord-Ouest. Over-excited persons quickly attacked this brave and uncompromising sailor. Only the Governor's courageous stand saved him from being lynched.

By this time also, the privileges of the new Compagnie des Indes (the Compagnie de Calonne) were abolished, and trade became henceforth totally free.

Outraged by all these events and developments, Conway resigned on 27 July 1790. He decided to return to France, and left Port-Nord-Ouest on 9 September on board the *Nymphe*. On his return, he published a book entitled *Tableau religieux et politique de l'Indoustan*, which narrowly saved him from the guillotine.

David Charpentier de Cossigny (1790–1792)

From the end of August 1790, Governor Conway was replaced by David Charpentier de Cossigny, who was then on duty on the island of Bourbon. He was the nephew of the famous engineer Cossigny, who had been dispatched to Isle de France, before the arrival of La Bourdonnais, to assess the value of that island. The engineer had stayed on Isle de France in 1732, and again in 1736 and 1772.

Upon arriving on Isle de France, David Charpentier de Cossigny was immediately faced with a difficult and delicate situation, with the latent anarchy threatening to cause chaos. The Assembly had the real power and for two years, Cossigny restricted himself merely to maintaining order on the island. From the beginning of his administration, he was faced with a tragedy which perfectly reflected the spirit of rebellion in the colony: in the midst of a rampaging crowd, Captain Henri de Mac Nemara, a friend and compatriot of Count de Conway, was murdered at Port-Nord-Ouest by drunk and overexcited soldiers, while he was on his way to the barracks after having been received by the Colonial Assembly.

Tension and unrest had already been rife for some time. However, Cossigny reacted to these serious incidents calmly and with moderation. He managed to restore order and maintained it until the end of his administration, up to the arrival of his successor, Count de Malartic.

Hyppolite de Maurès, Count de Malartic (1792–1800)

A native of Montauban, where he was born in 1730, Count de Malartic took part in Montcalm's campaign in Canada, and distinguished himself at his side on several occasions. On returning home in 1763, he was appointed Governor of Guadeloupe in 1769. After his recall to France, Malartic was promoted to Camp Marshal. In 1792, at the age of 62, he received the mandate to act as Governor of Isle de France and the French Establishments beyond the Cape of Good Hope. During the troubled period of his administration, Malartic managed to win over the most ardent patriots. In 1794, when France was proposing to abolish slavery on Isle de France, Malartic, though not fundamentally against the project, insisted, and backed by the settlers' firm support, that the decree should be accompanied by financial support to the inhabitants in order to avoid economic repercussions, which would only be disastrous for the colony. This resistance caused the outright expulsion of Messrs Baco and Burnel, who had come to Isle de France firmly resolved to enforce the said decree. It must be emphasised here that the troop's commander, Magallon de la Morlière, who refused to apply the decree by force, also played a prominent role in the turn of events.

This attitude made Malartic the real "father of the colony". Thanks to his clear vision, he spared the inhabitants from serious riots and, in the short term, saved the colony from riun. In 1798, he received two ambassadors sent by Tipu Sultan of Mysore, son of the great Hyder Ali Khan. Like his father, Tipu Sultan was a faithful ally of the French. These ambassadors came to request help from the Governor of Isle de France in supplying reinforcements to the Prince's army for the support of the French in India. In spite of his goodwill, Malartic was unable to fully accede to their request. Captain L'Hermitte was delegated to accompany them back to India onboard the *Preneuse*.

After eight years of loyal administration, Count de Malartic died during his mandate on Isle de France in July 1800. The death of this remarkable man, loved by all, plunged the colony into deep mourning. The Colonial Assembly paid him a vibrant tribute and he was given a magnificent funeral. A memorial was erected in his memory at the Champ de Mars, and his ashes were transferred there in 1801.

Count François de Magallon de La Morlière (1800–1803)

The successor of Count de Malartic was the Divisional General, François de Magallon de La Morlière, Commander-in-Chief of the troops based on Isle de France. These were the troops which had escorted the famous delegates of the Directoire, Baco and Burnel, who, as we recall, had come to apply the decree of the abolition of slavery with immediate effect, but had been forced to return to France empty-handed, owing to the firm opposition of Malartic. Being unconvinced about the need to oppose the colonists, Magallon de La Morlière had then avoided applying any sanctions against them.

Magallon de La Morlière calmly completed his three trouble-free years of administration until the arrival of his successor, General Decaen, who was appointed by Napoléon. He then returned to France where, before retirement, he was for seven years Commander of the 15th division under Napoléon, from 1807 to 1814.

FOLLOWING PAGES (TOP): Third Anglo-Mysore War (1790–1792). Defeat of Tipu Sultan by the English forces under the command of Lord Cornwallis. In March 1792, the British captured two sons of Tipu, Abdul Khaliq and Maïz ud Din, aged 10 and 8 years. They were detained as hostages in Madras for 18 months, awaiting the payment by their father, the "Tiger of Mysore", of 36 million rupees, claimed as war damages by the English.
Engraving by J Rogers, after a painting by H Singleton, 19th century.

FOLLOWING PAGES (BOTTOM): Fourth and last Anglo-Mysore War (1799). Tipu Sultan, ruler of Mysore and last ally of the French in India died in his palace on 4 May 1799 while defending Seringapatam against the English at the head of a devoted troop. During the attack, one English regiment was commanded by Arthur Wellesley, future Duke of Wellington, who subsequently led the allied troops which defeated Napoléon at the Battle of Waterloo in 1815.
Engraving by J. Rogers, after a painting by H. Singleton, 19th century.

FOLLOWING PAGES (RIGHT): Portrait of Tipu Sultan of Mysore (1749–1799).
Drawing by Alessan, engraving by Mochetti, 19th century.

Alessan. Mochetti inc.

Tippoo-Saib.

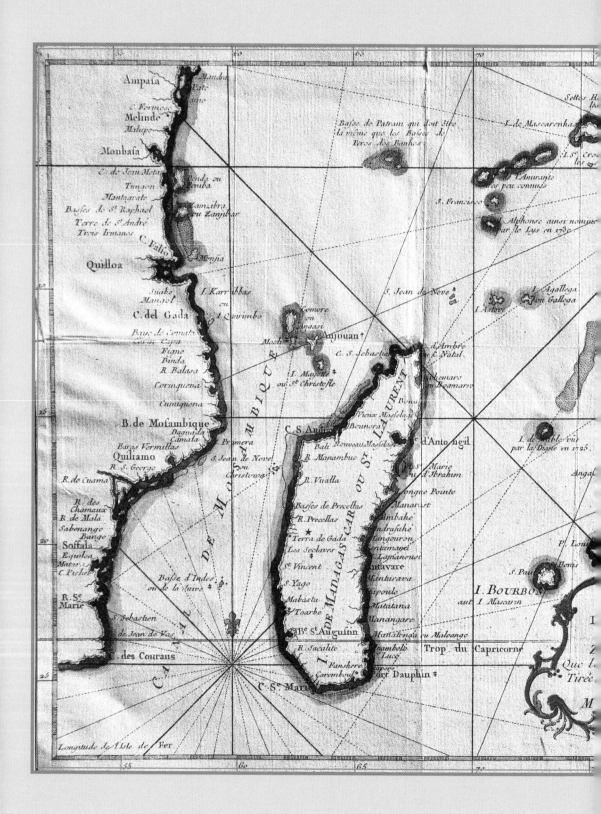

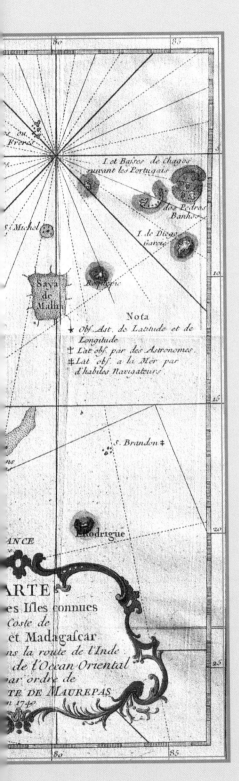

ISLE DE FRANCE: PORT OF CALL AND SAFE HAVEN

Some Famous French Visitors to Isle de France

- *Marquis Joseph Dupleix*
- *Jean-Baptiste d'Après de Mannevillette*
- *Abbot Nicolas de La Caille*
- *Jacques-Henri Bernardin de Saint-Pierre*
- *Count Louis Antoine de Bougainville*
- *Philibert Commerson*
- *Jean-François Galaup, Count de Lapérouse*
- *Pierre André de Suffren*
- *Viscount Paul de Barras*
- *Nicolas Baudin*
- *Jacques Gérard Milbert*
- *Jean-Baptiste Bory de Saint-Vincent*

The Corsairs' War in the Indian Ocean

- *Robert Surcouf*

Map drawn in 1740 by order of the
Count de Maurepas, Minister for
the Navy of Louis XV from 1723
to 1749.

*Extracted from Histoire Générale des
Voyages by Antoine-Francois Prévost,
1746.*

Located at the heart of the "Spice Route", Isle de France was, during the 18th century, the essential port of call for the vessels of the Compagnie des Indes. After their long and difficult navigation from Lorient or Saint-Malo, these ships could very safely put into port at Port-Louis before heading for Pondicherry. A pleasant port of call for passing travellers, the island later became the favourite port of call in that part of the world. Indeed, the long sea voyages were far from restful for travellers of that time. The on-board living conditions in confined spaces, in addition to the awful sanitation and weather hazards, exhausted the crews and put the ships under great stress. Moreover, the men could not rely on a healthy diet for sustenance, given the difficulties of preserving food properly; fresh meat, consisting of a few goats, pigs and chicken, was very quickly consumed owing to lack of storage space on board. They then had to fall back on tiresome salted meats, and on stocks of biscuits, which were often spoilt. Fresh water, poorly stored in wooden casks, quickly went foul, and thirst became an acute problem. On top of all this, the lack of vegetables and fresh fruit caused vitamin deficiencies; scurvy was a real scourge on all ships at the time.

The ships, being ill-equipped to resist the continuous onslaughts of bad weather over such long distances, quickly found themselves in very poor condition. Provisional repairs had to be carried out so that the vessels could make it to the next port of call. Moreover, a voyage to India involved rounding the Cape of Good Hope, with its frequent storms. And if the favourable southern monsoon season (between April and October) was missed, the ships would not escape the fearful storms in that region. Two months of navigation was sometimes enough for a ship fall to pieces, and it became absolutely necessary to stop in a safe harbour.

Isle de France was, therefore, most welcome after weathering the Cape. Crews and ships were certain of finding at Port-Louis whatever needed to be replenished. While the exhausted men recuperated and the ships, safely sheltered in the harbour, underwent repairs, the sick were taken to the hospital at Port-Louis, where they were given large helpings of tortoise broth, the miracle cure of those times, which soon restored them to health. Supplies of fresh wood and water were then stocked up before the ships set sail again, bound for the Coromandel coast.

This was also a major era of exploration and important scientific discoveries. Many expeditions set sail across the Indian Ocean and the southern Pacific not only in search of new territories, but also with the aim of studying the flora and fauna of distant lands, as well as the mores of primitive peoples. Scientist, geographers, artists and navigators pooled their knowledge and talents to serve the advancement of the sciences. Many

The areca tree was imported from India to Isle de France by the botanist Jean-Baptiste Fusée-Aublet, who lived on the island from 1752 to 1761.
Drawing by T Descourtilz, engraving by Pérée, c. 1845.

of these expeditions found Isle de France to be a port of call which proved as pleasant as it was welcoming.

During the 18th century, this small territory witnessed the passages or the sojourns of some great Frenchmen who, each in his own way, have contributed to the fame of France: Gentil de la Galaissière, astronomer; Marion-Dufresnes et Crozet, navigator and discoverer of several islands; Pierre Sonnerat, naturalist (and relation of Pierre Poivre); Abbot Rochon, astronomer and physician; Kerguelen-Tremadec, explorer; Pingré, astronomer; Surville, explorer; Péron, sailor and traveller; and naturalist Aubert Dupetit-Thouars. Others, even more famous, included Dupleix, d'Après de Mannevillette, Abbot de La Caille, Bernardin de Saint-Pierre, Bougainville, Lapérouse, Suffren, Baudin, Milbert and Bory de Saint-Vincent.

SOME FAMOUS FRENCH VISITORS TO ISLE DE FRANCE

Marquis Joseph François Dupleix (5 April–27 April 1722; 25 November 1754–mid-January 1755)

Isle de France was only a stopover for Dupleix, whose brilliant destiny played out on the Indian continent. Memories of him, however, remain linked to those of Mahé de La Bourdonnais on account of the disastrous conflict between both men during the Madras affair in 1746. However, this unfortunate affair must not cause us to overlook this figure's dazzling career. Dupleix is a name which resounds in the colonial history of France and immediately brings to mind a glorious record. Dupleix truly remains memorable as the great conqueror of India, a genius at strategy and a subtle politician, who, through diplomacy, became a nabob and whom the Indians respectfully called "Your Divinity". He became a nabob[24] in order to win the trust of the Indian princes, and thus won for France a wealthy empire in India.

However, the hagiography of his character has been queried by some historians, who only wished to see him as a merchant of the Compagnie des Indes; a skilful trader certainly, very self-confident and well organised, conducting the company's affairs as skilfully as his own. In fact, Dupleix was the worthy son of his father, who was a canny financier. In this particular area, Dupleix met expectations: as Director of the company's trading post at Chandernagor for eleven years, he conducted its commercial operations in a masterly fashion.

Thanks to his tireless energy and initiative, but even more so to his acute business sense, he managed to quickly develop this post's trading activities and regularly dispatched to the port of Lorient rich cargoes of

After 32 years in the service of the Compagnie des Indes, this great figure of French colonialism ended his life in disgrace, dropped by the Versailles Cabinet.
Drawing by Sergent, engraving by Mme de Cernel, 1789.

JOSEPH-FRANÇOIS, MARQUIS DUPLEIX

Commandeur de l'Ordre Royal et Milit.^{re} de St Louis, Commandant Général des Établisemens françois dans l'Inde, Gouv.^r pour le Roy des Ville et fort de Pondichery; né à Landrecy en 1697; mort à Paris le 11 9bre 1763.

goods, which were successfully sold. This trade, which he spread subsequently to Bengal and its surroundings, substantially increased the company's business turnover.

Appointed in January 1742 to the post of Governor of Pondicherry, a position which he was to occupy for 12 years, Dupleix was thus able to demonstrate that he was not only a skilled trader, but also an excellent strategist and a skilful politician.

His military skills soon became obvious when faced with Admiral Boscawen's fleet. After an attempt to attack Isle de France, which had been repulsed thanks to a ruse of Governor David and Baron Grant, Commander of the region of Plaines Wilhems, the English fleet had withdrawn to the Coromandel coast. On 20 August 1748, Boscawen decided to besiege Pondicherry, at the head of his 19 ships and 6,000 men.

Dupleix, who was personally in charge of the defence operations, assisted by the Marquis de Bussy, was able to resist brilliantly. His energy, reinforced by his determination and a clever strategy, soon defeated the English, who surrendered in October after a siege of nearly two months. This marked the beginning of a glorious period for the Governor of Pondicherry, who was awarded the Cross of Saint-Louis for this notable deed, as well as given the title of Marquis. Now invested with many privileges as well as almost unlimited powers, Dupleix was to nurture great ambitions from then on. This is when his gift for politics became clear; aware of the influence he could exert on the Indian potentates by taking advantage of their rivalries concerning the sharing of the Moghul empire, he conceived a plan for building an empire for France in India. With the assistance of his wife, Jeanne Albert[25], his first strategy was to ally himself, in 1750, with Princes Mousafer Jang and Chanda Sahib against the formidable troops of the powerful nabob, Anwar ud Din. This alliance led to the victory of Ambour, thanks to which these two princes respectively became "Soubab" of Deccan and Nabob of Carnat. The subsequent defeat of Naser Jang and his strong army brought Dupleix to the peak of his fame, wealth and power in India.

Thus it came about that, dressed as a Moghul dignitary, during a lavish ceremony, Dupleix received from the great Prince Salabet Jang the title of "Lieutenant-General for South Deccan and Carnatic", together with a mansabdar of 7,000 horses and the permission to display a special fish, the "mahemaraleb", on his standard. That title, one of the highest distinctions of the Moghul Empire, gave him the right to be preceded by 12 elephants, horsemen and peons during his official trips. He also had the honour of receiving from Mousafer Jang a headdress, belt and a small shield, as well

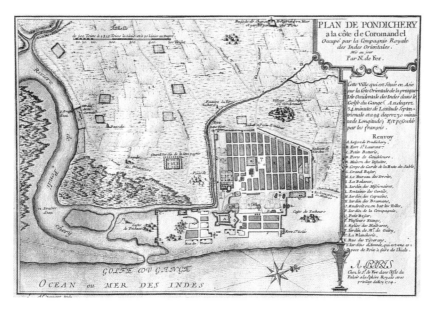

PLAN DE PONDICHERY
a la côte de Coromandel
Occupé par la Compagnie Royale
des Indes Orientales.
Mis au jour
Par N. de Fer.

OPPOSITE (FROM TOP):
Indian soldier made prisoner of
the English;
officer of the English army;
officer of Tipu Sultan's army;
soldier of the English army.

LEFT: Plan of Pondicherry on the
Coromandel coast.
Drawn by N de Fer, 1704.

BELOW (FROM TOP):
Warrior of the Marathi calvary;
warrior of the Rajput cavalry.

as a sword and dagger which had been given by Aurengzeb, the Grand Mughal, to the Nizam ul Mulk.

However, faced with the rise of French influence in India, the famous Englishmen, Colonel Robert Clive, Captain Stringer Lawrence, and Thomas Saunders, Governor of Madras, unceasingly harassed the French in the Carnatic region, by means of alliances with other princes of the region. This war of nerves was successful, and soon came the major defeats of the French at Trichinopoly and Srirangam.

Dupleix henceforth became entangled in endless conflicts; riots followed fights, and fights led to battles. His personal initiatives soon went against the interests of the Compagnie des Indes. The latter, finding itself drawn against its will into a colonial adventure with much wider implications than its own trading policy, was not prepared to support military campaigns which were undertaken without its consent, and which, moreover brought the company no tangible gains. It therefore decided to put an end to a situation which was threatening to lead it to certain ruin within a short span of time. Dupleix, however, ignored the order to put an end to hostilities, and persisted in the attempt to fulfil his political vision. He was accused of having overstepped his bounds and depleting the funds which had been entrusted to him, not only in expensive and fruitless wars, but also in a luxurious way of life, which, while intended to dazzle the Indian Princes, was somewhat lacking in discretion. Trapped by his own ambitions, he was dismissed from his post in 1754.

RIGHT: A nabob rides in a palanquin.
Drawing by P. Sonnerat, engraving by Poisson, from Voyage aux Indes Orientales et à la Chine (1774–1781).

OPPOSITE: Major General Lord Robert Clive, 1st Baron Clive of Plassey (1725–1774). Clive, who had been in Madras since 1744 as a simple clerk in the civil service, was in the city when Mahé de La Bourdonnais's squadron started its bombardment. Madras surrendered after several days, on 21 September 1746. Following his brave conduct during the siege, Clive was appointed ensign in the British armed forces. From then on, his career in India went from strength to strength. During the periods 1746–1753, 1755–1760 and 1765–1767, Clive became a key figure in the creation of British India. Clive's celebrity was at its height when, on 23 June 1757 at Plassey (near Kolkata), he and his troops defeated the troops of Suraj-ud-Daula, the ruler of Bengal, who was supported by French forces. With Warren Hastings, Clive established the military and political supremacy of the East India Company in South India and Bengal. In 1765, he obtained from the Great Mughal Shah Alam II a firman granting to the East India Company sovereignty of Bengal, Bihar and Orissa. This deed, together with two others obtained for the Carnatic and Deccan regions, made the East India Company rulers of India.
Engraved by WT Mote from the original painting in Kolkata. Published by Harding & Lepart, London 1836.

He returned to France in June 1755 onboard the *Duc d'Orléans*, after a stay of nearly two months at Isle of France. He landed at Lorient, with his luggage full of splendid riches, but in a rather more precarious financial situation. Discredited in the eyes of the company in spite of the numerous memoranda he wrote in his defence and tracked by a horde of creditors, the glorious Nabob Bahadour Zafer Jang ended his days in total oblivion. This was the ultimate irony for the man who had tried by every means to discredit his rival, Mahé de La Bourdonnais, by accusing him of embezzlement! Bernardin de Saint-Pierre, who praised the latter in the preface to one of the editions of *Paul et Virginie*, remarked: "Joseph Dupleix, his rival for fame and glory in India, and the most cruel of his persecutors, died shortly after him, having, by a reversal of fortune, experienced a similar fate in the last years of his life."

That ambitious man, who had reached the heights of success, had begun his career as a mere adviser to the Compagnie des Indes. Born at Landrecies in the north, where his father was a farmer general, he spent his whole youth in Britanny, at Brest and Morlaix. He was educated by the Jesuits at Quimper up to 1713, displaying a marked love of the sciences but also of art and poetry. However, Mr Dupleix senior, a practical and thrifty man, wished at all costs to turn his son into a merchant, the only profession which, according to him, would provide him with the means of acquiring an honourable fortune. In 1715, he made the young Dupleix set sail on a ship of the Compagnie de Saint-Malo. The young man made several voyages to India and America, acquiring a sound knowledge of trade and seamanship. Through his father, a major shareholder of the Compagnie des Indes, he was appointed by the company to the post of sixth member

of the Conseil Supérieur[26] War Commissioner at Pondicherry. He was then 25 years old.

Dupleix left the small island of Groix, off the coast of Lorient, on board the *Atalante*, on the same ship as the Chevalier Denis Denyon. The latter was on his way to Isle de France to take up a momentous position: he was to become the first French governor of the very new colony. A small contingent of men and women, mostly from Brittany, travelled with him onboard the *Diane*, sailing along with the *Atalante*. These were to be the inhabitants of Isle de France. A commissioner, two missionaries and a company of Swiss guards completed the group of first settlers. The voyage was very uncomfortable. The ships suffered constant battering from the bad weather which plagued the two frigates during the whole crossing.

After a few days' rest, these valiant pioneers set up the first facilities, with the help of Dupleix. However, his stay in the island lasted only for a little more than three weeks. On 27 April, he took to sea again, bound for Pondicherry, to take up his new responsibilities. A few years later, in June 1729, he bought a concession at Isle de France, in the region named "les Trois-Îlots", which he subsequently resold to Mr Routier de Grandval.

It was only after his 32-year career in India that Dupleix again landed on Isle de France, when he stopped over in 1754 on his way to Lorient. He had just been dismissed from his post of Governor of Pondicherry, and replaced by Mr Godeheu de Zaimont. When he had first left the little island in 1722 after spending a few weeks there, he was only 25 and looking forward to a very promising future. He was now coming back in disgrace, having lost all his glory... Dupleix was accompanied by his wife and a retinue of 60. They remained for a little over a month on Isle de France, as guests of Messrs de Rostaing and Hermans at Pamplemousses. On 3 December, the wife of his nephew, Mr de Kerjean, gave birth to a son. Dupleix was invited to be his godfather, and the christening was held at Pamplemousses, in the church of Saint-François.

Jean-Baptiste d'Après de Mannevillette (May 1751–early 1752)

A ship's captain of the Compagnie des Indes, d'Après de Mannevillette was a famous cartographer. He had already carried out several missions in the Indian Ocean in order to map of its topography. He arrived at Isle de France in May 1751, in command of the *Glorieux*. The Abbot de La Caille was on board up to the Cape of Good Hope, where he disembarked on a mission of scientific exploration. The Compagnie des Indes had given d'Après de Mannevillette the responsibility of mapping the exact position of Isle de France, and drawing up its precise outline. His meticulous calculations led him to spot a mistake of nearly nine leagues in the length of the island and, accordingly, he drew up a new map. These observations, subsequently checked by Abbot de La Caille, were found to be rigorously exact. D'Après de Mannevillette published the findings of his mapping works in *Le Neptune Oriental*, which later added a supplement: *Instructions sur la navigation des Indes Orientales et de la Chine*. This massive, well-documented work later proved a most useful guide for the French Navy.

D'Après de Mannevillette returned to France in July 1752, and was made a member of the Royal Academy of the Navy. In 1762, he became director of the map registration office at Lorient. D'Après de Mannevillette was one of the most reputed French cartographers of the 18th century.

Nicolas Louis de La Caille (April 1753–January 1754)

Interest in science during the Enlightenment led to the launch of many experimental expeditions throughout the world in a bid to increase knowledge. Thus, the Académie des Sciences of Paris undertook a project to install an observatory in the southern hemisphere in order to complete the celestial chart drawn up in 1677 by the famous English astronomer, Edmund Halley. The colony of the Cape of Good Hope was then chosen, not only for its ideal geographical position, but also because it had adequate facilities to assist such a venture. The task of preparing the expedition was entrusted to the Abbot de La Caille, one of the most brilliant astronomers and mathematicians of the time.

Strange indeed was the path taken by this cleric, who wore the habit of his calling but did not take on its usual responsibilities. Originally set on a priestly career, he first studied philosophy and, subsequently, theology. However, having come across the *Elements* of Euclid, Abbot de La Caille became passionate about mathematics and decided to devote himself entirely to that subject. Attached as an apprentice to the Observatory of the famous astronomers Cassini and Maraldi, he displayed exceptional gifts in that field. In 1738, he was given the task of drawing a topographic survey of the French coasts for the purposes of navigation, a mission which he accomplished with remarkable precision. He also drew a meridian line from Perpignan to Dunkirk, which earned him a nomination to the Académie Royale des Sciences in the field of Astronomy in 1741. He was then 28 years old. He was at the same time appointed Chair of Mathematics at the Collège Mazarin, where he set up an observatory for his own use: he spent most of his time there, improving his knowledge of astronomy and checking the calculations of ancient astronomers. After publishing the *Leçons Élémentaires de Mathématiques, d'Astronomie, de Mécanique et d'Optique*, Abbot de La Caille published the first part of his *Éphémérides* in 1746, as well as a theory about comets. Wishing to produce a treatise on astronomy for the southern hemisphere, a subject which had not been covered in any depth up to then, he expressed his intention of going to the Cape of Good Hope, and obtained the support of the Académie des Sciences for this project.

Abbot de La Caille set sail from Lorient on 21 November 1750 on board the *Glorieux*, which was under the command of d'Après de Mannevillette, and reached the Cape in April 1751 after stopping over in Brazil for a month. The Dutch East India Company provided him with men and equipment, and Abbot de La Caille undertook to build a rudimentary laboratory for his task. After just one year of observation, the astronomer drew up a catalogue in which the positions of 10,000 stars were marked (Halley's catalogue of 1677 only identified the positions of 550 stars). Abbot de La Caille also calculated the exact dimensions of the moon and of the planets, and also figured out the longitude of the Cape, a piece of data most useful to the Navy.

Abbot de La Caille's scientific turn of mind made him curious about everything, and, during his stay at the Cape, he did not fail to also show an

ABOVE : Abbot Nicolas Louis de La Caille. After a year of observation at the Cape, Abbot de La Caille drew up a catalogue of 10,000 stars, 9,450 more than the catalogue of the famous astronomer Edmund Halley.
After a painting by Ms Lejeunneux, engraving by Ms Devaux.

OPPOSITE : Hottentot woman.
From Voyage en Afrique, William Burchell *(1782–1863). Drawing by L Mansard, engraving by Choubard, 19th century.*

interest in natural history. He regularly sent many plant specimens to the Jardin du Roi (present-day Jardin des Plantes), as well as various collections of animal species. Driven by his passion for discovery, he showed unfailing dynamism and energy, refusing to be put off by any obstacle.

Abbot de La Caille went on scientific expeditions through the African bush with two huge chariots; one of them, hauled by 12 horses, was laden with beds, tents and food supplies, while the other, containing all his scientific equipment, was drawn by 10 oxen – a real feat at the time! However, in such a territory, the unorthodox nature of his convoy led him to request that he should be accompanied by an escort, in case he should be taken for some evil spirit...

In April 1753, Abbot de La Caille left for Isle de France on board the *Puisieulx*, with a mission to carry out a geodesic survey of the island. Governor Bouvet de Lozier provided him with seven soldiers to help protect him from attacks by runaway slaves. He was also given nine porters, as well as all the equipment necessary for such an expedition, including a pirogue (a canoe) to help him reach the small offshore islands. During his journey around the island, he was assisted by Mr Godin, an engineer, and Mr d'Esny, after whom the coastal region south of Mahébourg, Pointe d'Esny, was named. After two months of hard work, the Abbot de La Caille had collected all the necessary data which he would need later to draw an accurate map of the island, including its topography and outline. When Nicolas Bellin subsequently drew his own map, he used the famous astronomer's data.

The Abbot de La Caille remained for another nine months on the island, during which time he carried out observations on the island's relief, its fauna, its flora, as well as the crops to be found there. These observations, prefaced by a historical summary, are to be found in his *Journal Historique*, published in 1776.

After a short visit to the island of Bourbon, the astronomer returned to France on board the *Achille* in January 1754. In 1757, he published all the results of his work at the Cape, in *Astronomiæ Fundamenta*, a colossal piece of work which was to remain for a long time the main reference in the area of astronomy. This work was followed, in 1758, by a supplement containing solar tables. To this day, his memory remains linked to a small creek, not far from Souillac, called the Gris-Gris, named after his dog, a faithful member of his expedition. The Abbot de La Caille was Professor of Mathematics at the Collège Mazarin, member of Académie Royale des Sciences of France, of the science academies of Prussia and Sweden and of the Institute of Bologna.

Jacques-Henri Bernardin de Saint-Pierre (1768–1770)

Jacques-Henri Bernardin de Saint-Pierre was born on 19 January 1737 at Le Havre, where his father, Nicolas de Saint-Pierre was manager of the postal services. Nicolas pretended to belong to the aristocracy by claiming a family relationship with Eustache de Saint-Pierre, the famous mayor of Calais, who, with a few other burghers, managed to save that city after the siege of Calais by the English in 1347, by giving themselves up as prisoners. Thus, during an age in which high birth was a guarantee of consideration as well as the key to social success, this ruse led him to hope that his three sons would have brilliant futures. His youngest son, Bernardin, was the only one to fulfil this dream, thanks to a spectacular rise in the literary world. This success came so late, however, that the poor man did not live to see it. It was not until he was 50 years old that Bernardin de Saint-Pierre, after an unstable and eventful life, knew fame and fortune thanks to his famous novel *Paul et Virginie*, published in 1788. This tropical pastoral tale, somewhat neglected today, remains an undoubted literary masterpiece of its time, and made its author the fore-runner of the Romantics. This work was conceived and ripened in the exotic setting of Isle de France, to which fate had brought the future writer in 1768. It embodies, in fact, the ideas dear to Bernardin of the need for man to live "according to nature and virtue", the only conditions capable of bringing happiness in this world. His novel was the fruit of his long meditations about the ideal society, a subject which constantly troubled him during his youth.

Dreams of Glory

In addition to his very passionate nature, Bernardin possessed a most fertile imagination. Instructive texts, including the tale of the adventures of Robinson Crusoe, as well as the many hagiographies which he so enjoyed, contributed, since childhood, to the mind of this dreamer the concept of utopia which turned into a real obsession: the creation of a republic which would welcome all the wretched people of the world, regulated by "the laws of justice and liberty", and in which he would, of course, be the leader. His location of choice for this future Eden was none other than the shores of the Aral Sea in Russia! Being convinced of what the future held in store for him – the destiny of a hero and having, moreover, a tranquil faith in the powers of Providence, which were undeniable, according to him, he had no doubt about the success of this immense project. Thus armed with such candid optimism and coupled with a strong wish to become famous, he set out on a life of wandering, and

Bernardin de Saint-Pierre preached of the need for man to live "according to nature and virtue", the only conditions able to ensure happiness on this earth, according to him.
Drawing of Girodet-Trioson, engraving by Wedywood, 1829.

met with numerous encounters, which by themselves would have added up to a tale of adventure. For this royal engineer, before landing on the shores of Isle de France on a beautiful day of July 1768, faced some tribulations, and these are mentioned here to throw light on this curious character.

A Bold Adventurer

His time as a student was relatively short. After his training at the College of Rouen, he obtained, at the age of 20, a diploma in mathematics which allowed him to join the École des Ponts-et-Chaussées. However, because this institution had to close down for financial reasons, Bernardin was unable to complete his engineering studies and found himself without a qualification. He managed, by cunning means, it is said, to obtain an accreditation and enrolled as Officer-Engineer in the Rhine Army during the Seven Years' War.

Bernardin left for Dusseldorf in 1760. The campaign, which he had looked forward to, held some surprises for him. Having in mind idyllic images of heroes clothed in glory, he was horrified to discover the other side of the picture. He was deeply shocked by war, with its stream of horrors and pain. On the other hand, having an irritable and quarrelsome disposition, he found the rigours of the army unbearable, and was continually in conflict with his fellows and superiors, who were quick to suspend him and send him back to France. On his return to Paris, in March 1761, he found himself penniless and without any prospects. He came to join, as engineer-geographer, a group of engineer officers despatched to Malta to defend its Order against the Turks. However, as he had no documents with him to prove his status, he was taken for a schemer by the officers, who did not welcome him in their midst. Despised and ridiculed, he stayed wretchedly on the island before returning to Marseilles on a Danish ship, which, on top of everything else, nearly sank with all hands on board during a terrible storm.

After this unfortunate experience in Malta, Bernardin returned to Paris poorer than ever. The little money he had left was soon spent. He was soon on the brink of destitution. He desperately tried to earn a living by giving some tuition in mathematics, but could not earn enough to live decently.

Having withdrawn into miserable solitude, he began to dream of a better life. His old fantasy of creating a colony of happy people in Russia resurfaced. He would certainly need funds. Regardless, with the help of Providence, he would raise the money! Weren't perseverance and boldness needed to obtain fame and glory? He was certainly not lacking in these two qualities and so pursued his idea with dogged determination.

From then on, he left no stone unturned in pursuit of the fulfilment of this great quest, with the ultimate objective of charming Catherine II of Russia with his marvellous project. First step: Holland. At Amsterdam, he met Mustel, a French journalist who offered him a simple way to happiness: he offered Bernardin the hand of his sister-in-law and a job at 1,000 écus as editor of his newspaper. But, driven by his dreams and wishing to remain master of his own fate, Bernardin turned down that offer.

After borrowing money from Mustel, Bernardin went on to Lubeck, where the town's commander, the Chevalier de Chazot, lent him 200 pounds so that he could proceed to Saint Petersburg. De Chazot recommended him to his father-in-law, Mr Torelli, who was on his way to court, to which he had been appointed Director of the Academy of Arts. As soon as he arrived, Torelli let him down, and Bernardin de Saint-Pierre was stranded once again. There he was, alone in a foreign city, and his only resource being a tiny sum of money on which he could barely manage to live for a few weeks. But "Providence was watching", it would seem, because he came across a new saviour in Mr Duval, a citizen of Geneva who, by the strangest of coincidences, happened to be a court jeweller. The two men became friendly. Bernardin informed his friend of his project, and the latter did not hesitate to fund his trip to Moscow.

Duval also recommended Bernardin to General du Bosquet, who commissioned him as sub-lieutenant in the engineers' corps, and offered him an engineering diploma. Bernardin was then 24. He was thus decked out in the fine uniform of the Russian engineers when he made his debut at court, introduced by Mr de Villebois, Grand Master of the Artillery Corps.

Bernardin had prepared a memorandum on his colony project[27], most carefully wrought in order to capture the attention of the Empress, and with this in hand, he awaited his presentation before Catherine the Great. When her arrival was announced and she appeared in all her majesty amid the grandeur of the court, he rather lost his nerve, but nonetheless managed to rise to the occasion. He made an excellent impression on the Empress, who enjoyed his conversation, and, moreover, was far from impervious to his charms. The encounter was so brief, however, that in the rush of the moment, Bernardin hardly had time to describe his plans. However, the imperial attention, which he had the rare honour of being gratified, did not fail to attract a cohort of courtiers to him. He was flattered from all sides and was even given to understand that he might easily become the rival of Prince Orlov, Catherine II's favourite at the time. Disgusted by all these intrigues and lies, Bernardin decided to leave the court, not without having submitted his famous memorandum to the attention of Prince Orlov, never

doubting that the latter would be interested in his fabulous idea. To his great disappointment, the Prince did not deign to open the document.

With the commission of Engineer-Captain having been bestowed on him by the office of the Empress, Bernardin accompanied General Bosquet to Finland on a military mission. Here, he received another offer of marriage. This time it concerned Mademoiselle de la Tour, the General's niece. He courteously declined the offer, preferring once more to pursue his dream of fame, even if it meant facing the uncertain hazards of new adventures rather than living an anonymously quiet life, albeit secure in the knowledge that he would no longer have to earn his keep. He had by then, spent four years on in Russian territory, without succeeding in giving meaning to his life.

Stormy Love Affairs

New adventures awaited him in Warsaw. Received in the most brilliant salons, he met a Polish princess, Marie Miesnik, whose beauty dazzled him. It was love at first sight for the two young people. However, after a year of tender idyll, the fairy tale vanished into thin air: the beautiful princess was not to marry a Prince Charming of such modest condition. Noblesse oblige.

The ordeal was hard for Bernardin and he decided to return to France. He stopped in Germany on the way and reached Dresden in 1765, where he was a guest of Count de Bellegarde. In order to drown his sorrows, he took long solitary walks each evening on the banks of the Elbe. There, he attracted the attention of a mysterious stranger who, one evening, sent her page to fetch him in her coach. Bernardin was driven to a magnificent palace, where he was met by a marvellous creature, dressed in her most beautiful finery, who gave him a king's welcome. There, in a splendid atmosphere of luxury and magnificence, the lucky chosen one enjoyed all the delights of Cythère in the company of his beauty... This incredible escapade lasted for 10 days, and left Bernardin with the strange impression of having lived through a dream. The "Venus" was none other than a famous courtesan, whose fortune had been made by a court grandee.

Bernardin soon left for Berlin and tried to enlist in the army of Frederick II, requesting the status of major, but without success. He then met the king's adviser, Mr Taubenheim, who became a great friend of his. He even wished to marry him Taubenheim's daughter, Virginie, a graceful 15-year-old beauty whose virginal charm moved the Engineer-Captain to some degree. Was it her freshness and gaiety which later inspired him when he described the candid character of his novel's famous heroine? That is possible, but, meanwhile, the memory of his Polish princess was still too

Arch symbol of exoticism, the banana tree (*Musa paradica*) is a native of Ceylon, of Southeast Asia and the Philippines.
Drawing by C Vauthier, engraving by Schmelz, circa 1850.

raw to let him think of a new love. Having heard that his father had died, Bernardin planned to return to France in order to collect his share of the inheritance and he bade farewell to his host in April 1765.

In Pursuit of Utopia

After a short pilgrimage to Le Havre to revisit the places associated with his childhood, Bernardin returned to Paris and rented a room in the house of a priest at Ville-d'Avray. There, Bernardin wrote his travel memoirs, with which he subsequently tried to interest the Minister for Foreign Affairs, Mr de la Roche, but his many attempts remained fruitless.

Somewhat discouraged, he then thought of trying his luck in the colonies, and sought out the Baron de Breteuil, whose guest he had been in Saint Petersburg. The latter supplied him with an "engineering commission" for Isle de France and, remembering his desire to found a colony on the shores of the Aral Sea, offered him, under an oath of secrecy, an important mission to Madagascar. The idea was not only to rebuild the walls of Fort Dauphin, the painful vestiges of a first attempt at colonisation, but, chiefly, to pacify the small Malagasy tribes that were forever fighting one another. This was not to be done by violent means, but by giving an example of wisdom and virtue. Having become thus civilised, Madagascar would, at last, belong to France. In other words, they were relying on his philosophy to lay the foundations of a colony on that island. He thought his dream was coming true. The long-awaited opportunity was presenting itself at last.

Bubbling over with enthusiasm for this happy prospect, which went beyond his expectations, Bernardin joyfully accepted this heaven-sent mission. He was introduced to the person responsible for the project, Count de Maudave, a settler from Isle de France. From then on, the future administrator went to work enthusiastically to prepare the plans for his wonderful colony. He devised many schemes in the hope of leading these tribes to enlightenment so that they could discover the practice of virtue, the only state of being likely to produce happiness, according to Bernardin. To that end, he spent a fortune on expensive books on all the sciences in order to fulfil the needs of that noble cause.

When the great day arrived at last, Bernardin, accompanied by his dog "Favori", embarked at Lorient onboard the *Marquis de Castries*, which set sail on 18 February 1768. However, Bernardin de Saint-Pierre was to disengage himself from the project during the journey. It seems that a quarrel with Count de Maudave lay at the root of this sudden decision. The details of the quarrel remain unclear, but there are two versions of it. According to his biographer, Aimé Martin, Bernardin discovered during the voyage the whole truth about the projects of that settlement at Madagascar: in addition to the attempt at colonisation, Count de Maudave had, among other prospects, the intention of deriving benefits from the slave trade. It is thought that, outraged by this news, Bernardin showed his anger at not having been informed earlier of this particular aspect of the enterprise, and refused to join such a project which was so alien to his concept of universal happiness. He therefore decided to disembark at Isle de France.

However, according to another version which might be more compatible with Bernardin's temperamental personality, the tiff with Count de Maudave originated with an incident which Bernardin took to very badly. It must be stressed that Bernardin de Saint-Pierre was not easy to get along with. His over-sensitive and irritable temperament, made worse by the stresses of communal life in such a confined space as that of a ship, made him the ideal scapegoat on board, and jokes were often made at his expense. The incident involved a demonstration of physics which was conducted on the bridge following the mentioning in front of Bernardin of this fact: that the sun's rays, when caught through a lens, could set fire to any inflammable object, even at a distance. The example of the Roman fleet destroyed by Archimedes by this means was then quoted. Despite his status as an engineer, Bernardin was ignorant enough – and also pretentious enough – to scoff at this and asked Maudave to prove it to him. The latter duly obliged and deposited a little gunpowder in Bernardin's palm, took a lens, and, sardonically launched into the experiment which, of course, had the desired effect, causing the naive engineer to let out a yelp in pain. It was indeed a burning affront! "Ashamed and embarassed", Bernardin hardly had time to vow that "they wouldn't catch him out again", and amid the laughter of all those present, bolted to his cabin. Subsequently, Bernardin declared that he had not yet received his engineer's commission[28], and with this, he informed Count de Maudave that he did not intend to travel with him to Madagascar.

Isle de France, a Welcoming Land

The last stage of the voyage took place under very tough conditions. The *Marquis de Castries* had suffered serious damage during the crossing of the Mozambique Canal, where it had run into a storm which lasted for more than 24 hours. Moreover, an epidemic of scurvy broke out on board, claiming the lives of more than 10 victims. The rest of the crew was in a pitiful state. Later, in his *Voyage à l'Isle de France*, Bernardin would paint a terrifying picture of their arrival at Port-Louis on 14 July 1768: "[...] Imagine this stricken main mast, this ship with its flag at half-mast, firing

PAUL ET VIRGINIE DEMANDENT À UN HABITANT
LA GRÂCE DE SON ESCLAVE.

its cannon every minute, with some sailors looking like ghosts sitting on the deck, the hatches open and letting out a horrid stench, the steerage decks full of dying persons, the forecastles full of sick men who had been put outside in the sun and who died while they were talking to us [...]."

The Meeting with Pierre Poivre

As soon as Bernardin had landed, he went to meet Mr de Breuil, the island's Chief Engineer, who agreed to employ him. He then found lodgings in Port-Louis, in a small house where he occupied one room on the ground floor. The only furniture in this tiny cubbyhole were a chest of drawers, a hammock and some suitcases. That was where he studied the natural sciences in his spare time, under the obedient eye of his dog.

The Intendant of Isle de France at that time was Pierre Poivre, who, in collaboration with Governor Jean-Daniel Dumas, had been managing the affairs of the colony since 1767, when the island had come under royal administration. Bernardin knew about the Intendant's reputation and, from the very first meeting, the latter befriended the philosopher, whose intelligence and knowledge made a strong impression on him. His meeting with Poivre was indeed a turning point for him. He at last realised that his project of a colony founded on the principle of virtue was a mere utopia. The example of the Intendant gave him further proof that principles alone were not sufficient for governance. This man, although a fine person, had not managed, in spite of his careful administration, to establish order and harmony, even on such a small territory. One day, when Bernardin had presented to him his project for a colony, Poivre spoke these words, the wisdom of which had put a final stop to the engineer's mad dreams: "What you propose is impossible; to set up a perfect government, you would need a gathering of perfect men, of men like you, imbued with the same keenness to do good and, above all, with the will to be happy by the same means [...]. You must take society as it is today, with its corruption, its prejudices, and its independent spirit. They are tigers who must be turned into men; what charms will you use? [...] If there are but few men fit to speak the truth, do you think that there are many who are prepared to listen to it?"

Exploring the Island

In addition to these long philosophical conversations, Bernardin was also interested in botany, an area where the advice of the Intendant would be most useful. So he organised an expedition on foot around the island, with the aim of studying the tropical fauna and flora. To achieve this, he decided to follow the coast in order to survey and, at the same time, to discover the

An illustration from the novel *Paul et Virginie*.
Drawing by JM Moreau, engraving by JL Delignon, 18th century.

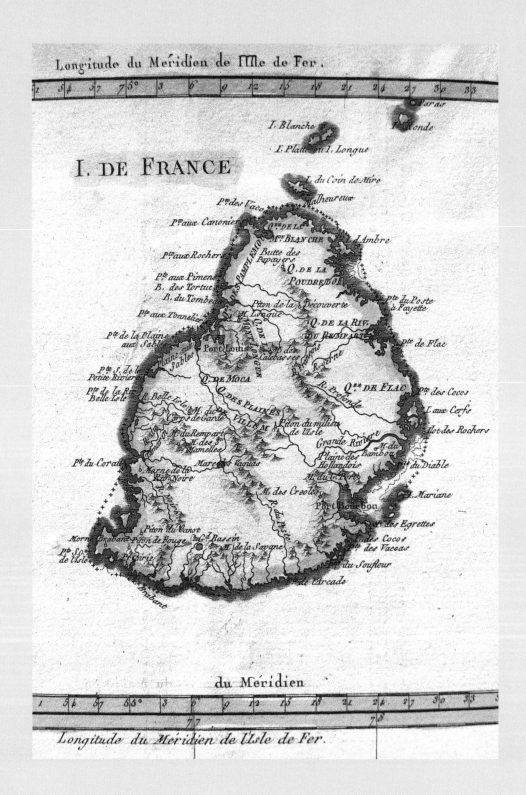

sites likely to provide strategic points for the defence of the island. With the help of the map drawn up in the past by the Abbot de La Caille and accompanied by a few porters as well as by his inseparable "Favori", he set off with his baggage through woods and rocky paths, forded rivers (on his porter's back) and climbed rocks under a scorching sun, stopping only in the late evening at the home of some remote settler, who then offered him a roof for the night. At dawn, the small troop set off again. Leaving from Port-Louis, he descended towards the south, past Tamarin, Le Morne and Souillac, then made his way to Le Chaland and Grand-Port, where he had the opportunity to observe a comet during three consecutive nights; he then went up the east coast via Flacq, passed through Poste Lafayette, Rivière-du-Rempart and at last reached Poudre d'Or. At that stage, he was compelled to leave the coast and make his way inland to Pamplemousses, the rest of the coast being arid and, moreover, without drinking water.

An account of this expedition can be found in his first book, *Voyage à l'Isle de France*, published in 1773, in which the author condemns the practice of slavery, denouncing its abuses. This deplorable institution existed in the colonies at that time, as well as in many countries. But compared to the inhuman cruelty that was practised on certain islands, the slaves at Isle de France were comparatively well-treated[29] and lived on good terms with the settlers and their families. Mahé de La Bourdonnais had trained them in various trades and created a constabulary from among them for the purpose of maintaining order in the colony. Pierre Poivre, for his part, had made some regulations in order to prevent certain abuses. There were certainly some bad masters, this cannot be denied, but it seemed that Bernardin de Saint-Pierre went out of his way to paint a picture darker than reality. The abuses which could be deplored were those committed against the "marrons", or runaway slaves. These escaped slaves, having fled to the forests and mountains, struck terror among the island's inhabitants. They regularly plundered and set fire to the plantations and did not hesitate to attempt to kill planters and their slaves. It was therefore necessary to take measures against these frequent attacks. These measures, however, were often cruel.

Be that as it may, the "marrons" drawn by Bernardin in his book, so kind to the two children lost in the forest, were too good to be true. In his book, he is hard on the settlers, whom he describes as rough and rapacious; he draws, to say the least, a disastrous picture of the society of Isle de France:

"They are totally insensible to everything that makes honest people happy. They have no taste for literature and the arts. Natural feelings are perverted. [...] Disorder reigns among all classes and has banished from that

Map of Isle de France drawn in 1782 by Mr Bonne, naval engineer and hydrographer.

131

island any love of society. [...] They are all disgruntled, all seeking to make their fortunes and leave as quickly as they can. Listening to them, each is planning to leave next year. Some have been saying this for 30 years."

There were, indeed, some inhabitants like these. They were adventurers of doubtful reputation who, having come to Isle de France in the hope of making their fortunes, were concentrated in the town of Port-Louis, where Governor Desroches had "a great deal of trouble" maintaining order among those "schemers" and "grabbers". One had to go to the regions of Pample-mousses, Flacq, or Grand-Port, Savanne and Black River, to find the "better class of people". In those peaceful and shady surroundings, settlers and their families made a living from the cultivation of their lands, far from the urban agitation of Port-Louis, where Bernardin found himself confined. The writer's somewhat arbitrary opinion was contradicted by that of the painter Milbert, who, while visiting Isle de France in 1801, fell under the spell of the wit and qualities of the Créoles:

"The Créoles add goodness to their other qualities of vivacity, eagerness, bravery; they like an independent life; their frankness is unequalled. [...] Their mind is naturally quick and penetrating. [...] many are well-educated, without ever having left their island."

Raymond d'Unienville too, in his book, *Hier Suffren*, refers to the level of culture of this refined society "where good manners are nurtured...". "They find time for the joys of the intellect. [...] Music is highly appreciated. The pianoforte can be heard during family evenings. [...] They keep up with the great trends of modern thought. On the bookshelves to be found in every dwelling, the works of Pascal and d'Aguesseau can be found alongside those of La Bruyère, Rousseau and Voltaire."

Bernardin also shared his thoughts on trade, agriculture and the defence of the island. The engineer finally raises doubts about the administration of Isle de France, and even of its very usefulness. He queries its status as a military base which, on account of the distance separating the island from the Indian Continent, requires, according to him, heavy surplus expenditure on maintenance. He was also shocked by the exorbitant sums needed to keep up the way of life of the colony, which, being incapable, according to him, of producing anything more than some meagre foodstuffs, depended entirely on the import of luxury goods: "I do not know of any other place on earth which spreads its needs so far. This colony imports its crockery from China, its linen and clothing from India, its slaves and cattle from Madagascar, some of its food from the Cape of Good Hope, its money from Cadix, and its administration from France." "[...] Of what earthly use is Isle de France? To grow coffee, and provide a stopping-place for our ships."

The unflattering picture which Bernardin de Saint-Pierre paints of Isle de France and the mores of its settlers might lead us to conclude that his memories of his stay in the island were rather bitter. That did not prevent him from thoroughly exploiting the exoticism and beauty of the island in his attempt to write a popular novel based on them, and of including in it, for the purposes of local colour, a couple of devoted slaves, though being himself so violently opposed to the practice of slavery. Even more paradoxical is the fact that *Voyage à l'Isle de France*, being presented in the descriptive style of a travel diary, displays none of the sensitivity of the future author of *Paul et Virginie*. Indeed, he observes nature through the dry eyes of the writer of a catalogue. He is content with drawing up an inventory, but describes none of its beauties, nor the emotions it might inspire. We cannot fail to notice that during his whole journey around the island, Bernardin never lingers to describe the slightest landscape. This indifference from a man who professed to be a lover of nature can only surprise us.

By contrast, Jacques Milbert, who, like Bernardin, made many trips to explore the island in 1801, was able to convey his sensitivity to the beauty which surrounded him. In his *Voyage Pittoresque à l'Isle de France*, he enthusiastically shares his emotions before a sunrise:

"The blue of the shadows, the shine of the rocks tinged with gold by the sun contrasted beautifully with the crimson of the clouds. He who has never seen the sun rise over our planet has missed a delicious source of emotion. The poet or artist who would scorn such a sight, should give up his pen or paintbrush for ever."

Was Bernardin de Saint-Pierre, who succeeded in moving generations of readers, capable of very deep emotions? We are led to ask ourselves that question when referring to some of his biographers, who agree that he was, above all, a selfish opportunist. However, whatever the man's faults, we must admit that his greatest talent was to skilfully use the resources of his pen to create a work whose sensitivity has moved millions of admirers. *Paul et Virginie*, in spite of the inevitable wrinkles it has collected in its two-century existence, continues to coax a tear in cottages all over the world.

Françoise Poivre, Bernardin's Muse?

Having landed at Isle de France by an unexpected turn of events, our Ponts-et-Chaussées engineer was not submerged with work in that faraway little island. His duties were light enough to allow him some leisure time, which he shared between his study of natural sciences and his visits to Monplaisir, Pierre Poivre's residence in the district of Pamplemousses. When the Intendant was held up by work, his young wife, intelligent and educated, proved a pleasant companion. Françoise Poivre was quite a beauty and the young engineer was not impervious to the charms of this 20-year-old. He courted her constantly, so much so that gossip spread. A regular correspondence began between them – the letters of the engineer, as well as those of Françoise, have been kept at the library of Le Havre among the author's archives. Judging by their number, it would seem that she quite enjoyed this correspondence and, while she did in some of her letters request him to stop writing, the tone of the requests, whatever some biographers may think, did not appear to be that of someone genuinely irritated at receiving the letters. Nevertheless, we are given to understand that Françoise Poivre was happily married and, while she may well have shown herself flattered by the attentions of this 30-year-old admirer, her intention, it would appear, was never to yield to the charms of the handsome Bernardin. However, the over-frequent visits of this suitor did finally end up annoying her husband, who broke up his friendship with the importunate man. Bernardin had to accept his fate. Withdrawing to his little house in Port-Louis, with his faithful "Favori" as his only companion, he began to find that time hung heavily on his hands. The Government granted him a small plot of land in a corner of the Champ de Mars, and he took pleasure in cultivating it himself, growing not only useful plants, but also a collection of rare species on which he lavished all his care. In spite of his passion for horticulture and his natural history studies, he did not forget the pretty Françoise and still sent her occasional notes. However, tired of a persistence which he was now finding to be in poor taste, Poivre then decided, in agreement with the new Governor, Desroches, that Bernardin be recalled to France. So, after a two-and-a-half-year stay at Isle de France, the latter left for good onboard the *Indien* in November 1770. Bernardin left behind his illusions and his dear "Favori", whom he had the sorrow of losing some time before his departure.

It is surprising, however, that this episode with Françoise Poivre was never mentioned by his most devoted biographer, Aimé Martin, who was also his secretary in Paris, and who usually waxed so eloquent about the events of his previous romances. It is true that, having subsequently married Bernardin's widow, Martin may have found it awkward that he should reveal the story of a failed courtship which would naturally have tarnished the image of the man for whom he otherwise had an apparently boundless admiration for. As for Bernardin himself, he never mentioned the Poivres in his *Voyage à l'Isle de France*. Why this silence, when he seemed to have so much admiration for the philosopher? Had his pride caused him to nurture a lasting grudge against the Intendant?

In any case, we can suppose that his love found expression through his famous novel. Even if the tender Virginie does not have the appearance of the beautiful Françoise Poivre, the passion she awoke in the young Paul, a passion painfully ended by the tragic death of the heroine, seemed to reflect the author's feelings.

The Origin of *Paul et Virginie*

As far as the novel itself is concerned, it must be remembered that certain events in the story are real. The wreck of the *Saint-Géran* did actually occur near Ile d'Ambre on 17 August 1744, while Mahé de La Bourdonnais was Governor of Isle de France. The shipwreck happened on the east coast of the island, 24 years before Bernardin de Saint-Pierre's arrival in the colony. Among the passengers on this ship were three young ladies, Jeanne-Hélène Niezen, Ms de Mallet and Ms Caillou. The last two were engaged to two of the ship's officers, Péramont and Longchamps de Montendre. Unlike the story told by the novel, the reason for their death during the shipwreck was not that they refused to take off their clothes at the request of a sailor in order to be able to swim ashore. According to the testimony of a survivor, they chose to stay on board with their fiancés, in the hope that they would all be rescued at dawn. The only character who refused to strip was the captain of the *Saint-Géran*, de Lamarre, whom one of his sailors tried to save at the risk of his own life, but who deemed it unseemly for someone of his status to reach the shore naked. Bernardin de Saint-Pierre simply merged the two anecdotes, attributing this modesty to the unfortunate Virginie. He succeeded in giving a sorrowful account of the famous scene where she "seeing that death was inevitable, placed one hand on her clothing, the other on her heart, lifted her eyes calmly to heaven, with the appearance of an angel ready to fly to the sky."

The Birth of a Writer

In June 1771, Bernardin reached Paris after a stop at the island of Bourbon, followed by another stop at the Cape of Good Hope. He had returned from Isle de France with a rich harvest of notes which he could use for his future writing. He was introduced to d'Alembert who found him an editor for his *Voyage à l'Isle de France*, and also introduced him to the literary salon of Louise de Lespinasse. There, he met the philosophers, with whose ideas he did not agree. His theories of a world where Providence takes first place were incompatible with the doctrine of the Enlightenment, which was founded on reason. Bernardin got a poor welcome from this group of atheists, who were rather suspicious of his love of virtue. His meeting with

FOLLOWING PAGES
"Childhood of Paul and Virginie";
"Adolescence of Paul and Virginie";
"The Triumph of Virtue";
"Tomb of Virginie".
Series of four etchings drawn by Jean Frédéric Schall and engraved by Augustin Legrand in 1791.

Rousseau was decisive. Bernardin henceforth avoided the salons and became friendly with Rousseau, whose love of nature he shared. His second book, *Études de la Nature*, was published by Didot the Younger in 1784, after 10 years in the making. This work, whose immense popularity exceeded the expectations of the author, seems an anachronism today. In it, Bernardin unfolds, with lavish complacency and surprising presumptuousness, a whole set of pseudo-learned ravings on the system of the Universe, whose perfection, according to him, provided ample proof of the role of Providence. The latter, besides, was supposed to have dispensed its benefits, to fulfil the needs of its noble creature, Bernardin himself. He thus threw himself with a calm boldness into speculations which were hazardous, to say the least, and which draw a smile today:

"Many fruits are designed for the mouth of man, such as cherries and prunes; others for his hand, such as pears and prunes, and others, much bigger, such as melons, are divided into segments and seem meant to be eaten by the family..."

Paul et Virginie was published in 1788, and enjoyed the triumph that we know about. The book, however, did not arouse enthusiasm when Bernardin was invited to give a first reading of it in Madame Necker's salon. The handpicked audience included the best minds, among whom was the famous Buffon, reputed among other things for his *Traité sur le style*. However, this respectable assembly did not pay careful attention, to say the least, and Buffon was even rude enough to fall asleep. This gloomy omen had added to Bernardin's conviction of the futility of his literary ambitions, and, discouraged, he had then decided simply to destroy his manuscript. It was the painter Joseph Vernet who, touched by the craftsmanship of the novel, encouraged him to have it published. Moved by the freshness and simplicity of the scenes, which were in perfect harmony, according to him, with the natural beauty of the tropical landscape, the artist convinced him that the novel would be successful. Sensibility triumphed over reason. The book was first published in the fourth volume of his *Études de la Nature*, and it was only in 1789 that the first separate edition came out.

The resounding success of this tender and naive work, pervaded by innocence and virtue, announced a clear tendency, in that century which had been imbued with the values of the Enlightenment, to return to simplicity and true feelings. Bernardin de Saint-Pierre, Rousseau's first disciple, was to be the initiator of the taste for exoticism which was to find tangible expression in *Atala*, Chateaubriand's first novel.

In 1791, Bernardin published *La Chaumière Indienne*, which was not very successful. Appointed by Louis XVI, in 1792, to the post of Intendant of the Jardin des Plantes and the Natural History conservatory, he had a greenhouse built, which still exists today, and which, at the time, had a fine collection of tropical plants. He also had the idea of creating a menagerie for the study of animal behaviour. The author's statue is now to be found at the heart of the present garden. His two young heroes are seated at his feet, leaning against the base of the statue, in an attitude of tender complicity.

Bernardin de Saint-Pierre married his editor's daughter, Félicité Didot. When the post of Intendant was abolished by the Convention in 1793, he retired with his young wife to his house in the Essone, to await the passing of the throes of the Revolution. In this peaceful retreat, he wrote *Harmonies de la Nature*, which was published in 1795. The previous year, 1794, saw the establishment of École Normale, where he was appointed Professor of Morality by the Directoire. His colleagues there included Monge, Laplace, Daubenton and Verney. This school was soon abolished and replaced in 1795 by the Institute, where he kept his Chair. However, his religious convictions were misunderstood by his colleagues, among whom he made a few enemies.

His young wife died in 1798, leaving two young children: Paul and Virginie. Being too old to look after them by himself, he got married again to Mademoiselle de Pelleport in 1800. He was 63, while she was barely 18. He then settled at Éragny-sur-Oise, where, thanks to the generous pensions

granted by Napoléon and his brother Joseph, he acquired a house with a large garden. Bernardin de Saint-Pierre was decorated with the Legion of Honour in 1806. He died on 21 January 1814, at the age of 74.

Bernardin de Saint-Pierre has left to posterity a lasting memory which will remain forever linked to the exoticism of a tropical island, where a hut in the shade of banana trees and the lullaby of distant waves on the shore were enough to provide lasting happiness. That image of a lost paradise, where two children can frolic at the heart of rich tropical vegetation, remains, to this day, a sweet "invitation to travel".

Many artists took their inspiration from the exotic scenes created by the writer and attempted to recreate this enchanting landscape. The extra-ordinary magic which permeates these remarkable compositions give us an idea of their talents. The most famous are undoubtedly the two series painted by Schall; one, published in 1791, consisting of etchings engraved by Augustin Legrand, and the other of lithographs, published in 1795, and engraved by Descourtis.

Count Louis Antoine de Bougainville
(8 November–12 December 1768)

"I am also staking my hope of fame on a flower!" Thus spoke Bougainville. He was about to leave Isle de France, where he had stopped after a journey of nearly two years around the world. Philibert Commerson, the tireless French botanist on his expedition, who had decided to remain on the island, had just presented him with "a wonderful plant with flowers of a splendid violet colour." Commerson had collected cuttings of this plant during a long visit to Rio de Janeiro, and had carefully tended them. It was the splendid result of his patient efforts that Commerson proudly held out to the man who gave him the opportunity of expanding his collections: "I have named it 'Bougainvillea' as a tribute to the great navigator that you are!"

Commerson could not know how true his words would turn out to be: for the ordinary person, the bougainvillea is the best-known legacy of Bougainville. Its clusters of brightly coloured flowers, which stream down in shimmering cascades in the midst of tropical stony grounds, remind us of these green and sunlit islands, fringed in white sand, which rest lazily in their peaceful turquoise lagoons. We can then conjure up the paradise where Bougainville landed, the beautiful island of Tahiti, which he rightly named "Nouvelle Cythère". He did not know at the time that the English seafarer, Thomas Wallis, had landed there 10 months before him.

Even if his name is associated today with magical islands, Bougainville remains the first Frenchman in the story of the great sea adventure to have

"Virginie resting". This work was exhibited in Paris at the 1796 Salon.
Lithograph by JL Simon, after a painting by Landon.

circumnavigated the globe and explored the Pacific with a scientific expedition, shortly before the famous Captain Cook. We also owe him the discovery of an island in the Solomon Archipelago in Melanesia, which still bears the name of Bougainville. A lawyer by training, but also very gifted in mathematics, Bougainville was the pupil of d'Alembert, and became famous at the age of 27 for his *Traité du calcul intégral*. This man of open and educated mind, friend of the Encyclopedists, was also an accomplished soldier, with a certain preference for the musket. As aide-de-camp and friend of General Montcalm, he was at his side during the siege of Quebec in 1759 and, earned a commission as colonel as well as the Cross of Saint Louis, all before he turned 30. In 1763, he joined the Navy as a ship's captain and was chosen in 1766 by Louis XV and his dynamic minister, the Duc de Choiseul, to head a mission of exploration in the Pacific Ocean. Besides its scientific observations, the expedition had another objective – the search for that legendary southern continent mentioned in the ancient maps.

This mission was timely for Bougainville, as it would compensate for the failure of his attempt to found a colony on a group of desert islands not far from the Strait of Magellan, which he had named the "Malouines" in honour of a native of Saint-Malo, Nicolas Duclos-Guyot, the ship's captain who assisted him in this enterprise and who had first discovered the islands. The aim was not only to provide a safe haven for some Acadian families who had fled to Saint-Malo from Canada after the capture of

Branche S.C.

Bougainville

Quebec, but also to ensure that France would have an economic and military base at the entrance to the Pacific Ocean. However, after occupying these islands for three years, France had to face the claims of England, which declared that these lands, which they had named "The Falklands", belonged to them, while Spain, for its part, maintained that the islands had always belonged to the Spanish crown as dependencies of its possessions in South America. Faced with this dispute, and wishing to avoid any conflict, France abandoned the territory, which was finally restored to Spain. In compensation, Louis XV had considered appointing Bougainville Governor of Isle de France and the island of Bourbon, but the latter declined the offer. However, Bougainville enthusiastically agreed to take the leadership of this expedition in the southern seas.

At the end of the expedition, Bougainville stopped at Isle de France. On 8 November 1768, the *Boudeuse* and *Étoile* dropped anchor at Port-Louis harbour. The fleur-de-lys flag flying proudly at the Place d'Armes touched the hearts of the travellers by reminding them of the presence of the French on this remote little island. They were warmly welcomed by Pierre Poivre who, while still in Paris before the departure of the expedition, had been linked to the project. As a botanist and an enlightened traveller, he had been approached for some advice and it was he who recommended that his friend the botanist Philibert Commerson, should accompany the expedition. It was also at Poivre's instigation that the famous "cucurbite", an enormous still invented by Poissonnier for distilling seawater so that it could become drinkable, was installed on each of the ships. This greatly contributed to the success of the expedition.

Bougainville and his friends were the guests of the Intendant at Monplaisir, and the latter of course took them round his marvellous exotic garden, at which the visitors could only marvel. This tropical paradise, where fruit trees harmoniously grew alongside rare essences and flowering shrubs from every continent, provoked the admiration of Commerson, who easily let himself be convinced by Pierre Poivre to stay on at Isle de France. Bougainville took the opportunity of his stay at Pamplemousses to visit the Hermans' smithy, which made a strong impression on him: "There are few as fine in Europe and the iron they manufacture is of the finest quality. It is hard to imagine how much perseverance and ability were required to set up such an establishment, and the amount it must have cost."

He also met Bernardin de Saint-Pierre at a dinner, to which Governor Dumas and the engineer Hermans were also invited. Bernardin, who had only been at Isle de France for a few months, presented himself at his worst

ABOVE: The bougainvillea flower. It owes its name to the famous navigator Louis Antoine de Bougainville (OPPOSITE), the first Frenchman to circumnavigate the globe.

France Maritime, engraving by de Branche, 19th century.

145

PHILIBERT COMMERSON
Médecin Botaniste et Naturaliste du Roi,
Chevalier de l'Ordre de St. Michel,
Membre de l'académie des Sciences.

and Bougainville felt a strong dislike for this character, whom he described as "theatrical, embittered and over-sensitive".

After a pleasant month on the island, Bougainville set sail on 12 December, headed for the Cape. Isle de France, so criticised by Bernardin, had made a marvellous impression on him. In addition to Commerson, four other members of the expedition decided to stay on the island, among them the astronomer Véron, who wished at all costs to witness the extremely rare phenomenon of the transit of Venus in front of the sun, which, according to Halley's calculations, would occur the year after, on 3 June 1769.

At the Cape, Bougainville was amazed to discover the giraffe, zebra and wildebeest, of which he had sketches drawn to be presented to Buffon in Paris. On 16 May 1769, after a voyage lasting two years and three months, he dropped anchor in the bay of Saint-Malo. With Bougainville was Aoturu Pontaveri, a young Tahitian chieftain who had expressed the wish of visiting France, and had insisted on joining the expedition. This specimen of the "good savage", much vaunted by Rousseau, created a sensation in Parisian drawing salons. Being intelligent and perfectly sociable, he quickly adapted to high society, and, strangely, was fascinated by the opera, which was his favourite source of entertainment during his stay in Paris.

From his travels, Bougainville brought back a harvest of discoveries which would enrich Buffon's *Histoire Naturelle*. In 1772, he published his *Voyage Autour du Monde*, which was a great success. The details he described on the mores of wild tribes contributed new elements to Diderot's *Encyclopédie*. The latter, however, in a pamphlet entitled *Supplément au Voyage de Bougainville*, blamed the Europeans for having come to disturb the simple happiness of the Tahitian people by introducing them to the misdeeds of civilisation and stealing their land. Diderot attacked Bougainville directly, through the invective of an old man:

"And you, chief of the robbers who obey you, quickly withdraw your vessel from our shore: we are innocent, we are happy and you cannot ruin our happiness. [...] We follow the pure instinct of nature; and you have tried to erase its character from our souls. [...] We have no wish to exchange what you call our ignorance for your useless enlightenment; we possess everything which is necessary and good for us. [...] Go and get excited in your own country, worry as much as you like; leave us in peace: do not pester us with your artificial needs, nor your fanciful virtues."

That theory of the "good savage" dear to the philosophers was queried by Bougainville, but even more, later, by Lapérouse who powerlessly witnessed the massacre of his friend, the ship's captain Fleuriot de Langle, together with 10 members of his crew. These two men, both raised on the ideas of the

Philibert Commerson (1727–1773). After the death of his wife, Antoinette Beau, the famous French botanist Commerson, joined the Bougainville expedition in 1766 and embarked on the vessel *Étoile* "with his valet Jean Baré". It was in fact his female companion Jeanne Barret disguised as a valet. The trick was discovered when the ship stopped at Tahiti. She became the first French woman to perform a circumnavigation of our planet. On the way back, the couple disembarked at Isle de France in 1768. Commerson stayed for three years at Isle de France with his friend Pierre Poivre. He died of exhaustion in 1773 on his return from Madagascar and Bourbon, where he had worn himself out in research work on the botany of these islands. After his death at Isle de France, his companion Jeanne married, in 1774, at Saint-Louis Cathedral, Port-Louis, to Jean Duberna, a French officer.
From the book of Dr FB de Montessus, drawing by P Pagnier, printed by Lemercier, Paris, 1889.

Enlightenment, lost their illusions when faced with the "good savage" in action. They never forgave the philosophers for spawning theories, unsupported by experience, without leaving the comfort of their study. On his return to France, Bougainville participated in the American War of Independence, but after being defeated by Hood in the Battle of the Saintes in Martinique, he was court-martialled and disgraced. In 1792, he refused the title of Vice-Admiral and retired to his farm in Normandy. He was a suspect during the Reign of Terror and was imprisoned, but freed after two months. Later, Napoléon recognised his merits, and honoured him by successively appointing him Senator in 1799, Grand Officer of the Legion of Honour in 1804, and Count of the Empire in 1808. Bougainville died at the age of 82 in Paris. He was given a state funeral at the Panthéon.

Jean-François Galaup, Count de Lapérouse (21 August 1772–April 1778)

Lapérouse became a legendary figure on account of the mystery which, for many years, surrounded the disappearance of his expedition, the hopes raised by the searches for him, and, finally, the remains discovered on the island of Vanikoro, which bore witness to the painful tragedy which occurred there. This drama, still rooted in our memories, helps to keep alive the memory of this great navigator with humanistic ideas, who was chosen by Louis XVI to lead the second French scientific expedition across the Pacific Ocean after Bougainville's in 1767. Lapérouse stayed for six years at Isle de France in the peace of a lush property which he had bought at Mesnil, not far from Curepipe. This was a happy stage of his life, as he had the joy of meeting there a lovely 17-year-old Créole, Éléonore Broudou, whom he later married in Paris.

Born in the Tarn, near Albi, in 1741, Lapérouse began his career in the royal Navy at the age of 15. He sailed on several ships as sub-lieutenant before being attached to the Chevalier d'Arzac de Ternay, under whose command he participated in two campaigns in Canada during the Seven Years' War, on board the *Zéphir*. The Chevalier de Ternay soon became friendly with this likeable young sub-lieutenant, and took him under his wing. So, when Chevalier de Ternay was appointed Governor of Isle de France, Lapérouse accompanied him and landed at Port-Louis on 21 August 1772, on board the *Belle Poule*. Lapérouse stayed on the island for nearly six years, during which he undertook several missions abroad on behalf of individuals or on behalf of the Governor. Thus, in 1773, the Chevalier de Ternay put him in command of the store ship *Seine,* with a mission to obtain respect for the honour of the French flag along the coasts of Coromandel and Malabar. It was indeed important that the French presence in the area should be reinforced, with the aim of supporting the company and thus protecting its trade interests, which were being threatened by the Marathi states and the great independent Indian princes, of whom some were allied to the English. During this mission, Lapérouse found himself in a battle against a Marathi fleet which he came across north of Surat, and on which he inflicted a bloody defeat. As a result of this feat, Lapérouse was made a ship's lieutenant.

On Lapérouse's return from India in 1775, he and his friend, ship's lieutenant Charles Mengaud de la Hague, bought a property of 156 arpents (about 65 hectares) at Eau-Coulée, adjacent to a river at Mesnil, not far from Curepipe. This purchase brought him closer to the beautiful Éléonore Broudou, whose parents had a property in the neighbourhood of Rivière-la-Chaux, at Mahébourg. Lapérouse had met this young lady soon after his arrival at Isle de France and had fallen madly in love with her. However, his engagement plan was not approved by his family, who were thinking of marrying him to Mademoiselle de Vésian, who came from the ancient nobility of Albi. In spite of his 36 years, Lapérouse submitted to the demands of his father, who remained inflexible.

Lapérouse left Isle de France in April 1778 with a broken heart. Éléonore joined her mother at Nantes 15 days later and, in desperation, prepared to become a nun, while Lapérouse enlisted for the American War of Independence in the squadron of Vice-Admiral Count d'Estaing in the West Indies. However, love did triumph at last, and the two lovers got married five years later in the Church of Sainte-Marguerite in Paris. Lapérouse was then 42 and Éléonore, 28. Little did they know then that their happiness would only last for two years.

In 1785, the Minister for the Navy, the Marquis de Castries, wishing to reinforce the influence of France in Europe and to rival the prestigious exploits of Captain Cook, decided to mount a large-scale scientific expedition around the Pacific Ocean. Having obtained the enthusiastic support of Louis XVI, who was passionately interested in geography and the sciences, the Minister then put forward the services of Lapérouse to the King. The latter's success in the American War of Independence, together with his high level of education and his naval expertise, made him an ideal candidate for this vast project. The expedition, which gathered the best scientists and researchers, aimed not only to explore new lands, but also to collect all the observations they would deem useful to science. The equipment envisaged was very sophisticated for the time: in addition to naval clocks and chronometers, the scientists would have the benefit of a

OPPOSITE: Warrior of Nuku-Hiva, Marquesas Islands, French Polynesia.

BELOW: Woman of Cape Turnagain, Oceania.

JEAN FRANÇOIS GALAUP DE LA PÉROUSE,
Chef d'Escadre des Armées Navales de France,
Né à Alby en 1741

portable observatory, which would not only allow them to make exact hydro-graphic measurements, but also to calculate longitudes with precision.

When the many preparations were at last completed, Lapérouse took command of the *Boussole*, while his friend Fleuriot de Langle assisted him on the *Astrolabe*. The ships left Brest harbour on 1 August 1785 to shouts of "Long live the King!".

The outcome of the expedition was tragic. After nearly three years of circumnavigation, the reports of which were regularly despatched to the Ministry for the Navy, as agreed with the King, Lapérouse set sail from Botany Bay (now Sydney, Australia) in March 1788. He headed for the friendly islands of New Caledonia, the Santa-Cruz islands, the land of the Arsacides (of Surville) the Gulf of Carpentaria, the west coast of Australia, in the hope of reaching Isle de France by December 1788 and, from there, to France to be reunited with his dear Éléonore. But alas, the expedition was never to return.

The first searches were undertaken in 1791 by d'Entrecasteaux, who was previously Chief Commander of the French naval forces of the Indian Ocean and Governor of Isle de France, but to no avail. It was not until 1826 that the Irish Captain Dillon, having stopped in an island of the archipelago of Santa-Cruz in Melanesia, discovered among the inhabitants of a village what seemed to be relics of the expedition: axes, swords, knives and various utensils, and also the silver handle of a sword which had probably belonged to Lapérouse. They declared that these objects came from the neighbouring

Lapérouse (OPPOSITE) met Éléonore Broudou (ABOVE) on Isle de France and fell in love. They married in Paris in 1783.

LEFT: Warrior of Sandwich Islands where Lapérouse called at and paid tribute to the famous Captain James Cook.
From Voyage Autour du Monde, *William Beechey (1796–1856). Engraving, 19th century.*

FAR LEFT: Woman of Sandwich Islands.
From Voyage Autour du Monde, *Louis de Freycinet (1779–1842). Engraving, 19th century.*

RIGHT: Before his departure in June 1785, Lapérouse received his last instructions directly from Louis XVI. Depicted in the background is the Minister for the Navy, the Marquis de Castries and Captain Claret de Fleurieu.
After a painting by Nicolas Monsiau, engraving by Pigeot.

BELOW: Islander of Romanzoff archipelago in the Lapérouse Detroit.
From Voyage Autour du Monde, *Otto Von Kotzebue (1787–1846). Engraving, 19th century.*

OPPOSITE: Natives of the island of Vanikoro. Lapérouse and his unfortunate companions most probably fell prey to their ravenous appetites.
Engraving by Pardinel.

island of Vanikoro (now Vanuatu). Thus, Dillon learnt from an old native of that island that, a long time ago, two big ships which had been caught off their guard by a violent cyclone had been wrecked off the coast of Vanikoro. According to him, the survivors who managed to reach the shore were massacred by the cannibal natives. A bronze bell as well as numbered cannons were discovered and purchased by Dillon from the inhabitants of the island. These pieces, when subsequently identified by Barthélemy Lesseps, one of the members of Lapérouse's expedition who had been put ashore at the port of Kamchatka with a mission to bring the latest dispatches to Paris, confirmed the hypothesis of a shipwreck.

During his exploration of the Pacific Ocean in 1828, Dumont d'Urville, having heard of the discoveries of Dillon, stopped at Vanikoro. The natives showed him the site of one of the wrecks, from which he managed to recover a large anchor and some numbered cannons. Before leaving this wind-swept island, d'Urville erected a cenotaph to the memory of Lapérouse and his companions. Thanks to research more recently carried out in 1996 by Ron Coleman, historian and naval archaeologist at the Museum of Queensland, it has been possible to locate the precise position of the two wrecks, which were about a kilometre of each other. The archaeological works, concentrating on the site of the *Boussole* wreck, made it possible to work out the circumstances of the tragedy. Various objects were recovered, including dishes of "blue-and-white" porcelain from China.

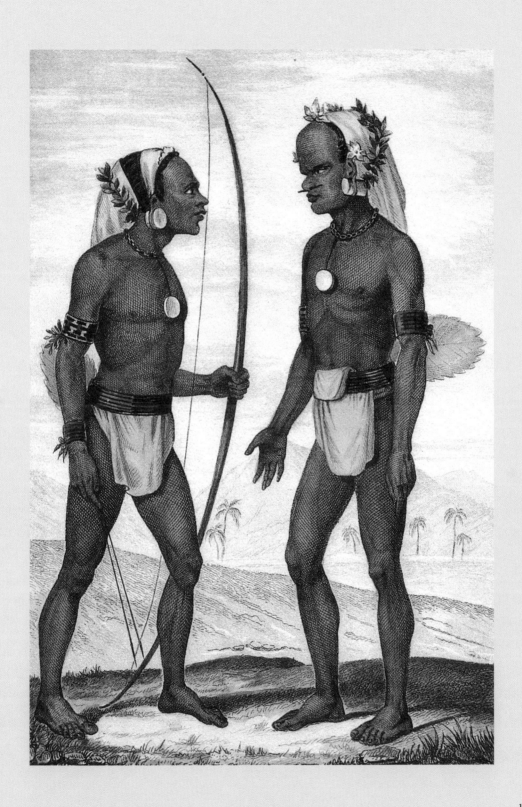

Viscount Paul de Barras (1776–1779)

Born in Fos-Amphoux in the county of Var in 1755, Viscount de Barras arrived at Isle de France in 1776 with a commission as officer with the Pondicherry regiment. He stayed for some time with Governor Antoine Guiran, Chevalier de La Brillane, who was a family friend. He went to Pondicherry in May 1779 and took part in the battles against the English led by Governor de Bellecombe and Bailli de Suffren. Barras returned to Isle de France in 1779, only to learn that his friend, the Governor, had died. He decided to return to France, where he chose to go into politics.

Barras went from success to success and, in 1792, he was elected a deputy of the Convention and made Commander-in-Chief of the armed forces of Paris (which had about 40,000 men). At the head of this army, Barras played a leading role in the downfall of Robespierre the "Incorruptible" by ordering his arrest in 1794 and putting an end to the Reign of Terror.

After the siege of Toulon, in 1795, Barras appointed Napoléon Bonaparte Commander-in-Chief of the armed forces of Paris. At the head of his army, Bonaparte put down the uprising against the Convention. Barras subsequently became a prominent member of the Directoire and appointed Bonaparte Commander-in-Chief of the French army in Italy. After the coup of 18 Brumaire in Year VIII of the French Republican calendar (corresponding to 9 November 1799) by Bonaparte, the latter proclaimed himself First Consul and forced Barras to resign. Barras went into exile in Brussels, then in Rome. In 1810, Bonaparte, by then Emperor of the French, had him imprisoned in Montpellier. Barras only returned to Paris after the Bourbon Restoration in 1814, although he had voted for the execution of Louis XVI. Barras died at Chaillot in 1829.

Pierre André de Suffren de Saint-Tropez
(October–December 1781; November–December 1783)

We could allow ourselves to adopt the expression used about Malherbe regarding his bold use of the French language, and declare, concerning the glorious sailor Suffren: "And at last, Suffren came!" and, with him, all of France's hopes of recovering the vast empire which Dupleix had built up for it in India; an empire which England had quickly seized from it during the Seven Years' War (1756–1763). Only tiny fragments remained of the immense territories which had previously been conquered, spreading from the river Narbada, in central India, to Cape Comorin in the extreme south: a few lodges at Surat, Calicut and Mahé, on the Malabar coast, which had been returned at the time of the Treaty of Paris (1763), and its four main trading posts on the Coromandel coast: Chandernagor, Pondicherry,

OPPOSITE: Viscount Paul de Barras. *Drawing by Raffet, engraving by Léon Mauduison, published by Furne and Coquebert, 19th century.*

SUFFREN.

Yannaon and Karikal. This bold sailor did all he possibly could to try and dislodge the English from India during the hostilities triggered by the American War of Independence. In one year of campaigning (1782–1783), he won many victories and, if peace had not been concluded in 1783, and above all, if he had had more means, he would probably have succeeded in this undertaking; for this ebullient southern figure, all of a piece, was a practical and determined man. In spite of his appearance resembling "an English butcher", to quote the unflattering description of a British officer, and his often scruffy clothing, he knew how to be very effective in battle. His competence was not to be measured by a powdered wig, a lace ruffle or silk stockings. He was a fighter first and foremost, and his objective was to win. Everything else was incidental.

However, although he was able to resist the formidable fleet of Admiral Hughes, thanks to his tireless energy and his bold initiatives, Suffren did not manage to destroy it completely. He certainly distinguished himself during that campaign, but it did not bring any substantial changes to the political situation in India. Being more concerned with supporting America, France concentrated its forces in the Atlantic, to the disadvantage of its Indian possessions. In the end, Suffren was to have exerted himself only for the sake of fame, "this smokescreen for which we do so much," he confided to his friend, Madame d'Alès. Still, that does not diminish the military genius he displayed throughout the campaign. Napoléon, in his *Mémorial de Sainte-Hélène*, wrote nostalgically about this excellent strategist whom fate did not put in his path: "Oh! Why didn't this man live until my time, or why was I not able to find someone of his calibre? I would have made our Nelson of him, and our affairs would have taken a different turn."

Born at Saint-Cannat, near Aix-en-Provence in Bouches-du-Rhône, on 17 July 1729, Pierre André de Suffren showed an early taste for the sea. In 1743, he joined the École des Gardes de la Marine, at only 14 years old. Blessed with a quick intelligence and a bold and energetic temperament, he quickly climbed the ladder to reach the ranks of ship's captain in 1772, after serving for four years in Malta.

In 1778, France became involved in the American War of Independence and sent Admiral d'Estaing's squadron to support the "insurgents". Suffren was in command of one of the ships, the *Fantasque*, and three frigates. He distinguished himself in Newport harbour by spreading such panic in the English ranks that they decided to scuttle five frigates and two corvettes rather than let the vessels fall into French hands. This bold and sudden action gave the French their first victory. He contributed to the rout of the English in the West Indies with his zeal and dynamism. Meanwhile, the

OPPOSITE: Portrait of Pierre André de Suffren de Saint-Tropez with his signature. Appointed Squadron Commander, Suffren was "Bailli" of the Order of Malta and ship's captain in the French Royal Navy. *France Maritime, 19th century.*

157

English forces had not remained idle on the coast of Coromandel in India. They attacked the French trading posts once again; they captured Chandernagor, and attempted to besiege Pondicherry. Hyder Ali Khan, Prince of Mysore and father of Tipu Sultan, was an ally of the French. He did his best to protect Pondicherry by land, but requested that France should send reinforcements by sea.

The squadron of Count Thomas d'Orves, despatched by the Governor of Isle de France, Viscount de Souillac, had not been able to resist the forces of the English Admiral Hughes and had been compelled to retreat to Port-Louis. Moreover, the Dutch Cape Colony, faced with the threat of a siege by the English, begged for support from France. The English Commodore George Johnstone and his troops were already on their way towards southern Africa. It became imperative that France should reinforce its forces in the region, in order to curb the appetite of the English, because, if "Perfidious Albion" conquered the Cape, it would spell the end of French power in India, and at the same time, of Isle de France and Bourbon. Suffren was to be the man to the rescue. Having distinguished himself during the American campaign not only by his grasp of naval strategy, but also by his daring, he was chosen by the Marquis de Castries for this mission. Suffren was still smarting from the setbacks suffered during the American campaign, and was driven by a strong desire to tackle the English again. The coming operations would give Suffren the chance to make his revenge upon the English.

Suffren left Brest in March 1781 at the head of a division of five vessels. His first destination was to be the Cape, before joining the squadron of Count d'Orves at Isle de France, and then he was to head for the Coromandel coast. But he had to make haste to catch up with the squadron of Commodore Johnstone, which was ahead of Suffren on the way to the Cape. Suffren found the English squadron just when he came within sight of the Cape Verde Islands, at the level of the island of Santiago. The English fleet was sitting there, at anchor in the bay of La Praya. He had an ideal opportunity to launch his first attack. The *Héros* entered the bay, followed by the *Annibal*, while the rest of the fleet kept aside. Once they were within cannon's reach, it was action stations for all. Taken by surprise by this unexpected attack, the English fought back the assault of the French as best they could, but had to give up after a stiff resistance of 90 minutes.

The battle had been tough. Suffren lost two of his squadron's captains, and his largest ship, the *Annibal* (holding 74 cannons), took a battering. He towed it to the Cape, and very fortunately reached well ahead of Johnstone, in spite of his burden. Suffren and his men were just in time as, with a

OPPOSITE: An Indian rajah in his court.
Drawing by Philippoteaux, engraving by Saunier, 19th century.

Philippoteaux del   Saunier sc

Brahmine   Bayadère   Femme du Raja   Esclave   Raja

garrison of only 400 men and a few cannons, the Cape would have been far from able to defend itself and would have fallen into English hands. Once the troop reinforcements had disembarked, the squadron remained at the Cape for a few weeks in order to carry out the most urgent repairs before sailing to Port-Louis.

When Suffren reached Isle de France on 25 October 1781, Viscount de Souillac came onboard the *Héros* to greet him. The Governor of Isle de France was welcomed onboard by 11 cannon shots and the repeated cry of "Long live the King!". Suffren, wearing ceremonial dress with a cocked hat, powdered wig and the Cross of Malta on his chest, then proceeded to Government House, followed by his captains. Lodging at Monplaisir at Pamplemousses, he tasted the tropical charm of its shady gardens, where subtle aromas wafted from beautiful exotic plants, planted long before by Pierre Poivre. Brilliant parties were organised in his honour. He was a guest at the best tables, where he enjoyed spicy Créole dishes, and relaxed for a moment amid the gaiety of these society frivolities, where there was no shortage of pretty women. But Suffren had not called at Isle de France to let himself go amid the pleasures of this "Calypso Island", as he liked to call it. He had other concerns. Count d'Orves' squadron was quite ready to set sail for India and was only waiting for him. But the *Annibal* was in very poor condition, and Suffren was not prepared to leave his best ship behind. The repairs took a long time and forced him to stay for six weeks on the island. While his officers, to his great fury, courted pretty women, he spent the best part of his time between blacksmiths' forges, rope-making and other workshops in an effort to speed up repairs. Meticulous and demanding, he insisted on personally controlling everything, and was far from reluctant to take an active part in the works himself when necessary. Here is a colourful description of Suffren by Raymond d'Unienville: "Suffren was everywhere, he motivated, stimulated, livened up everyone and everything by his presence [...] He left others to caper and enjoy sweetmeats in the company of the ladies of the capital. For the time being, he acted like the big caulker, with hands black with tar, feet standing in dirty water, scruffy-looking under his straw hat, with a cigar in his mouth, his chest drenched in sweat – closer to the workers than to the gentlemen officers of the squadron, mostly Bretons, who remained dumbstruck, or smiled sarcastically at this bawling and exuberant Moco [...]"

Thanks to the support of the settlers of Isle de France and Bourbon, the squadron was at last ready with everything necessary. The signal for departure was quickly given: 28 vessels were on the move, leaving Port-Louis harbour in proud array. A regiment made up of volunteers from Isle

OPPOSITE: "Suffren was everywhere, he motivated, stimulated, livened up everyone and everything by his presence. He left others to caper and enjoy sweetmeats in the company of the ladies."
Drawing by Marck, engraving by Pardinel .

LEFT: Suffren's squadron in action off the Cuddalore coast against the powerful squadron of Admiral Hughes, on 20 June 1783. A year before, on 27 July 1782, Suffren was warmly received by the French ally in India, Hyder Ali, the Sultan of Mysore and father of Tipu.
Drawing by Jugelet, engraving by Ed. Chavane.

de France was on board one of the ships. At the very start of the voyage, Count d'Orves, being very ill, handed over command of the squadron to Suffren. The latter remained in command following the death of the Count a month later, just as the squadron was approaching the Coromandel coast.

Suffren quickly launched his first offensive against the squadron of Admiral Hughes before Sadras. The outcome was a first defeat for the English, soon to be followed by several more.

Indeed Suffren was to challenge the proud English frigates to bold battles on five occasions: after Sadras, Providien, Negapatam, Trincomalee and finally at the Battle of Cuddalore. However, these battles were only half-victories, as, in spite of the relentlessness shown by the French, they mostly ended in the flight of the English, or by a change in the wind, which parted the opponents, or by a dangerous position which forced the French to give up the struggle. However, the superiority of the French squadron always prevailed. It must be emphasised that, for as long as the hostilities lasted, Suffren constantly received support from the Governor of Isle de France, Viscount de Souillac, who supplied him with all the reinforcements he required and encouraged him by writing to him regularly.

After the Battle of Cuddalore, Suffren was well on the way to fulfilling his most cherished dream: to expel the English from India once and for all, but, while he was looking forward to fresh confrontations, a dispatch from Admiral Hughes informed him that a peace treaty had already been signed at Versailles on 20 January 1783, restoring to France its five trading posts on the Coromandel coast.

The long campaign was over. The game had been won. Rewarded by the title of "Bailli" which he had received after the victory of La Praya, Suffren sailed at full speed towards Isle de France, where he received a triumphant welcome. A crowd of boats pressed around the squadron in the harbour and, when he appeared on the deck of the *Héros* in full uniform and waved his cocked hat at the crowd, they were ecstatic! As he was landing on the quay, following Governor Viscount de Souillac, he received a 21-gun salute and shouts of "Long live the King!" and "Long live Suffren!". Splendid receptions were organised in his honour, specially the one held at the residence of Mr Le Roux de Kermorseven in the region of Pamplemousses, where Suffren praised the Isle de France regiment.

On 29 November, he sailed from Port-Louis harbour towards the Cape and then on to Toulon, where more honour and glory awaited him. As soon as he reached Versailles, he was received by Louis XVI and the Marquis de Castries. He was awarded the Order of the Saint-Esprit and the title of Vice-Admiral. He later requested the title of Marshal of France, but this request was refused by the Marquis de Castries, which left some bitterness in the heart of this valiant fighter, who could certainly have expected more gratitude from his motherland for such glorious exploits.

This formidable warrior, ironically, was not to die in battle. His end remains shrouded in mystery to this day. Many rumours have circulated about the circumstances of his death and some hypotheses have been suggested. One theory is that Suffren died on 8 December 1788, from wounds received during a duel with a mysterious opponent. But this has never been proved. The epitaph on his tomb reads, which, by itself, summarises his talents as a strategist: "Suffren, single-handed, dismantled the English fleet."

Nicolas Baudin (15 March–25 April 1801; August–September 1803)

Nicolas Baudin was a native of Ile de Ré, where he was born in 1754. He began his sailing career in the merchant navy but was very quickly appointed a lieutenant in the royal Navy. From 1792 to 1793, he undertook two botanical voyages on behalf of the Muséum d'Histoire Naturelle (the former Jardin du Roi) to the Far East, including to China, to the Sunda islands and to India. Another expedition, from 1796 to 1798, took him to the West Indies and South America, from where he returned with an important cargo of young shoots of bushes and plants of various species, which enriched the museum's collection. On Baudin's return, the famous botanist Jussieu commented most enthusiastically: "Never have such considerable collections, all fully alive and so well chosen, been brought to Europe".

ABOVE: Nicolas Baudin called at Port-Louis in August 1803. He became seriously ill and died on the island in September that same year.
From Voyage Pittoresque Autour du Monde *by Captain Dumont d'Urville, Paris 1835.*

When Bonaparte decided to organise a scientific and naval discovery expedition in order to explore the coasts of New Holland (Australia), Baudin was deservedly chosen to lead it. That expedition gathered the best scientists of the time, selected by the Bonaparte himself. It comprised not only of astronomers, geographers, botanists, zoologists and anthropologists under the direction of Jussieu and Lacépède, but artists and painters chosen from among the most talented. Equipped with state-of-the-art materials, its objective was to explore the west and south coasts of the Australian continent and collect all data useful to science. Two corvettes, the *Géographe* and the *Naturaliste,* had been equipped for the expedition. The first was under the command of Nicolas Baudin, promoted to the rank of ship's captain in view of this mission, while the second was entrusted to Frigate Captain Emmanuel Hamelin[30]. The two ships left the port of Le Havre on 19 October 1800 and, after a long and arduous journey lasting nearly five months, reached Isle de France in mid-March 1801. Being in a precarious state of health on landing, several members of the scientific team and crew chose to stay at Isle de France until the return of the expedition. Among these were the astronomer Frédéric de Bissy; the botanists André Michaux and Jacques Delisle; the zoologists Désiré Dumont and Bory de Saint-Vincent; the artists Louis Lebrun, Michel Garnier and Jacques Milbert.

On 25 April 1801, after over a month and a half at Port-Nord-Ouest, the two corvettes raised anchor and reached the southwest coast of Australia on 1 June 1801. From there, they sailed towards the island of Timor to the north, then south towards Van Diemen's Land (Tasmania), whose separation from the mainland had long ago been identified by d'Entrecasteaux during his search for Lapérouse in 1793. The expedition remained there for three months and explored several small islands in the area, where they had the opportunity of studying the mores and customs of some primitive tribes, which are now extinct. Following this stop, which had yielded a rich harvest of observations, Baudin, being anxious to do his best to fulfil his mission, took the initiative of going up the east coast of Australia. There, he came across the English explorer Matthew Flinders, who had also been sent by his country on a mission to reconnoitre the coasts of that continent. However, travel conditions became more and more difficult. Scurvy and dysentery were rife on board the two ships, and the crew, often short of food supplies, were exhausted. Having decided to continue the journey at all costs, Baudin persisted. But soon, the overwhelming number of deaths and the repeated complaints of the members of the scientific expedition finally overcame his obstinacy, and forced him to make for the English colony of Port Jackson, where the sick were taken ashore to receive medical care.

After a five-month stay in this colony, where the expedition had received a considerate welcome, the *Géographe* and the *Naturaliste* headed south again, before the two corvettes parted company at Bass Strait. While the latter sailed for France, the former went up the west coast towards the north of Australia. It travelled alongside the *Casuarina*, a small schooner which had been purchased at Port Jackson, and whose command had been entrusted to Lieutenant Louis Claude de Freycinet.

After having reconnoitred the Gulf of Carpentaria in the north and explored the coast of Witt's Land in the northwest of the continent, Baudin, whose crew members were exhausted, and who was faced with a daily increase in the numbers of sick men, at last decided to make for Isle de France, which he reached on 8 August 1803. It was his turn to become ill. He was admitted to hospital at Port-Nord-Ouest, but in spite of the devoted care with which he was tended, his health deteriorated and he died a month later, on 16 September 1803. In recognition of his worth, Isle de France honoured him with a ceremonial funeral.

The expedition was then taken over by Lieutenant Pierre Millius, and three months later, on 16 December 1803, the *Géographe* left Port-Nord-Ouest for Lorient, its hold laden with the most important collections of plant, mineral and animal species ever brought back to France. These included the famous Australian marsupials, with several species of kangaroo, many varieties of birds, including a cockatoo with black plumage dotted with white spots, which was named "Baudin", and two black emus, captured on King Island, north of Tasmania. These joined the menagerie of Joséphine, the wife of Napoléon, in her park, La Malmaison near Rueil.

While that expedition proved valuable for the natural sciences and considerably enriched the collections of the Jardin des Plantes, it was, on the other hand, one of the most deadly in human terms. Besides the deaths among the crew members of the two ships, only six of the twenty-four members of the scientific team returned safe. Among them were the zoologist François Péron and the artist Charles Alexandre Lesueur who, after much labour, wrote and illustrated *Voyage aux terres australes sur le Géographe et le Naturaliste*, the first volume of which was published in 1807. Dying suddenly in 1810 at the age of 35, François Péron left the series unfinished. It was completed by Claude de Freycinet in 1816.

Jacques Gérard Milbert (14 March 1801–24 February 1804)

The enforced stopover at Isle de France of Jacques Gérard Milbert, a talented landscape artist, has given us a rich collection of illustrations of the landscapes and the main administrative centres of the island at that time.

OPPOSITE (FROM TOP): "View of the town of Port-Napoléon from Pouce Mountain";

"View of the town of Port-Napoléon from Fort Blanc."

Drawings by Jacques Milbert, made during his stay on the island from 1801 to 1804.

BELOW: Portrait of
Bory de Saint-Vincent
(1778–1846).
*Drawing, from life, and engraving by
Ambroise Tardieu in 1826.*

OPPOSITE (FROM TOP): View of Trou-
Fanfaron at Port-Napoléon; the
Church of Pamplemousses; the
watchman's dwellings.
*After Jacques Milbert's drawings
published in* Voyage Pittoresque à L'île
de France, *1812.*

The work of Milbert, which reflects the appearance of Isle de France at the dawn of the 19th century, thus constitutes an iconographic document of exceptional value.

Jacques Milbert was a native of the south of France, who studied painting in Paris with Mr de Valenciennes. After a visit to England, he was appointed professor of draughtsmanship at the École des Mines in Paris. Thanks to his connections with Mr Vincent, a prominent artist and Member of the Institute, he took part as head draughtsman in the expedition of Nicolas Baudin to discover the Southern Lands. Having taken ill during the stopover of the *Géographe* at Port-Nord-Ouest, Milbert found himself obliged to stay at Isle de France to receive medical care. Disappointed at being unable to proceed with the voyage, he decided to make the most of his time to undertake an in-depth survey of the island. He journeyed over the island in every direction to collect information and draw sketches to illustrate his notes. Milbert marvelled at the island's landscapes, which inspired his most beautiful compositions. He remained on the island for three years.

On his return to France, Milbert published his observations in *Voyage Pittoresque à l'Isle de France, au Cap de Bonne Espérance et à l'île de Ténériffe* in 1812. The work consists of two volumes, accompanied by an atlas containing 42 lithographs of the most beautiful landscapes of Isle de France. After describing the historical background, Milbert provides us not only with richly detailed descriptions of the fauna and flora of the island, but also of the life and customs of the inhabitants. He held fond memories of this land and the warm welcome of the settlers, whom he held in high esteem. In the preface of *Voyage Pittoresque*, Milbert addresses them with these words: "Thank you, honest and generous inhabitants of Isle de France, who have welcomed me so generously! I found among you that frank hospitality which always accompanies the noblest feelings: when I was parted from the objects of my affection and forced against my will to remain on your island at the beginning of a journey during which I was meant to explore other territories, you alleviated my anxieties and made my regrets less bitter."

Jean-Baptiste Bory de Saint-Vincent (14 March 1801–16 March 1802)

This traveller, zoologist, botanist and geographer was a native of Agen. He specialised in the study of botany and entomology. In 1794, Bory de Saint-Vincent intervened in favour of the zoologist Latreille, who had been sentenced to deportation, and won the case. As a result, he won a circle of friends among the naturalists at Bordeaux, who valued him for that action. Thanks to their backing, he was chosen as head zoologist of the Baudin expedition to the Southern Lands. Bory de Saint-Vincent was, therefore,

also among those who joined the *Géographe* and the *Naturaliste*, after resigning from the regiment in which he was a sub-lieutenant.

He left Le Havre on 19 October 1800. Like Milbert, Bory de Saint-Vincent was too ill to continue with the expedition to Australia and stayed on Isle de France to receive medical care. He stayed there for a year, during which he studied the fauna and flora as well as the geological structures. He also took the opportunity of visiting the island of Bourbon, to study its tropical nature and famous volcano. All his observations, especially those concerning the island of Bourbon, were published in the *Voyages dans les quatre principales îles des mers d'Afrique*.

On his return to France, he enlisted in the Grande Armée and participated in all the campaigns of Napoléon Bonaparte, under the orders of Davout, Ney and Soult. He was decorated with the Legion of Honour after being promoted to head of battalion. A faithful follower of Bonaparte, he was not liked by Louis XVIII and, as a result of the Bourbon Restoration, had to go into exile in Belgium. There, in collaboration with other scientists, he published *Les Annales générales des Sciences physiques*, followed on his return to Paris by *Dictionnaire classique de l'Histoire naturelle*, in 17 volumes, which were successively published between 1822 and 1831.

After a spell in prison for being unable to refund his debts, he organised official expeditions to Greece in 1828, and to Algeria from 1840 to 1842. His observations on these two countries were published from 1844, and post-humously, from December 1846 to 1867.

THE CORSAIRS' WAR IN THE INDIAN OCEAN

From the start of the American War of Independence, France considered reinforcing its strength in the Indian Ocean, and a decree from the Cabinet in Versailles, dated 24 June 1778, authorised privateers to equip ships. The first vessel to depart from Isle de France on 17 April 1780 was the *Philippine*, whose owners were the Pitot brothers. Its captain was Deschiens, a famous corsair, or privateer, whose persistence earned him the nickname "Rabid Dog" from his English opponents. But corsair activity increased mainly between the wars of the Revolution and the Empire, that is, approximately between 1793 and 1808. While England deployed its formidable forces in the Indian Ocean, where it carried out a systematic blockade, France found itself in a precarious situation. Its navy was in the middle of a crisis. Since the Revolution, it had lost its most experienced squadron leaders, as well as its best admirals, who had formerly been recruited from among the nobility and who had won fame during the American War. Such men included d'Estaing,

During his expedition across the island of Bourbon, Bory de Saint-Vincent did not fail to be inspired by these Créoles in their palanquin. *Drawing after Patu de Rosemond.*

de Grasse, Suffren, de La Motte-Picquet and de Vaudreuil. France needed time to develop a new generation of leaders.

Meanwhile, France could only rely on its corsairs to maintain respect for the tricolour in that region. Their main mission was to weaken England's power by attacking its trade. On the other hand, Isle de France, as well as the island of Bourbon, were not only being neglected by France at that time, but were also being strangled by the English blockade. The islands' inhabitants faced frequent food shortages, as they were unable to produce enough for their own needs. So the corsairs, encouraged by incentive bonuses, and also certain of finding shelter there, stocked the islands' stores all the foodstuffs they seized from the enemy. Port-Louis became their main base. The most famous corsair, whose reputation has inspired many legends, was undoubtedly, Robert Surcouf, nicknamed "King of the Corsairs".

The King of the Corsairs, Robert Surcouf

This giant of the seas, who struck terror in the hearts of the English, stayed on Isle de France at various periods of his life, especially between 1789 and 1808. However, it was only from 1793 that he made the island his real home port. Between his various comings and goings for the purpose of privateering, he must have spent a total of three to four years on Isle de France.[31] His warehouses and his lodgings were opposite the Town Hall, in the building situated at the corner of Desforges Street (now Sir Seewoosagur Ramgoolam Street) and Pope Hennessy Street. Surcouf must have walked all over the streets of Port-Louis[32], not only at the time of the governors of the

SURCOUF.

Convention and the Directoire, but also of the Consulate and the Empire. Bold and reckless, this sturdy native of Saint-Malo, with his strong personality, picked some quarrels with two of the most famous governors, Count de Malartic and General Decaen.

Surcouf was born at Saint-Malo on 12 December 1773. He first landed on Port-Louis in June 1789. He was then aged a little over 16, and had enrolled as ship's boy onboard the *Aurore*. He sailed round the Indian Ocean for two years until September 1791, when he returned to Lorient to visit his family. In 1793, he again found himself on Isle de France, where he heard of the declaration of war against England. He then considered staying in the area to engage in the slave trade[33]. That activity, which, for him was merely a means of earning his living, gave him no satisfaction. He really had one dream: to join the corsairs' war. He soon had an opportunity when ship owners Malroux and Levaillant, worthy citizens of Isle de France, offered him the command of a 180-ton brig, the *Modeste*, which they wished to equip for privateering. This small vessel, renamed the *Émilie*, was then fitted with four cannons and a crew of 30 strong men, all driven by a frantic desire to hunt down the English. Surcouf was now quite ready to weigh anchor. He only needed to obtain a "lettre de marque" from Governor

OPPOSITE: Robert Surcouf, "King of the Corsairs", made Isle de France his home port in 1793.
Printed by Lemercier, engraving by A Maurin, 1835.

BELOW: Attack of the HMS *Triton* by the corsair the *Hasard* under the command of Robert Surcouf.
Drawing by L Garneray, engraving by Pardinel, 1837.

Malartic. The latter, however, hesitated. The corsairs' war had already brought enormous riches to Isle de France. More captures might provoke the indignation of the English, who might then, according to him, attempt a landing on the island. So, after a lot of dithering, he decided not to give this permit to Surcouf, but instead granted Surcouf "navigation leave"[34] on a food supply mission to Seychelles, a status which did not allow him to attack the enemy in the name of France. The impetuous Surcouf disregarded this and managed, with unparalleled recklessness, to capture no fewer than four English vessels, including the *Triton*, a superb vessel belonging to the East India Company. After this fine achievement, he returned to Isle de France, as proud as Artaban, at the head of a rich convoy whose holds were overflowing with foodstuffs. This was a real boon for the colony, which was then in the throes of its worst famine. But, while the settlers greeted him with applause as soon as he landed at Port-Louis, his welcome by Governor Malartic was less enthusiastic. As Surcouf had broken regulations, his prizes were confiscated. Disgusted by what he considered to be rank injustice, Surcouf demanded that the case should go to court. Unfortunately, he lost his case. Greatly piqued, he returned to France towards the end of 1796, and lodged an appeal with the Directoire and the Conseil des Cinq-Cents. After long discussions in support of the validity of his claims, he was granted half the value of his booty. Encouraged by this turn of events, he returned to Isle de France onboard the *Clarisse* in December 1798.

From there, Surcouf went off in pursuit of the English in the Bay of Bengal, where he captured a good number of their vessels, before returning to Port-Louis in February 1800. His prizes, legal this time, provided him with a comfortable income, enabling him to purchase a new ship, the *Confiance*. More spacious than the *Clarisse*, this elegant sailing ship was also faster, and wonderfully suitable for privateering. On board were 17 cannons and a crew of 204, including 159 Frenchmen, 25 volunteers from Bourbon, and 20 sons of Isle de France settlers. Among the most fearless names on board were Drieu, Dumaine, Louvel, Desveaux, Fournier, Fontenay, Roux, Viellard, Lenouvel, Millien et Dutrône. They all had a blind faith in their leader and were convinced that their mission would be successful.

The Capture of the Kent

During a voyage to India, on 7 October 1800, Surcouf and his companions succeeded in the boldest corsair attack of the time, a feat which forged for the bold Breton the reputation for courage and fighting spirit for which he is still remembered. This exploit was the capture of one of the most powerful vessels of the East India Company: the *Kent*.

LEFT: Capture of the *Kent*, one of the most powerful vessels of the East India Company, by Surcouf, who was in command of the *Confiance*, on 15 Vendémiaire of Year IX (7 October 1800).
Painting by Louis Garneray, typogravure by Goupil, Paris, 19th century.

This splendid ship was under the command of Captain Rivington. Three times larger than the *Confiance*, the 1,200-ton vessel was armed with 38 large-calibre cannons, twice the number possessed by its opponent. The *Kent*, in addition to having a well-trained crew, had picked up the crew of the *Queen*, another English ship, which had been lost in a fire in Brazil, thus bringing its military strength to 437. Among them were General Saint-John and his officers. In comparison with this powerful monster, the *Confiance* seemed very small, with only 18 cannons and 190 men, to be risking an assault.

Undaunted, Surcouf approached the enemy boldly. Relying on his strength, Captain Rivington was not unduly worried. Who would dare challenge this formidable force, deep within the Bay of Bengal, near the mouth of the Ganges, and, what was more, in what the English regarded as their own "territorial waters"? He decided, nevertheless, to make a few preparations, almost as a matter of principle. Rivington was so sure of his power that he even invited a few distinguished ladies to come up on deck to witness the show. General Saint-John was also present. "My lord, and you, my ladies," declared Rivington, "be my guests to watch the capture of a French corsair, or to watch him sink if he refuses to surrender." By skilful and clever manoeuvres, Surcouf, braving the fire power of the enemy, managed to come close to the rear of the ship and soon found himself at the giant's starboard flank. The flag of the Saint-Malo corsairs had already been hoisted. The French flag followed. The French then doubled their efforts, while Rivington lost some of his fine confidence. The two ships fiercely fired cannon salvoes at each other, at point-blank. The French suffered some damage, but lost no lives. The *Confiance* was now touching the powerful stern of the *Kent*. The sailors, in a swift gesture, cast the boarding hooks. The small frigate was now strongly attached to the starboard flank of the enormous ship. Surcouf immediately gave the order to fire. Then came a mighty broadside which made many victims around the enemy's lower battery. The *Kent* instantly counter attacked. As soon as the smoke subsided, the English, persuaded that they had knocked out the corsair, were amazed to find that fierce-looking men, armed to the teeth with cutlasses, swords and axes, were about to clamber aboard to throw themselves on them. "All aboard!" yelled Surcouf with his stentor's voice. This was followed by a frenzied stream of sailors pouring onto the deck, driven by a thirst for victory, hurling themselves furiously from all sides at the stunned enemy. From the top of the sails, seamen hurled grenades into the midst of the English troops massed on the deck. A horrible massacre ensued. The English resisted with the exemplary courage for which the units of the Royal Navy are well known. But the persistence of the French was such that the British troops soon began to weaken. Captain Rivington then took the lead to encourage them to fight on. At that very moment, Surcouf, followed by his men, jumped onto deck. Soon, fierce hand-to-hand combat began. The corsair fought like a lion and, in the midst of that terrible fray, never lost sight of his objective: victory at all cost.

The hatred and ferocity of the French caused four times as many casualties among English. But victory was not yet assured. Surcouf then decided to seize the enemy's cannon placed on the forecastle in order to halt the advance of the English soldiers, who, like a column of ants, were constantly flooding in from the poop deck. With a terrible crash, the powerful cannon spewed a volley of shots, mowing down the enemy ranks. The English, horrified at the turn of events, were at wits' end. In a burst of energy, Captain Rivington harangued the troops once more. At that moment, a French seaman named Avrier threw a grenade and grievously struck Rivington, who fell as if thunderstruck. Twenty other soldiers who were close to him were seriously wounded. Surcouf seized the opportunity of the spreading confusion to strike even harder.

Resistance soon weakened and the last combatants threw down their weapons. The *Kent*'s deck was won. At that moment, the *Kent*'s second-in-command, who was posted at the battery, risked a desperate attempt at resistance, but, quick as a flash, Surcouf and his men overran the place and soon became masters of the ship. "The *Kent* is ours! Long live France!"

A Six-Year Pause

Shortly after his return to Saint-Malo in April 1801, Surcouf got married on 28 May to Marie Blaize de Maisonneuve, the daughter of a rich ship owner of Saint-Malo. In March 1802, the Treaty of Amiens was signed and Surcouf experienced a warrior's forced rest. This was far from displeasing to his young wife, who shared some sweet years of happiness with her husband, between the peaceful life of Saint-Malo and the splendour of Parisian receptions. His stay at Saint-Malo, which started in 1801, was to last for a little over six years. Surcouf turned into a businessman and was busy managing the enormous fortune he had won "by the edge of the sword". He became a ship owner in partnership with his father-in-law and, short of being able to engage in direct action, continued to harass English merchants vicariously through his ships. The *Caroline*, the *Confiance* and the *Napoléon* were the most famous corsair ships of that period.

The Titans' Struggle

In spite of the glorious exploits of its corsairs, France did not manage to completely crush the powerful fleet of His British Majesty. Many naval defeats, including that of Abukir, had already demonstrated this. The French navy, indeed, did not fare well under the Consulate.

In spite of the efforts made by the Navy Minister, Denis Decrès, to extract it from this crisis, there were not enough ships and those available were often poorly equipped, lacking not only weapons, but also men. To crown it all, there occurred a sudden turn of events:

"Perfidious Albion", deeming that the conditions of the Treaty of Amiens were not being fulfilled by France, decided, in reprisal, to place an embargo on all French ships which found themselves in British ports, while French merchant ships at sea simultaneously came under attack. These hostile acts, perpetrated without notice, did not fail to provoke general indignation in France. That was when Napoléon, then First Consul, expressed a wish to meet Surcouf.

The meeting took place at the castle of Saint-Cloud. The rank of ship's captain was offered to Surcouf so that he could apply his skills in the service of the French naval forces in India. Surcouf was very flattered, but requested that he be allowed to function independently from the squadron commander, Admiral Linois. Taken aback and somewhat irritated by this lack of compliance, the First Consul, as Surcouf prepared to take his leave, asked him:

– "Monsieur Surcouf, you know the state of the war at sea better than anyone else. What is your opinion of it?"

BELOW: Napoléon Bonaparte, the First Consul in his "Colonel de la Garde" uniform at La Malmaison Castle, near Rueil.
Engraving by Geoffroy from the original painting by Jean-Baptiste Isabey, 1802.

– "You are asking me a very serious question, General, but Lloyds provides me with the arguments for drawing a conclusion. From 1793 to 1797, England has lost 1,800 more ships than we have. I conclude from this that, as our fleets have suffered disasters, it must have been the corsairs who accounted for this difference in favour of our nation. For the last six years, the number of English ships lost has followed the same proportions as before, while our losses have tripled. If you were to calculate what amount of money the corsairs have cost England, you will find that your corsairs have well avenged the defeat of Abukir."

– "Well! What conclusion do you draw from these facts?"

– "If I had the honour of being, like yourself, at the head of the Government of France, I would leave all my regular fleets of ships in their harbours, I would never fight the British fleets and squadrons, but I would send out to sea a multitude of frigates and light ships, which would soon destroy English trade, and would put England at your mercy. England relies on its trade for a livelihood, and it is only through its trade that it is possible to hurt it."

– "What you are saying, Monsieur, is very serious, and yet you must be right, and you have quoted the figures to prove your point, but I cannot, for the very honour of France, destroy its military navy. Keep at it, you and your friends, continue to serve your motherland as you have done up to now, and you will reach the goal you propose, which is the one to which each true Frenchman should aspire!"

In 1804, Napoléon awarded this exceptional sailor the title of Chevalier of the Legion of Honour.

The Devil's Return

In 1806, fired by the spirit of adventure which still possessed him, Surcouf threw himself into the construction of a new ship. It was a splendid three-master of 300 tons with a provocative name, to say the least: the *Revenant*. Six years had gone by since the corsair sailed the seas, and he was missing the ocean. The symbol he chose to adorn the prow of this ship was very revealing: a man coming out of his shroud. It was the Devil's resurrection! Equipped with 20 cannons and 192 men, the *Revenant* left Saint-Malo on 2 March 1807 and sailed at full speed to Isle de France.

When Surcouf reached Port-Louis in June 1807, a crowd of admirers and onlookers gathered on the quay to greet him. He met the new Governor, General Decaen, who gave him a warm welcome. After some preparations, which kept him on the island for two months, he set sail in September for the Gulf of Bengal: he engaged in a fresh campaign against the English, and captured more ships. He returned to Isle de France in January 1808, escorted by his many prizes, with holds full of foodstuffs for the colony. A delirious crowd awaited him at the harbour and gave him a true hero's welcome. Times were hard for the inhabitants of Isle de France. Having to bear the English blockade, which was even more strictly enforced around the islands, they had come to rely only on the corsairs for their subsistence. They thus took Surcouf for a saviour and pinned all their hopes on him. He also did actually help them generously with loans to improve their lot.

When a Corsair Gets Angry

While he was busy winding up his business on the island before his final departure for Saint-Malo, Surcouf entrusted the *Revenant* to his cousin, Joseph Potier de la Houssaye. The opportunity of a great prize was soon to present itself in the shape of a large and richly laden Portuguese ship, the *Conceçao*, which was due to pass by Isle de France on its way from the Cape of Good Hope. Surcouf immediately gave his cousin instructions to seize it. But, to his utter amazement, General Decaen intervened officially and temporarily forbade the *Revenant*'s departure. Wishing, in fact, to take the initiative of this promising capture himself, he only provided Potier with his "letters of marque" after despatching two frigates from the French navy to intercept the *Conceçao*. Most ironically, not only did the frigates fail in their mission, but it was, moreover, the *Revenant* which brought the Portuguese galleon back to Port-Louis, where the inhabitants had a triumphant welcome in store for the corsair ship.

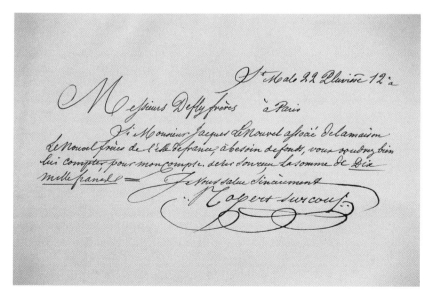

LEFT: Signed message from Surcouf, dated 12 February 1804.

Although forced to put on a brave face, Decaen did not forget this humiliation and devised his own revenge on the corsair. Taking advantage of the powers provided by his status, he launched his first attack, which was to requisition the *Revenant* "for the purpose of using it for the service of His Majesty the Emperor". He renamed it the *Iéna* and officially put someone else in command. Surcouf thus found himself not only banned from his own ship, but was reduced to the mere rank of ship's lieutenant! This was too much for Surcouf, who rushed towards the residence of the Governor in a boiling fury, determined to assault him.

The prompt intervention of his friends prevented him from carrying this out. A meeting between the two was arranged, but in spite of Surcouf's protests, Decaen did not budge. Surcouf then arranged to return to France. He bought a new sailing ship, the *Sémillante*, which he renamed the *Charles*, and in agreement with some Saint-Malo ship owners, proposed to return to Britanny with an escort of his prizes. Decaen intervened and demanded that the corsair should take the captain of the *Conceçao* as well as two of his officers onboard. Surcouf, fearing that these prisoners might stir up a mutiny once they had reached the high seas, did all he could to persuade the Governor of the risks of this request, but the latter remained inflexible. Surcouf had only one solution: to apply his shrewdness. At dawn on the day of his final departure from Isle de France, on 21 November 1808, just before weighing anchor, he had the Portuguese put ashore on the port's pilot boat. This trick provoked the fury of Decaen, who then launched his second attack. He issued a sequestration order on all of Surcouf's property on Isle de France. But he had underestimated Surcouf's connections. As soon as he returned to France, the corsair took immediate action by approaching the Minister for the Navy and the Colonies, Admiral Decrès, who ordered the Governor of Isle de France to return Surcouf's property.

Surcouf, however, did not bear a grudge against General Decaen for very long. When the latter was imprisoned, during the Restoration for having joined Napoléon's side during the Hundred Days, the corsair acted magnanimously. It was indeed thanks to his interventions in high places, as well as his constant support during Decaen's trial, that the former Governor was finally freed. The adversaries became firm friends.

Peaceful Retirement

Surcouf was only 36 when he finally returned to Saint-Malo in 1809. His hectic career as a corsair, which began when he was 22, was finally over. He then found himself the owner of colossal wealth which he would be able to enjoy in peace. He was the wealthiest ship owner of France, and continued to equip vessels, not only for privateering, but also later for trade and whale-fishing in the Antarctic. He divided his time between his businesses at Saint-Malo and his property of Riancourt, at Saint-Servan, where he enjoyed his favourite pastime: hunting!

Suffering from a painful stomach disease which slowly wore him down, Surcouf died on 8 July 1827, at age 54. His body, placed on a black-draped rowing-boat, was taken across the bay of Saint-Malo, where a huge crowd had gathered to pay him a final tribute. He was buried at the cemetery of Rocabey to a salvo of muskets, as a memento of the "good old days" of the corsairs' war. During his short career as a corsair, he single-handedly captured 47 enemy ships, including the *Triton* and the *Kent*, two jewels of His Majesty's Navy. But Surcouf was not the only one to achieve glorious feats. Jacques Perroud from Bordeaux, who was awarded the Legion of Honour and the Poleaxe of Honour by Napoléon, was also a prominent corsair then. Many other corsairs distinguished themselves, and effectively weakened English trade with China and India. It would be unfair not to name the more valiant of them: Carosin, Harel, Henry, Hodoul, Laboulaye, Courson, Épron, Vaillant, Malroux, Thréouart, Coutence, Ferretier, Pinaud, Desjean-Hilaire and Surcouf's brother, Nicolas. We should not forget the most fearless among them: Dutertre, Lemême and, not least, the remarkable François Fidèle Ripaud de Montaudevert, a friend of Tipu Sultan. De Montaudevert never stopped fighting the English in the Indian Ocean, in America or in India with Suffren, but he was fatally wounded while in command of the corvette *Sapho* during the siege of Bayonne in 1814.

BELOW: Louis Garneray (1783–1857) was engaged as a corsair with Surcouf and Dutertre up to 1806. A prisoner of the English for eight years, he started painting and became well known as a marine painter, then as a writer. He painted the scene depicting the capture of the *Kent* by Surcouf, which is exhibited at the Museum of Saint-Malo.
Drawing by Biard.

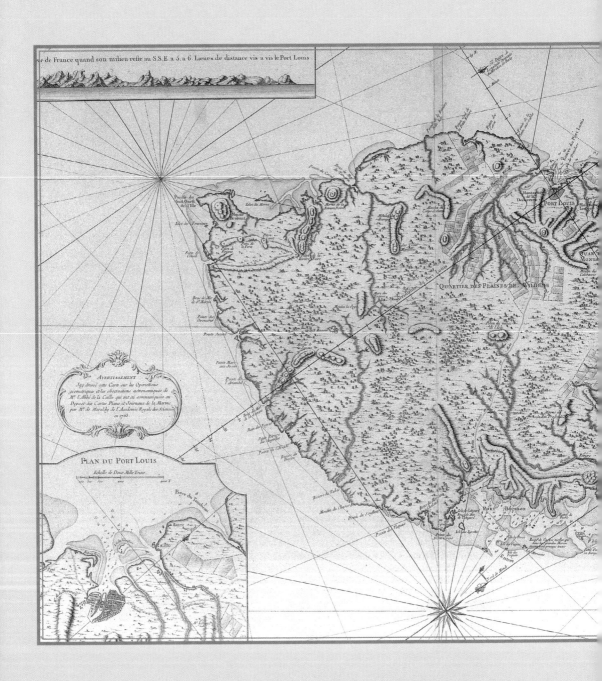

...le de France quand son milieu reste au S.S.E. a 5. a 6. Lieues de distance vis a vis le Port Louis.

AVERTISSEMENT
Jay dressé cette Carte sur les Operations
geometrique et les observations astronomiques de
Mr. l'Abbé de la Caille qui ont été communiquées au
Depost des Cartes Plans et Journaux de la Marine
par Mr. de Moralby de l'Academie Royale des Sciences
en 1763.

PLAN DU PORT LOUIS

Echelle de Deux Mille Toises

PORT LOUIS

QUARTIER DES PLAINES DE WILHEMS

PORT BOURBON

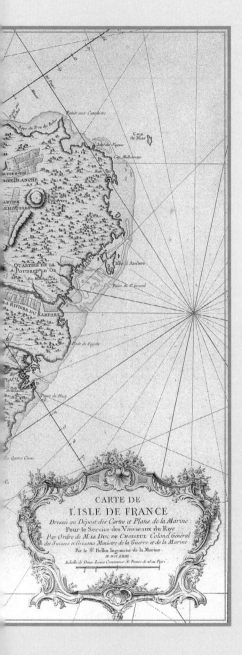

PORT-LOUIS: NAVAL BASE

- *Table of the Commanders-in-Chief of the French Naval Forces*

The Most Famous Commanders

- *Vice-Admiral Count de Rosily-Mesros*
- *Vice-Admiral Marquis de Saint-Félix de Maurémont*
- *Rear-Admiral Magon de Médine*
- *Vice-Admiral Marquis de Sercey*
- *Vice-Admiral Count Durand de Linois*
- *Rear-Admiral Baron Hamelin*

Other Great Figures of The French Navy and Their Activities on Isle de France

- *Admiral Count d'Estaing*
- *Rear-Admiral Count Villaret de Joyeuse*
- *Vice-Admiral Count Morard de Galle*
- *Vice-Admiral Baron Willaumez*
- *Vice-Admiral Denis Duke de Crès*
- *Rear-Admiral Baron L'Hermitte*
- *Rear-Admiral Bouvet de Maisonneuve*
- *Admiral Baron Roussin*
- *Admiral Baron Duperré*

Map drawn up in 1763 by
Mr Bellin, marine engineer, for the
Duke de Choiseul, Minister of War
and of the French Navy.

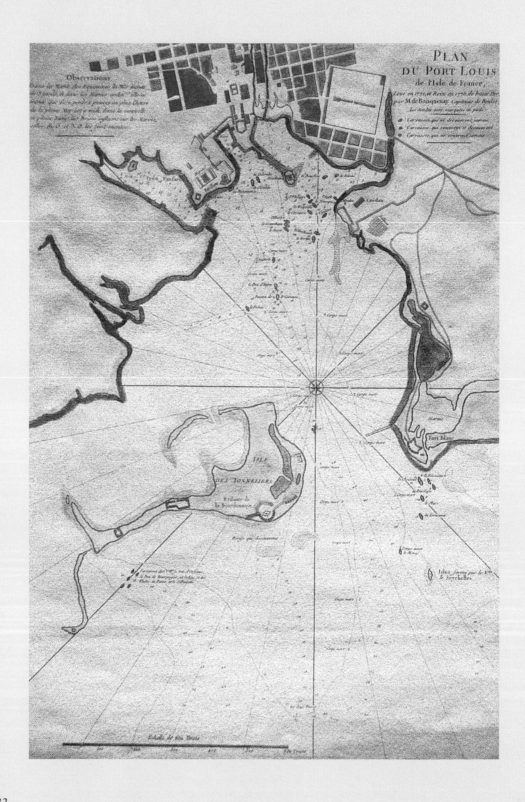

During the second half of the 18th century, the countries of Europe were troubled by endless conflicts: after the Wars of the Austrian Succession (1744–1748) and the Seven Years' War (1756–1763), came the War of American Independence (1778–1783), followed by the wars of the French Revolution and the Empire (1795–1815).

These wars had inevitable repercussions in the Indian Ocean, where France and England, busy carving out empires for themselves in the Indian peninsula, never stopped fighting merciless battles. English naval supremacy was being increasingly confirmed, and the many shows of force of the English on the Coromandel coast soon convinced the French of the necessity to reorganise their defences in the region. The loss of Pondicherry, the trading post where the majority of their squadrons gathered until the end of the Seven Years' War, had finally proved to them how precarious that base was. In contrast to the English, who were able to obtain supplies and reinforcements quickly during confrontations and to carry out repairs at Madras or in Bengal, the French, on the other hand, had to fight on for long periods without the possibility of obtaining reinforcements. The retreat of Count d'Aché in 1763, when he was compelled to leave Pondicherry in the enemy's hands, had amply demonstrated this.

In 1778, during the first hostilities triggered by the American War of Independence, it was the Chevalier de Tronjoly's turn to retreat to Isle de France, leaving Pondicherry to the English once more. Two years later, Thomas d'Orves, having been unable, through lack of men, equipment and food to effectively support Hyder Ali Khan's troops, also had to retreat.

It therefore became even more obvious that Isle de France had an essential role to play in these struggles for power. Its strategic location, coupled with the quality of its harbour, which was much more suitable than Pondicherry's open harbour, gave it all the assets required to become the main supply base for the French forces in India. As soon as the island had been taken over by the royal Government in 1767, Choiseul, Minister for the Navy, being aware of these advantages, understood the compelling necessity of transforming it into a real bastion capable of supplying France with the reinforcements needed in wartime. Choiseul then entrusted Pierre Poivre with the mission of restoring to Isle de France, which had become somewhat lethargic, the essential dynamism required to fulfil its first vocation as a naval base, as indicated in this letter to the future Intendant:

"It has fallen to Isle de France, owing to its location, to take the leadership of all the European establishments in Eastern India. This island is crucial to their trading posts; its harbours, its population, its healthy climate, its food production, as well as its geographical position, as are its many assets

OPPOSITE: Many ships sank in the harbour of Port-Louis during cyclones in the 18th century. Their wrecks are probably still there. *Map of the port drawn in 1775 by fire-ship Captain Mr. de Boisquenay.*

for even more successful defences and attacks. In wartime, it can substitute well-equipped ships and fresh troops for forces and vessels weakened by a long sea crossing [...]"

Poivre had then taken all the steps he could to reach the objectives set by the Minister and had entrusted Mr Tromelin, a highly skilled sailor and brilliant engineer, with the task of equipping Port-Louis for these purposes. Begun in 1772, the huge works Tromelin had undertaken were completed in 1779, just in time to welcome the squadron of the Chevalier de Tronjoly, who returned to Port-Louis for safety, before the squadron was taken over by Count Thomas d'Orves two years after.

Having been equipped as a naval base, and being moreover well protected from the winds by its ring of mountains, Port-Louis henceforth offered not only a safe haven, but now also had the capacity of sheltering whole squadrons: those of Suffren and Thomas d'Orves, amounting to a total strength of 28 vessels, fitted in comfortably during Suffren's visit in 1781, while he was on his way to India with the objective of recapturing Pondicherry and the trading posts lost in 1778. From that time, Port-Louis reached the highest point of its strategic military importance, fulfilling La Bourdonnais' dream of long ago. The successive captures of Pondicherry in 1793, and then in 1803, finally sealed the destiny of Isle de France as the French naval base in the Indian Ocean.

Table of the Commanders-in-Chief of the French Naval Forces in the Indian Ocean, based at Isle de France (under the orders of the Governor)

1777	**François Lollivier, Chevalier de Tronjoly** Ship's Captain		1793	**Jean-Marie Renaud** Lieutenant
1779	**Comte Thomas d'Orves** Frigate Captain		1795	**Charles Magon de Médine** Lieutenant
1785	**Antoine de Bruni, Chevalier d'Entrecasteaux** Ship's Captain		1796	**Marquis de Sercey** Rear-Admiral
1790	**Count Henri de Mac Nemara** Ship's Captain		1802	**Charles Durand de Linois** Rear-Admiral
1790	**Count de Rosily-Mesros** Ship's Captain		1807	**Jean Dornal de Gui** Ship's Captain
1791	**Marquis de Saint-Félix** Vice-Admiral		1809	**Emmanuel Hamelin** Ship's Captain

THE MOST FAMOUS COMMANDERS

Vice-Admiral Count François Etienne de Rosily-Mesros
(1771–1772, 1773, 1781–1783, 1785, 1790–1791, 1792)

Born at Brest in 1748, François Etienne de Rosily-Mesros began his naval career at the age of 14 as a naval guard. He was the son of Count François de Rosily, the Fleet Commander and commander of the Navy at Brest. François Etienne de Rosily-Mesros saw action at sea from 1762, and had the opportunity of calling at Rio de Janeiro, Newfoundland, Santo-Domingo and the West Indies.

By 1770, at the age of 22, he was a sub-lieutenant on board the *Abrewack*, under the command of Captain Kerguelen on a mission along the French coasts. He then moved to the *Berrier*, still with Kerguelen. He landed at Isle de France for the first time in August 1771. He remained with Captain Kerguelen, whose new mission was to discover the Southern Territories, and embarked on the *Fortune* in January 1772.

As they thought they had discovered the Southern Territories, Rosily was sent in a rowing boat to reconnoitre. By the time he returned, the *Fortune* had vanished. Rosily was miraculously rescued by Captain Saint-Allouarn on board the *Gros-Ventre*, and remained on board that vessel for eight months, during which he called at New Holland (Australia), the island of Timor, and Batavia (now Jakarta).

After returning to Isle de France, Rosily decided to go back to France. Upon hearing about a new expedition to the Southern Territories, which was again to be led by Captain Kerguelen, he went back to Isle de France to meet him there. He was then given the command of the corvette *Ambition* and took to sea again in August 1773. After 14 months at sea, he returned to France because of ill health. At the end of 1774, he visited the ports of England, Scotland and Ireland, and brought back to France navigation instruments which would be useful to the French Navy.

In 1778, Rosily was promoted to ship's lieutenant and carried out several trips in the English Channel in command of the *Coureur*. In order to save the ship *Belle Poule*, which was commanded by Fleet Commander de La Clocheterie, he did not hesitate to engage in battle against the English vessel *Aréthuse* and even attempted to board it. However, as his ship was sinking, Rosily was compelled to lower his flag and to be taken prisoner. He remained in England for nearly two years.

Rosily received the Cross of Saint-Louis for this act of bravery, and on his return to France, he undertook several naval construction missions in Brest and in the Gulf of Gascony.

In 1781, Rosily returned to Isle de France and, in command of the frigate *Cléopâtre*, joined the fleet of the Bailli de Suffren in March 1783, off the coast of Trincomalee. On his return to France, Rosily was promoted to the grade of captain in 1784. He came back to Isle de France in May 1785 in command of the *Vénus*, and left again on mission to the coasts of Madagascar, Arabia and Persia, where he corrected major cartographical mistakes. He was then dispatched to the Gulf of Bengal and the China Sea.

He did not return to Isle de France until 1790, where he found that spirits there were overheated by news of the French Revolution. During this period Count Henri de Mac Nemara, head of the French Navy in the Indian Ocean, was murdered in a most cowardly manner by drunken and over-zealous soldiers as he was making his way to barracks after a hearing at the Colonial Assembly. After this murder, Captain de Rosily-Mesros was appointed head of the French Navy in the Indian Ocean by Governor Charpentier de Cossigny. He did not remain for long in this post and was replaced by Captain Marquis de Saint-Félix. He returned to France and, after several missions, went back again to Isle de France in 1792 in command of the *Fidèle*. There were prestigious passengers on board: the new Governor, Hyppolite de Maurès, Count de Malartic, as well as four delegates of the National Assembly.

In 1793, Rosily was promoted to Rear-Admiral and on 1 Vendémiaire Year V (September 1796) he was appointed Vice-Admiral. He then performed several missions to the ports of Genoa, La Speza and Antwerp. Between these voyages, Rosily provided General Napoléon Bonaparte with valuable information for the latter's expedition to Egypt. Some historians even surmise that the General may have offered to make Rosily commander of the fleet carrying his troops to Egypt, but Vice-Admiral de Rosily is believed to have declined this offer for family reasons.

During the famous naval battle of Trafalgar, he was blockaded within the port of Cadiz by the English and unfortunately could not join the fray.

In 1810, Vice-Admiral de Rosily became a member of the Council of Enquiry, after the swift surrender of the island of Bourbon in 1809. He was President of the Council of Naval Construction in 1811, and, in 1814 reorganised the corps of hydrographic engineers. In 1827, he was appointed Honorary Director-General of the Navy depot. He retired in 1831 and died in January 1832. Rosily was a member of the Academy of Brest, of the Academy of Sciences of the Institute and of the Office of Longitudes. He was Grand Cross of the Order of Saint-Louis, of the Royal Order of Dannebrog (honorary Danish order founded by King Christian V in 1671), and Grand Officer of the Legion of Honour.

OPPOSITE: Vice-Admiral Count de Rosily-Mesros.
Engraving by A Maurin, printed by Lemercier, 1835.

DE ROSILY·MESROS .

ARMAND PHILIPPE GERMAIN, MARQUIS DE SAINT FÉLIX,
Vice-Amiral Commandeur de L'ordre Royal et Militaire de Saint Louis.

Vice-Admiral Armand Philippe Germain, Marquis de Saint-Félix de Maurémont (1772–1779; 1791–1794)

Born in the Lot at Carjac, this great sailor arrived at Isle de France in 1771 onboard the corvette *Heure-du-Berger*. He was 34. From 1772, the Intendant Poivre sent Saint-Félix to sea in search of the famous island of João de Lisboa. After a long voyage during which he found not a single trace of the island, he became convinced that it did not exist, but could not prove it.

In 1774, Saint-Félix was ordered to take to Madagascar the Hungarian adventurer Beniowsky, who intended to establish a colony there. Then, in 1775, he was sent onboard the *Atalante* on a mission to the Malabar coast, to chase away the pirates who plagued the area and were a threat to the trading-post of Mahé, which was reputed for its pepper trade. In May the following year, Saint-Félix married Marie-Anne de Guermeur de Penhouët, with whom he had several children.

During a visit to France in 1780, Saint-Félix was appointed to Suffren's squadron, which he joined at the Cape of Good Hope in June 1781. When Suffren stopped at Isle de France to pick up reinforcements, Saint-Félix remained there for a few weeks before catching up with Suffren's Indian campaign, during which he was successively in command of the *Fine*, *Brillant* and *Artésien*. Being utterly exhausted after three consecutive battles against Admiral Hughes' famous squadron, during which he showed exceptional courage and fearlessness, Saint-Félix obtained leave from Suffren to return to Isle de France. He thus came to be involuntarily mixed up in the cabal of the Bailli's officers, instigated by Tromelin. They also subsequently requested leave to return to Isle de France, but for reasons which Suffren judged to be unfounded.

When peace was signed with England, Saint-Félix returned to France. He spent a few years there before going back to Isle de France, in 1791, to take up the post of Commander-in-Chief of the French naval forces in the Indian Ocean. After two successive campaigns in India, during 1792 and early 1793, he returned to Port-Nord-Ouest. Following a complaint filed against him by his crew, he came up against the Jacobin Circle, the "Chaumière", which unjustly blamed him for having misguidedly wished to attack some English ships. Full of bitterness, he then retired for some time on his property along the Black River. Appointed Vice-Admiral in 1793, he immediately left for a campaign in India, but returned in mid-August, fearing an attack on the island by the English. A week later, he received an order from the Regional Assembly to take to sea once more against the English in India. Although he was not convinced of the soundness of that decision, he returned to sea on 21 August. When he was

OPPOSITE: Vice-Admiral Marquis de Saint-Félix.
Lithography by P Riviére, Toulouse.

MAGON.

forced by bad weather to return to Port-Nord-Ouest shortly after, on 27 August, his return was immediately construed by the Regional Assembly as an act of rebellion. Exasperated by this turn of events, Saint-Félix resigned from his post, a gesture which did not fail to create a bad impression on minds which were somewhat excited in the year 1793. So, sensing growing hostility against him, Saint-Félix left for the island of Bourbon in November 1793. He was immediately suspended from his duties by the Colonial Assembly and then relieved of his command by the Civil Commissioner.

Through their influence, the Jacobins forced Governor Malartic to have Saint-Félix arrested at Saint-André. He was brought back to Isle de France in May 1794 and was imprisoned in the tower of Saint-Louis Cathedral at Port-Nord-Ouest. When tried by a Commission of Enquiry appointed by the Colonial Assembly, he was acquitted in November of that same year because the accusations brought against him could not be proved. As soon as he was freed, he settled in his property along the Black River, where he spent a few peaceful years. However, being afflicted by constant health problems, he finally returned to France for good. He left on Isle de France his second son, Philippe de Saint-Félix who married Thérèse Pas de Beaulieu, and raised a family. On Saint-Félix's return to France, Napoléon granted him a comfortable pension, and Louis XVIII subsequently awarded him the Grand Cross of Saint-Louis. He passed away at Carjac on 10 August 1819.

Rear-Admiral Charles René Magon de Médine (1784–1798)

Son of Governor Magon de la Villebague[35], Charles René Magon de Médine joined the State Navy in Brittany. In 1777, at the age of 14, he enlisted as a midshipman. From that time, he criss-crossed the oceans, acquiring experience which was soon to allow him to participate in battle as a member of the squadron of Count d'Orvilliers, and then that of Count de Grasse.

After being made prisoner by the English, and later freed, Magon returned to the Indian Ocean campaign for several years. During one of his many stops on Isle de France, Magon married the widow Reine Françoise de Langlade, in 1784 when he was 21.

Having been appointed lieutenant, Magon's main mission was to protect Isle de France and Bourbon, as well as the French establishments in India, against English attacks. On his return to Isle de France, he was promoted to the rank of captain and naval adviser to Governor Malartic. Subsequently, in 1795, Magon became head of the French naval forces in the Indian Ocean, a post he held for two years until the nomination of Rear-Admiral de Sercey. After the latter's arrival, Magon sided with the Governor and the Colonial Assembly against the agents of the Directoire, Baco and Burnel,

OPPOSITE: Rear-Admiral Magon de Médine, son of Isle de France Governor, René Magon de la Villebague.
Engraving by A Maurin, printed by Lemercier, 1837.

who had come to Isle de France to see to the application of the decree of the Convention on abolishing slavery. Baco and Burnel were sent back to France. Magon's stand caused him to be demoted as soon as he returned to Rochefort in 1798. In spite of that, after the intervention of Admiral Bruix, he was reintegrated into the Navy and promoted to head of division. He served in the squadron of Villaret de Joyeuse at Santo-Domingo where, at the head of five vessels, he chased the English out of the fort and seized it. Appointed Rear-Admiral, he was allocated to the squadron of Admiral Villeneuve in the West Indies.

In 1805, while in command of the *Algésiras*, he served under the Spanish Admiral de Gravina. After a tough battle, in which he once again displayed exemplary courage, he was wounded in the head and chest, and died from his wounds very shortly after.

Vice-Admiral Pierre César Charles Guillaume, Marquis de Sercey (1796–1802; 1805–1811)

From the young age of 13, this native of Bourgogne accompanied his uncle, the Marquis de Saint-Aubin, to Santo-Domingo. Sercey took part in many expeditions to the Leeward Islands and to India, during which, he stopped at Isle de France. When the explorer Yves Kerguelen was despatched in search of the Southern Lands, Sercey was a member of the expedition on board the *Gros-Ventre*, under Captain Saint-Allouarn. After serving on the *Amphitrite* under the Marquis de Grasse-Tilly, Sercey was appointed lieutenant and then put in command of the *Belle Poule*, under the orders of Count du Bouexic de Guichen, Lieutenant-General of the naval forces. Sercey was only 29 when he received the Cross of Saint-Louis. Promoted to the rank of captain in 1790, he was sent on a mission to Santo-Domingo, where, during the slaves rebellion, he saved the lives of thousands of settlers by taking them on board the ships of his squadron. Sercey was appointed Rear-Admiral in 1793, but on his return to France, he was dismissed from his duties for being a *ci-devant* aristocrat, and imprisoned.

After the execution of Robespierre, Sercey was freed and restored to his rank and promoted Commander-in-Chief of the French naval forces in the Indian Ocean. In June 1796, he arrived at Isle de France, with the Directoire agents Baco and Burnel on board. He participated in their dismissal, siding with the Colonial Assembly and Governor Malartic. A year later, he married Victorine Suzanne Cailleau de Courtemain at Port-Louis. Based at Isle de France, he spent nearly seven years protecting the French establishments in India and supporting France's allies, the Dutch, who were constantly under threat from the British forces. He returned to

ABOVE: Vice-Admiral Lord Nelson (1758–1805). Like Vice-Admiral Magon on board the *Algésiras*, the English squadron commodore, Vice-Admiral Nelson died on board the *Victory* in October 1805 at the Battle of Trafalgar. A real genius at the strategy of naval warfare, the English Admiral, with inferior forces, inflicted a stinging defeat on Napoléon's navy, who gave up for good his plan to invade England. The French and Spanish lost 23 ships and 4,400 sailors, whereas the English only lost 448 sailors.
Engraving by T Woolnoth from an original by Hoppner, 19th century.

OPPOSITE: Vice-Admiral Marquis de Sercey, Peer of France.
Engraving by A Maurin, lithography by Lemercier Printers, Paris, 1836.

Lith de Lemercier à Paris

Vᵗᵉ Maurin
1836.

SERCEY.

France in 1802, and there, being dissatisfied with the conditions imposed upon him by Decrès, the Minister of the Navy, Sercey applied for retirement and returned to Isle de France, his second country, to settle there in 1805. But when the island was conquered by the English in 1810, Sercey could not bear to submit to their government and returned to France with his family after selling his property.

Sercey was made Commander of the Legion of Honour in 1804, and Grand Officer in 1814. That same year, he was appointed Vice-Admiral and, in 1816 Commander of Saint-Louis, and later Grand Cross of the Legion of Honour in 1820. Sercey passed away in 1836 at the age of 83.

Vice-Admiral Count Charles Alexandre Léon Durand de Linois (1791–1793; 1803–1805)

A native of Brest, Linois joined the Navy as a volunteer in 1776, at the age of 15. After taking part in the American War of Independence, he was promoted to the rank of lieutenant in 1791. From 1791 to 1793, Linois was based at Isle de France in the squadron of Saint-Félix, who was Commander-in-Chief of the French naval forces in the Indian Ocean. On his return to France, he was captured by the English after a battle outside Brest. As soon as he was set free, Linois was promoted to the rank of captain. Taken prisoner again in 1795, he was released and appointed head of division and then Rear-Admiral three years later.

In 1801, Linois defeated an English division in the harbour of Algésiras in Spain. As a reward for this exploit, Linois received a sword of honour from the First Consul Napoléon Bonaparte. A year after, Linois was promoted Commander-in-Chief of the French naval forces in the Indian Ocean. On 6 March 1803, he left Brest harbour with Captain-General Decaen who had been appointed Governor of Pondicherry. When he reached his destination, the English, who had resumed hostilities in spite of the Treaty of Amiens of 1802, refused to return the town to the French, who were then compelled to head for Isle de France, where Decaen's appointment as Governor of Isle de France and the island of Bourbon was confirmed.

Linois remained based on Isle de France for two years, during which he spent most of his time chasing after the English. With only four ships in his squadron, Linois managed to capture 23 enemy vessels. However, being in constant disagreement with Decaen who blamed him for his lack of fighting spirit, Linois eventually requested to be recalled to France. While he was on his way to France with the *Marengo* and the *Belle Poule* in 1806, these two ships were captured off Cape Verde

OPPOSITE: Death of Rear-Admiral Magon. During the famous naval Battle of Trafalgar, in October 1805, this son of the governor of Isle de France was in command of the ship *Algésiras*, at the head of a squadron of three ships. After putting on full dress uniform in order to motivate his sailors, he was severely wounded in the chest and head. These wounds quickly proved fatal. On hearing of his death, Napoléon is reported to have said: "With money and wood, I will have other ships but the loss of Rear-Admiral Magon is beyond repair." His name, along with those of other distinguished brave officers, is engraved on the Arc de Triomphe in Paris.
Drawing by Alfred Paris, engraving by V Rouq, late 19th century.

BELOW: Vice-Admiral Count Durand de Linois.
Engraving by A Maurin, 1835.

by the English after a stiff fight. Linois was captured and kept prisoner for eight years. After his liberation in April 1814, he was appointed Governor of Guadeloupe. The island was captured by the English during his administration. Having been blamed for this loss, he was tried, court-martialled and acquitted in 1816. Having been allowed to retire, he was appointed Honorary Vice-Admiral in 1825 and Grand Officer of the Legion of Honour in 1831. He died at Versailles in 1848.

Rear-Admiral Baron Jaques Félix Emmanuel Hamelin (1809–1810)

After several years in the merchant navy, this young sailor, a native of Honfleur, joined the State Navy in 1792, at the age of 24. After four years' service in the Mediterranean and Atlantic Ocean, Hamelin was appointed frigate captain. His reputation as a seafarer was already well established when he was chosen by the Consulate to command the *Naturaliste*, one of the two frigates of Nicolas Baudin's expedition to explore the Southern Lands, which stopped at Isle de France in 1801, and again on the way back in 1803.

In September of that year, Hamelin was appointed captain, and on his return to France, head of division at Le Havre. In 1808, Hamelin was sent on board the *Vénus* to support the French command at Isle de France, and to replace Linois. He reached the island in March 1809, after capturing several prizes on the way. In the night of 16 to 17 September 1809, he fought a glorious battle against the powerful English frigate, the *Ceylon*, which he captured off the coast of Isle de France.

On 22 August 1810, Decaen ordered Hamelin to join Duperré and his squadron, who were locked in battle with the English in the harbour of Grand-Port (Port-Impérial). Hampered by opposing winds, he was delayed but reached the area just in time, however, to stop the *Iphigenia* in its tracks and order the English Captain Lambert, to surrender. On his return to France, Hamelin was made a Baron of the Empire. Promoted to the rank of Rear-Admiral, he was entrusted with the command of a division of l'Escaut's squadron.

Baron Hamelin was appointed Commander of the Brest squadron in 1813, Chevalier of Saint-Louis and Major-General of the Navy at Toulon in 1818, then Commander of the naval forces in the Mediterranean in 1822. In 1828, Hamelin was made a Grand Officer of the Legion of Honour. Later, in 1832, Hamelin was appointed Inspector-General of the Navy, then Director of Maps and Plans. He died in 1839 while still occupying that position.

OTHER GREAT FIGURES OF THE FRENCH NAVY AND THEIR ACTIVITIES AT ISLE DE FRANCE

Admiral Count Charles Henri d'Estaing (1759–1761)

Born on 24 November 1729 at Ravel Castle (an ancient royal fortress dating from the 12th century, whose first owner was Pierre de Ravel) in Auvergne, Charles Henri d'Estaing was the son of Charles François d'Estaing, Marquis de Saillans, and his first wife, Marie-Henriette Colbert, a descendant of the brother of Jean-Baptiste Colbert, who was Louis XIV's famous minister.

D'Estaing began a military career in the infantry in 1745 and reached the rank of brigadier of the king's armies in 1756. After taking part in the battles of Lawfeld and Rocourt in 1747 and 1748, he was dispatched to India under the command of Lally-Tollendal with the troops which had embarked with the Count d'Aché's fleet. During the Seven Years' War, d'Estaing was taken prisoner by the English at the siege of Madras in 1758. After being freed on parole, he decided to change his army corps and, in 1759, obtained Choiseul's permission to serve in the French Navy. D'Estaing then moved to Port-Louis at Isle de France, where he fitted out two corsair vessels at his own expense, the *Condé* and the *Expédition*.

D'Estaing left Port-Louis in command of these two ships, and went to war in the Persian Gulf and the East Indies. He went from success to success in all his undertakings. D'Estaing successfully carried out brilliant and devastating raids on several British trading posts and returned to Isle de France with substantial booty after four months' campaigning at sea. On his way home to France, d'Estaing was captured and again taken prisoner by the English. He then faced the risk of being hanged by the British authorities for failing to keep his parole. However, in view of his high social rank, Versailles intervened and d'Estaing was freed in 1762.

On his return, d'Estaing was appointed Lieutenant-General of the naval forces by Choiseul in July 1762. In October of the same year, he was promoted Fleet Commander and Viceroy of Brazil, with the mission of conquering that country. But the signature of the Treaty of Paris in 1763 took d'Estaing by surprise and the fleet was disarmed.

In 1764, d'Estaing was appointed governor of Santo-Domingo and administered this French possession for two years. Made a knight of the Order of the Holy Spirit in 1768, he was then appointed Vice-Admiral of the Seas of America and Asia in 1777. D'Estaing then played an active part in the American War of Independence supporting General Washington with the famous Marquis de La Fayette.

ABOVE: George Washington (1732–1799). Commander-in-Chief of the insurgents' army during the American War of Independence from 1775 to 1783, and first President of the United States from 1789 to 1797. In 1778, Louis XVI sent Vice-Admiral Count d'Estaing, in command of a squadron of 12 vessels and 4 frigates, to assist in the American struggle against the English. When d'Estaing reached New York on board the *Languedoc*, he found that the city was defended by 12,000 soldiers commanded by General Henry Clinton, and realised that it would be most imprudent to land. A meeting was convened between General George Washington, d'Estaing and General La Fayette to establish a new attack strategy. At this meeting, the siege of Newport was decided upon and d'Estaing sailed with his squadron to Rhode Island. The siege was a failure, but it was during this action that Captain André de Suffren, commanding his vessel *Fantasque* and three frigates, distinguished himself. By his bold and sudden actions, he managed to spread panic within the enemy's ranks. The English even scuttled five frigates and two corvettes rather than let them fall into French hands.

Drawing by Marck, engraving by Birtonnier, published by Pourrat, Paris, 19th century.

HAMELIN.

D'ESTAING.

In April 1778, d'Estaing left the port of Toulon on board the *Languedoc* at the head of 12 ships and 4 frigates and sailed towards America in order to help George Washington and the insurgents. However, he was not able to defeat the naval forces of Admiral Howe with his fleet. After an unsuccessful attempt to recapture Saint Lucia in the Caribbean, d'Estaing brilliantly seized the islands of Saint Vincent and Grenada, having defeated Admiral Byron.

When d'Estaing asked for reinforcements, Versailles sent him three squadrons, commanded respectively by the Marquis de Grasse-Tilly, Count de la Motte (called la Motte-Piquet) and the Marquis de Vaudreuil. D'Estaing was now at the head of a fleet of 42 vessels (26 ships, 13 frigates, 1 store ship, 1 schooner and 1 cutter).

After several unfruitful manoeuvres, he was ordered to return to France. But, learning that the insurgents were again in trouble in Georgia in America, he decided to disregard the order and carry on fighting. In October 1779, he was unable to capture the port of Savannah in Georgia despite a successful landing of 3,000 soldiers, in consultation with General Benjamin Lincoln. The assault was probably badly prepared and too hasty. It is evident that the Franco-American coordination must have had significant weaknesses, for the attack was a failure. Meanwhile, the English had recaptured Georgia and seized Charleston in South Carolina. Vice-Admiral d'Estaing then returned to France, leaving the Marquis de Grasse-Tilly in command of the fleet. He was then strongly and officially blamed by all his subordinates for his inexperience and incompetence in battle.

In July 1784, at the first General Assembly of the French branch of the Society of the Cincinnati, which took place at the Paris residence of Count d'Estaing, he was elected its first President. Subsequently, the Vice-Admiral was appointed to the Assemblée des Notables and made commander of the National Guard at Versailles. In October 1789, d'Estaing resigned from his post. He tried in vain to become the Minister of the French Navy, but only got the title of Admiral.

In 1793, d'Estaing was summoned to the trial of Marie-Antoinette, the Queen of France, where he maintained a moderate position and did not condemn the Queen. In 1794, he was arrested on the charge of having supported an alleged conspiracy. D'Estaing refused to defend himself at his trial and, after having given his service record, he uttered this memorable sentence: "When you will have cut my head, send it to the English, they will pay a high price for it." On 28 April 1794, Admiral Charles Henri d'Estaing, Marquis de Saillans, Count d'Estaing and Viscount de Ravel, was condemned to death and beheaded.

Rear-Admiral Count Louis Thomas Villaret de Joyeuse (1774–1781)

After a duel, during which he fatally wounded his opponent, Villaret de Joyeuse, a native of Auch, resigned as guard of the king's household and enlisted in the Navy in 1773, at age 25. In February 1774, he joined his relative, Governor d'Arzac de Ternay at Isle de France, where he must have met Lapérouse. He remained there for seven years, during which he was very active in the Navy and served as officer under the orders of Lieutenant de Saint-Félix, then under Captain Tronjoly and under Colonel de Bellecombe, at the island of Bourbon. He was the captain of a fire-ship at Isle de France, when Suffren included him in his squadron before leaving Port-Louis for India in December 1781. Villaret de Joyeuse distinguished himself throughout the Bailli's famous campaign, at the end of which he was made a lieutenant, in July 1784.

On returning to France in 1785, Villaret de Joyeuse was promoted to the rank of captain and pursued a remarkable career in the Navy. After an expedition to Newfoundland under the orders of the Marquis de Sercey, Villaret de Joyeuse was raised to the rank of Rear-Admiral in 1793.

At the head of his squadron, Villaret de Joyeuse fought a heroic battle off Finistère against Admiral Howe's squadron, long to be remembered for the glorious resistance of the *Vengeur*, which finally sank. Having engaged in politics on top of his other activities, he was involved in the Council of the Five Hundred, and contributed to improving conditions for crews, and emphasised the usefulness of the activities of Surcouf in the Indian Ocean.

Appointed head of squadron for a grand expedition against Santo-Domingo in 1801, he took the lead of 40 vessels and 12,000 men, and sailed towards Santo-Domingo to repress the massive slave revolt led by General Toussaint Louverture. He was unfortunately unable to achieve all his goals. In spite of the expedition's failure, Napoléon appointed him Captain-General of Martinique in 1802. Like Captain-General Decaen at Isle de France, he suffered from the stranglehold of the British blockade until his surrender in 1806. In spite of this setback, Villaret de Joyeuse, who was already Chevalier de Saint Louis and Grand Cross of the Legion of Honour, was awarded the title of Count by the Emperor, and in 1811, was appointed Governor of Venice, where he died a year later.

Vice-Admiral Justin Bonaventure Count Morard de Galle (1776; 1781–1790)

This exceptional sailor was born at Goncelin in the Dauphiné in March 1741. Morard de Galle was the son of an infantry captain whose aristocratic roots can be traced to the 11th century. At the age of 11, he enlisted in the

MORARD DE GALLE.

king's household police. He joined the navy in 1757 as a guard. He first served on the brig *Écureuil*, then on the *Hermine*, which was shipwrecked in 1761. He then served on the frigate *Fleur-de-Lys* in the American fleet. He took an active part in two battles. Morard de Galle was then appointed Garde du Pavillon, a title given to the élite among the navy guards. He went on to serve on the ship *Sceptre* and then on the *Christine*.

In 1765, on board the *Héroïne*, he distinguished himself in the campaign against the Mediterranean Barbaresque pirates. Promoted to sub-lieutenant on board the *Etna*, he took part in the bombardment of Larache on the Atlantic coast of Morocco. During this campaign, Morard de Galle undertook the mission of blowing up one of the pirate vessels which had taken refuge under the protection of the coastal batteries. He went into action in the middle of the night and attached a *chemise soufrée* (canvas dipped in combustible material) to the side of the enemy ship. The success of this bold mission was heralded half an hour later by a terrifying explosion.

First on board the *Lunette*, then on the supply ship the *Normande*, Morard de Galle reached Port-Louis at Isle de France in 1776. After several campaigns on the coasts of Africa and India, he was appointed ship's lieutenant in 1777. In 1781, he joined the fleet of Suffren, who put him in command of the *Annibal* after the death of Captain Trémignon at the battle of La Praya. Morard de Galle was also wounded during that battle. After a short stay at Isle de France in October of the same year, he again joined the fleet of the famous Bailli and sailed towards India in command of the *Pourvoyeuse*.

In 1782, Suffren decided to put Morard de Galle in command of an important English prize: the *Hannibal*. Morard de Galle then took part in the Battle of Sadras, during which he behaved in a highly commendable manner. However, he did not perform particularly well while in command of that vessel during the Battle of Trincomalee on 3 September 1782. Then, to Suffren's surprise, he, together with Captain Saint-Félix and Captain Lalandelle, requested leave to return to Isle de France on grounds of ill-health. Nevertheless, he was promoted to ship's captain on the recommendation of the Bailli and received the Cross of Saint-Louis. Once his health had been restored at Isle de France, he returned to combat with Suffren in India and took part in the Battle of Cuddalore in June 1783. On his return to Isle de France, he married Louise de Maudave, daughter of Count Louis Fayd'herbe de Maudave. He left Isle de France in 1790.

In 1792, Morard de Galle was promoted to Rear-Admiral, and later Vice-Admiral in 1793. He was unexpectedly relieved of his command and imprisoned by order of the revolutionary André Jeanbon, who was responsible for the navy within the Comité de Salut Public. Morard de

OPPOSITE: Vice-Admiral Count Morard de Galle.
Engraving by A Maurin, printed by Lemercier, 1837.

FOLLOWING PAGES (LEFT, FROM TOP): Property of Mr Quirivel; view of Mr Roussel's property.
Drawing and engraving by Jacques Milbert, 1812.

FOLLOWING PAGES (RIGHT, FROM TOP): View from the interior of the forest; view of the mountain of Calebasses.
Drawing and engraving by Jacques Milbert, 1812.

Galle was reinstated in 1795 and then served under the command of Rear-Admiral Bouvet, taking part in the Irish expedition of 1796. A senator in 1800, he became secretary of the Senate in 1803. Grand Officer of the Legion of Honour in 1804, he was awarded a noble status and given the title of Count in 1808. He died in 1809 at Guéret in the Creuse.

Vice-Admiral Baron Jean-Baptiste Willaumez, Peer of France (1778–1780; 1794–1795)

From age 14, this Breton sailed as ship's boy aboard the *Bien-Aimé*, under Bougainville. He first landed at Isle de France in May 1778. During one of his many campaigns, he found himself on the *Louise* off the coast of Flic-en-Flac. The ship was wrecked and Willaumez had to swim ashore.

Chevalier de Tronjoly, then head of the French naval forces in the Indian Ocean, gave Willaumez the responsibility of the signal station on Signal Mountain (near Port-Louis), a duty he carried out successfully until February 1780. Willaumez then returned to Lorient and served on several ships under the orders of the most famous commanders of the time, such as Latouche-Tréville, Lapérouse and Bruni d'Entrecasteaux.

Willaumez was on board the *Recherche* in 1791, when the Convention launched an expedition to search for Lapérouse. He was promoted to the rank of lieutenant and subsequently awarded the Cross of Saint-Louis. After the failure of the expedition and the death of d'Entrecasteaux and Kermadec, who had assumed command, Willaumez was among the men imprisoned by the Dutch at Batavia, the port where the expedition had been compelled to call. After four months in captivity, he was freed, along with many officers and scientists who had taken part in the adventure. They then embarked on a Dutch ship, which brought them to Isle de France in April 1794, during the troubled period of the Revolution. The English were still in the area, threatening the island and restricting the free movement of ships on the ocean. Captain Jean-Marie Renaud, who was head of the French naval forces at that time, then decided to attack the enemy. He despatched a small squadron in their pursuit. This included Willaumez, at the head of around 50 soldiers. The battle raged off Flacq and Grand-Port. After 136 men were killed or severely wounded, the English fled.

On his return to Brest in February 1795, Willaumez handed over to the Minister for the Navy the precious documents of the d'Entrecasteaux expedition, which, by a clever trick, he had managed to hide at the bottom of a tea chest. In May 1796, he was despatched to Batavia, in order to search for the remnants of the expedition. Thanks to Willaumez, about a hundred

ABOVE: Vice-Admiral Baron Willaumez, Peer of France. *Printed by Chardon.*

breadfruit tree plants, which had been tended for two years by the gardener La Haye, were successfully retrieved and, in 1797, reached their intended destinations, the French colonies of Isle de France, Martinique and Cayenne (in what is now French Guiana).

On his return to France, Willaumez worked hard, with Fleurieu and Rossel, to write a report of the d'Entrecasteaux expedition. He was appointed Rear-Admiral and Peer of France by Napoléon in 1805. Later, the Minister for the Navy Decrès rejected the suggestion of the Emperor, who wished to see Willaumez replace Linois at Isle de France. Despite this disappointment, his star continued to shine and an array of titles and decorations continued to be awarded to him by successive sovereigns. Indeed, Louis XVIII appointed him Vice-Admiral and Charles X made him Commander of the Order of Saint Louis and Grand Officer of the Legion of Honour. After being responsible for inspections and enquiries into military harbours, he was appointed President of the Navy Minister's Council of works by Louis Philippe. He wrote many reports and drew up plans, which the Navy were later to use as references. He died at Suresnes on 18 May 1845. Willaumez is considered one of the key figures in the history of the French Navy.

Vice-Admiral Denis Duke de Crès, Minister for the Navy (1791–1794)

Decrès joined the Navy at the age of 17. After eight years at sea, he was appointed lieutenant for having fought in the West Indies with the forces of the Marquis de Grasse-Tilly during the American War of Independence. Appointed commander of the *Cybèle* and Major-General within the division of Saint-Félix, he accompanied the latter as aide-de-camp on a mission to the island of Bourbon. Saint-Félix, having had some problems with the Colonial Assembly, asked Decrès to take his letter of protest to Isle de France. The letter caused such an outcry that Decrès was nearly murdered. On his return to France in February 1794, he was responsible for justifying the position of his leader, the Marquis de Saint-Félix, and for persuading the Convention to send reinforcements to Isle de France. To his utter amazement, he was arrested and deprived of his noble titles. He managed to avoid imprisonment and retired to the bosom of his family in Haute-Marne. For one year, he waited quietly for the situation to calm down.

In 1796, Decrès was appointed head of division, then Rear-Admiral in 1798, and distinguished himself at the Battle of Abukir. Later, in Malta, he was surrounded by the English, but by dint of obstinacy, managed to break through their blockade. Relentlessly pursued by the English, Decrès was

ABOVE: Breadfruit (*Artocarpus*). This fruit is a native of Polynesia. It is closely associated with the famous mutiny of the *Bounty*; Captain Bligh having, among other actions, deprived his crew of water in order to water young breadfruit plants he had on board, intended for the English West Indies.

207

DECRES.

finally captured and taken prisoner. His detention was short, however, and, as soon as he returned to France, he pursued a brilliant career. After a short term as Prefect of Lorient, Decrès was appointed squadron commander, then, in 1801, Minister for the Navy, a post in which he remained under Napoléon for 13 years until March 1814. In spite of the enormous difficulties of the French navy during that period, which were mainly due to the exile or dismissal of its best leaders during the Revolution, Decrès fulfilled his duties quite adequately. However, it was under his administration that, in 1810, Isle de France was conquered by the English. Indeed, tired of waiting for reinforcements which never arrived, Decaen had been forced to surrender when faced by the enemy's naval forces. Many historians have attributed responsibility for the fall of the colony to Minister Decrès. Yet, as early as 1804, Decaen, being concerned about the future of the island, had dispatched his brother to Napoléon, who was then engaged in the Austerlitz campaign, to try and obtain a fleet and more troops, in order to be ready in case of an attack on the island. Orders had been transmitted to Decrès, who does not seem to have paid much attention to them. Decaen repeated his request in 1808, but, once more, in vain. Why this indifference on the Minister's part? Some historians have attributed this attitude to a personal grudge against the island's settlers, a feeling which stemmed from the attack he had suffered in 1792, while he was Major-General in the division of Saint-Félix. Others have asserted that his attitude came from spite at the rejection of his proposal of marriage to the daughter of a rich settler of Isle de France, with whom he was very much in love. Another theory is that he nursed a secret dislike of General Decaen, who had, in the past, attempted to discredit him in the eyes of the Emperor. Be that as it may, it was under his ministry that the beautiful Isle de France fell under the power of His British Majesty.

Rear-Admiral Baron Jean L'Hermitte (1796–1801)

This sailor, born at Coutances, began his career from the early age of 14 in the State Navy. After 13 years at sea, during which L'Hermitte acquired great experience, he was made a lieutenant in 1793. From 1793 to 1796, he captured and sank over a hundred enemy ships and boats in the English Channel and around the coasts of Norway and Ireland. In 1796, he arrived at Isle de France in the squadron of the Marquis de Sercey, in command of the *Vertu*. After a battle against two English frigates, Sercey put him in command of the *Preneuse*. L'Hermitte remained based at Isle de France for nearly five years, and undertook several heroic missions.

In 1798, while still in command of the *Preneuse*, L'Hermitte was ordered to take the ambassadors of Tipu Sultan back to Mangalore. When L'Hermitte

OPPOSITE: Vice Admiral Decrès. Minister for the Navy under Napoléon for 13 years, from 1801 to 1814.
Engraved by L Lauta, 19th century.

L'HERMITTE.

LEFT: Taking advantage of stormy weather, Captain L'Hermitte attacked and captured two English frigates in the port of Tellicherry, on the coast of Malabar, southeast of India.
Drawing by L Garneray, engraving by Pardinel.

OPPOSITE: Rear-Admiral Baron L'Hermitte.
Engraving by A Maurin, 1836.

was close to the Indian coasts, taking advantage of stormy weather, he attacked and seized two English frigates in the harbour of Tellicherry.

L'Hermitte remained in campaign for three months in Indian waters and captured about 40 enemy boats, before returning to Isle de France in May 1798. Being pursued by five English vessels, he anchored the *Preneuse* safely in the entrance of Black River and, after setting up seven cannons at the entrance to the channel, he kept the English squadron at bay for three weeks. Worn down by L'Hermitte's resistance, the English gave up.

L'Hermitte soon went back to war in the Mozambique Channel, where he attacked five English vessels in the Bay of Saint-François. Although he sustained serious damages, L'Hermitte managed as best he could to make for the open sea and headed for Isle de France. After about ten days at sea, he was attacked off the west coast by two English vessels, the *Adamant*, under the command of Admiral Pellew, and the *Tremendous*, under Captain Hotham. L'Hermitte fought like a lion in spite of the many wounded and sick on board. Under the enemy's devastating fire, the *Preneuse*, driven close to the reef at the Baie du Tombeau, was sinking, and L'Hermitte was compelled to lower his flag. Admiral Pellew ordered lifeboats to be sent to rescue his opponent. L'Hermitte, who was seriously wounded, was taken to the *Adamant*. He was so weak that when he came aboard he could hardly stand. Admiral Pellew raised the French flag in his honour, and, according to Garneray, welcomed L'Hermitte with a guard of honour of officers standing at attention. Admiral Pellew then came forward and said: "Captain,

please allow me to shake the hand of the bravest warrior I have ever met, I have no hesitation in so declaring!" L'Hermitte, as custom required, handed over his sword. "I accept it as the sword of a hero, and it will never leave me." said the Admiral. Then, unsheathing his own sword, Pellew offered it to the French captain, adding modestly: "I can only offer you in exchange the sword of a good and loyal sailor. Please accept it as a token of the high esteem in which I hold you." With respect and courtesy, he then invited L'Hermitte to lean on his arm and conducted him to his cabin.

On being freed in 1801, L'Hermitte returned to France, where he was congratulated by the First Consul. Appointed ship's captain in 1802, then head of division, he went to war on the American coast and sank or captured about 50 enemy vessels. He was made Baron and Rear-Admiral in 1807, then Maritime Prefect of Toulon in 1811. He retired in 1815. In 1826, L'Hermitte died at Plessis-Piquet near Paris, at the age of 60.

Rear-Admiral Pierre Henri Bouvet de Maisonneuve (1803–1811)

This exceptionally brave sailor was born on the island of Bourbon in 1775. His father, a ship's captain who was born at Saint-Servan, had married Marie Etiennette Perier d'Hauterive, who inspired the famous poet of Bourbon, the Chevalier de Parny. From the age of 12, the young Bouvet used to accompany his father on missions at sea. In 1795, he enlisted for service on warships, then spent several years on corsair ships which had their base at the port of Nantes. He was captured by the English on several occasions, but always managed either to escape or to benefit from an exchange of prisoners. On his return from a campaign in Guadeloupe with his cousin, Bouvet de Précourt, he was appointed lieutenant and posted to the division of Linois, which he joined at Isle de France in August 1803. He was then 28 years old.

After a campaign off the coast of Sumatra, Bouvet returned to Isle de France, then to Bourbon where he married Henriette Perier d'Hauterive, his first cousin. After the a mission, during which he was shipwrecked and taken prisoner in Bombay by the English, he returned to Isle de France. There he launched into the building of a corsair vessel, the *Entreprenant*, with which he captured many prizes. This success prompted him to build a larger, faster corsair ship which he also named *Entreprenant*.

During his many comings and goings between Isle de France and Bourbon to supervise works on this ship, he was captured and taken prisoner by Captain Willoughby, whose squadron was skulking in the area in order to set up a blockade around the islands. The clever Bouvet managed to strike a bargain with the English captain and thus obtained his freedom.

OPPOSITE: Admiral Edward Pellew, 1st Viscount Exmouth (1757–1833). On board the *Adamant*, Admiral Pellew received Captain L'Hermitte, who was seriously wounded while in command of the *Preneuse* off Baie du Tombeau. *Original painting by Sir T Lawrence, engraving by H Robinson, London, 1835.*

BELOW: Rear-Admiral Bouvet de Maisonneuve, the real victor in the Battle of Grand-Port.

He then completed the construction of his ship at Port-Louis, and returned to fight in the Indian Ocean, where he again engaged in the corsairs' war.

Recognising his talents, Decaen appointed Bouvet frigate captain and, in February 1810, he was put in command of the frigate *Minerve* within the division of Duperré, which consisted of four ships. On 14 August 1810, the English Captain Willoughby, on the *Néréide*, launched an attack at Port-Impérial (Grand-Port), and occupied Ile de la Passe, where he lay in ambush, waiting for the French squadron on its way to Port-Napoléon (Port-Louis). While Bouvet was cruising off Port-Impérial on 20 August on the *Minerve*, he fell into the trap and, preceded by the *Victor*, entered the harbour. Seeing that the *Victor* had struck its flag, Bouvet ordered it to follow him, and the two vessels made for the furthest part of the bay, closely followed by Duperré and the rest of his division. There ensued a battle which lasted from 23 to 26 August. Duperré was severely wounded at the beginning of hostilities and Bouvet took command; he moved to the *Bellone*, while Roussin took over the *Minerve*. Bouvet led the French to victory, constantly exhorting his men to fight with determination. Three English frigates were destroyed after a brave struggle. At the approach of the Hamelin division sent as reinforcement by Decaen, the fourth frigate, *Iphigenia*, surrendered, together with the fort of Ile de la Passe, which had been occupied by the English. Thanks to Bouvet, the battle was a triumph. As a reward for his bravery, Decaen appointed him head of a squadron of four ships and put him in command of the *Iphigenia*. On 12 September 1810, the indefatigable Bouvet fought a memorable battle off the coast of Bourbon against the *Africaine*, an English ship, which was obliterated. Later, after the capture of Isle de France in December 1810, he resided there before leaving for good in April 1811. He successfully carried out other missions in the Atlantic and the English Channel, before retiring in 1822 after receiving from the Napoléon III the order of Officer of the Legion of Honour. Bouvet died in 1860 at Saint-Servan, where the Emperor ordered a statue in his honour.

Admiral Baron Albin Reine Roussin, Minister for the Navy, Peer of France (1803–1808; 1810)

Born at Dijon on 21 April 1781, Roussin began his naval career as a ship's boy at age 12. Being dynamic and enterprising, he quickly climbed the hierarchy and became a sub-lieutenant in 1803, at 22. Having embarked on the *Sémillante* in Linois' division, he landed at Isle de France on 16 August 1803, at the same time as General Decaen. He accompanied Linois on his campaigns and frequently distinguished himself. When the latter returned to France in 1808, Roussin was promoted to lieutenant and was posted on

OPPOSITE: Admiral Baron Roussin. After the Battle of Grand-Port in August 1810, Roussin was presented to Napoléon at Morlaix in March 1811, where he was received very warmly by the Emperor.
After a painting by Charles Larivière, Palace of Versailles, 1841. Anonymous engraving, 19th century.

the *Iéna*, under Captain Morice. Captured by the English during a campaign in the Persian Gulf, he benefited from a prisoner exchange and returned to Isle de France in January 1810 on board the *Minerve*, where he assisted Captain Bouvet de Maisonneuve within the Duperré division.

At the Battle of Grand-Port, on 23 August 1810, Duperré, having been seriously wounded in the face, was forced to abandon his battle station, and was replaced by Bouvet on the *Bellone*. Lieutenant Roussin was thus left in command of the *Minerve*. The latter displayed both courage and initiative, rising to the occasion and endeavouring without respite to help win the struggle. When the guns of English frigate *Néréide* were finally reduced to silence, Roussin was sent on board to take it over, and it was he who discovered the apparently lifeless body of Captain Willoughby, wrapped in a Union Jack and seriously wounded in the eye. He then ordered that Willoughby should be taken aboard the *Bellone* along side Duperré in order to receive first aid. Roussin's bravery throughout this battle was recognised by General Decaen, who promoted him to frigate captain.

When the English conquered Isle de France a few months later, in December 1810, Roussin promptly returned to France, where he pursued a brilliant naval career. Promoted to ship's captain in 1814, he successfully carried out important missions to Brazil and Portugal, where he negotiated with Emperor Don Pedro I and Don Miguel, respectively. He became Rear-Admiral in 1822, then Vice-Admiral in 1831, and a Peer of France the year after. After serving as French ambassador at Constantinople, he reached the summit of his career when he was appointed Admiral and Minister for the Navy in 1840, a post which he held until January 1843, first in the government of Adolphe Thiers, and then that of François Guizot. Roussin died in Paris on 22 January 1854, at the age of 73.

Admiral Baron Victor Guy Duperré, Minister for the Navy, Peer of France (1809–1810)

This La Rochelle native left for India in 1791 at age 16. He sailed around the seas of the world for nine years before obtaining his first command position on the *Pélagie*. Duperré was appointed ship's lieutenant in October 1805, and embarked on the *Veteran*, under the orders of the Emperor's brother, Jérôme Bonaparte, en route for a campaign at the Cape of Good Hope, and on to the West Indies and Brazil. He was soon appointed frigate captain, and sailed for a campaign in the West Indies, in command of the *Sirène*. On his return, he defeated an English squadron near Glénans.

OPPOSITE: Portrait of Admiral Baron Duperré.
Lithograph of Delpech.

Promoted to ship's captain, he was despatched to Isle de France, which he reached in May 1809 on board the *Bellone* after capturing several prizes

Duperré.

along the way. Another fruitful campaign kept Duperré for a further six months in the Gulf of Bengal. On his return to Port-Napoléon in January 1810, Duperré remained there for three months before going out to sea again, bringing with him two captured frigates, the *Minerve* and the *Victor*. While cruising in the Mozambique Channel, he captured the *Ceylon* and the *Wyndham*, two vessels of the East India Company. On his return to Isle de France on 20 August, while rounding the southeast coast, he received a message from the fort at Ile de la Passe informing him of the enemy's presence off the islet of Coin de Mire. He then decided to call at Grand-Port but while he was about to enter the channel, a vessel displaying the French flag, which was at anchor close to the Ile de La Passe islet, hoisted the Union Jack and immediately opened fire. It was the *Néréide*, Captain Willoughby's ship! The English had taken possession of the islet, and lured the French into a trap. Taken by surprise, Duperré, who was not placed at the head of the convoy, followed the movement begun by Bouvet, who had already entered the port and who had decided to assemble his division there. On 23 August, three English frigates arrived as reinforcements and the battle began. Duperré was seriously wounded in the first few hours of fighting. Bouvet, who was in command of the *Minerve*, went over to the *Bellone* in order to direct operations. After fierce fighting, during which three English frigates were destroyed, the French were victorious. Duperré was looked after alongside Willoughby in the house of Mr de Robillard (the present National History Museum, Mahébourg). In October, when Duperré had recovered, he heading for Port-Napoléon, followed by his squadron. He received a triumphant welcome from the island's inhabitants. This naval victory did not stop the English from landing in the north of Isle de France four months later, and becoming the masters of the small colony.

On his return to France, Duperré was appointed Rear-Admiral in 1811 and commander of the light squadron of the French naval forces in the Mediterranean, then those of the Adriatic. During the Hundred Days, he was Maritime Prefect of Toulon and protected that port against the Anglo-Sicilian alliance. He obtained the surrender of Cadix in September 1823, at the head of a squadron, and was promoted to the rank of Vice-Admiral in October. Three years later, in 1826, he was appointed commander of the naval forces in the West Indies, after ridding those waters of pirates. He was Maritime Prefect of Brest when Charles X, in July 1830, entrusted him with a mission to conquer Algiers. His success in this mission earned him a promotion to the rank of Admiral and to the peerage of France. He was later appointed Minister for the Navy, and kept this post for three terms before retiring in 1843. He died three years later and was buried at Les Invalides.

OPPOSITE: The Battle of Grand-Port. "Calm, which had fallen after the ceaseless boom of artillery, had freed the tide's ebb and flow to bring with it, around our ships, the bodies of hundreds of victims who had been struck dead while bravely defending the cause." *After a painting by Gilbert, engraving by Chavane.*

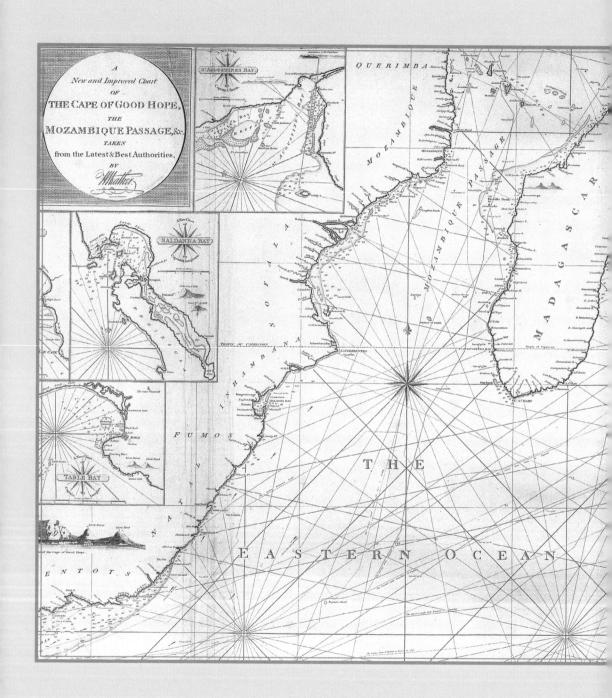

A
New and Improved Chart
OF
THE CAPE OF GOOD HOPE,
THE
MOZAMBIQUE PASSAGE, &c.
TAKEN
from the Latest & Best Authorities,
BY
W. Heather

St AUGUSTINES BAY.

SALDANHA BAY

TABLE BAY

QUERIMBA

MOZAMBIQUE

MOZAMBIQUE PASSAGE

MADAGASCAR

SOFALA

INHAMBANA

NATAL

FUMOS

ENTOTS

TROPIC OF CAPRICORN

THE

EASTERN OCEAN

THE END OF FRENCH COLONISATION

General Decaen, the Last French Governor

The Battle of Grand-Port

The Conquest of Isle de France by the English

Royal Navy Map used by the English during the months preceeding the conquest of the island by British forces in December 1810.

The future of Isle de France did not seem very bright at the beginning of the 19th century. Being involved in the wars of the Empire, France seemed to have other priorities than the needs of its two small colonies. Having already been very neglected since the Revolution, the colonies were no longer receiving food supplies nor financial and military support. They had to rely on their own resources to survive, but the situation was precarious. The crops, regularly destroyed by cyclones, were insufficient to feed a population and the people were constantly threatened by famine. In order to survive, there was only one way out: to attack English merchant ships to obtain food for the settlers. The Colonial Assembly therefore decided to encourage the corsairs' war. From 1793, spurred on by Governor Malartic, and later by General Decaen, many corsair ships left Port-Nord-Ouest with the aim of bringing back to Isle de France, the food they would seize from the enemy. Since then, the island therefore became the main home port of the corsairs, who, encouraged by incentives, regularly poured rich cargoes of pulses, food and goods of all kinds into the port's warehouses. These abundant riches were most welcomed by the colony. They not only helped to save the settlers from famine, but also to replenish the empty coffers of Isle de France as, while the island enjoyed a certain prosperity thanks to the corsairs, it remained very vulnerable in terms of its defences.

This deficiency was becoming all the more worrying because the English, being harassed from all sides by the corsairs' ships, and seeing their trade in India threatened with ruin, decided, from 1808, to destroy once and for

LEFT: "View of Pieter Both Mountain from Monplaisir."
After Louis Auguste de Sainson.

OPPOSITE: The verandah, a favourite place in which to relax, while enjoying the delightful scenery, sheltered from the sun's rays.
Drawing, from life, by Potémont, engraving by Frichon and L Chapon.

all with the "corsairs' nests" which Isle de France and the island of Bourbon had become. Gradually, strangled by the blockade set up by the enemy as soon as hostilities had resumed in 1803, despite the Treaty of Amiens in March 1802, Isle de France was thenceforth under threat. Being too vulnerable to resist the English onslaught which was being prepared and could occur at short notice, Isle de France could only have escaped this quandary if it were to have received the troop reinforcements which, despite General Decaen's urgent and repeated requests to Napoléon, never reached the island in time.

Thus it came about that, on 3 December 1810, after a heroic struggle, Isle de France had to bend its knee before its most formidable enemy. Although the name Mauritius replaced the beautiful one of Isle de France, nothing, however, will prevent the French spirit from living on there.

GENERAL DECAEN, THE LAST FRENCH GOVERNOR (1803–1810)

Comparing General Decaen to La Bourdonnais, Adrien d'Épinay, son of the famous French barrister and politician of that name, wrote: "These two men have left their mark, one at the beginning, and the other at the heroic end of the beautiful colony of Isle de France [...]."

This was due justice to the memory of General Decaen, who does not need further praise, although his name is all too often associated in public memory with the loss of the island. It is worth recalling here to what a dire situation the island had been reduced to when he was sent to administer it. It was partly owing to his great skills that the settlers were, in the short term, rescued from famine and poverty. The General, it must be emphasised, was a man of considerable worth, and it is likely that, under other circumstances, and especially with greater means at his disposal, his administration would not have ended in failure. Be that as it may, in spite of the feeble resources which were available to him, Decaen greatly contributed to the development of Isle de France by his wise and timely initiatives.

Charles Mathieu Isidore Decaen was a native of Calvados in Normandy, where he was born on 13 April 1769. He was the son of a lawyer. Decaen enlisted as a volunteer in the artillery corps of the Navy at the age of 18, but left the service after three years to study law. He enlisted again at the outbreak of war in 1792 and was promoted captain for Calvados. That was how Decaen came to serve under future famous generals of Napoléon: Kléber and Hoche in Vendée, as well as under

BELOW: Napoléon (1769–1821). In May 1808, Napoléon wrote to his Navy Minister, Vice-Admiral Decrès, in these terms: "We should not leave our colonies during such a long time without news. General Decaen rightly complained that, long after Tilsit, he was not aware of the peace treaty which he haphazardly learned from an American vessel. However, there are thousands of means to inform him, from America to Isle de France or from our ports to Isle de France".
Engraving by Vallot from an original painting by Jacques Louis David in 1812.

OPPOSITE: Captain-General Charles Decaen, the last French Governor of Mauritius.
Lithography by Prodhomme, engraving by L Lauta.

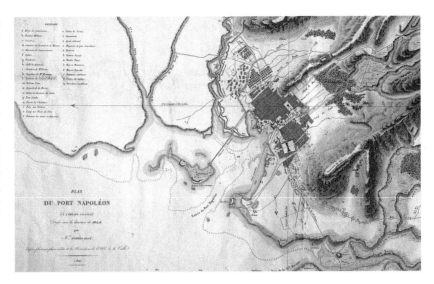

Desaix and Jourdan. Appointed divisional general under the command of General Moreau in Germany by a Consulate decree of August 1800, Decaen contributed to the victory of Hohenlinden. In July 1802, Napoléon appointed him Captain-General of the French establishments in India, at Pondicherry, on the basis of his reputation for courage and his military prowess.

The five ships in the expedition departed from Brest in March 1803. Decaen reached Pondicherry on 22 July in order to reinstate French sovereignty and take up his duties. He and his family were on board the *Marengo* of the squadron of Rear-Admiral Linois, Commander-in-Chief of the French naval forces in the Indian Ocean.

However, in spite of the agreements spelt out in the Treaty of Amiens, the English kept their hold on Pondicherry, and the powerful English squadron which was patrolling the harbour tried to prevent the French vessels from entering it. In the face of this hostile behaviour, Decaen then decided to implement the plans of the Minister for the Navy and to establish his headquarters at Isle de France.

On the morning of 17 August, the future Governor entered Port-Louis harbour on board the *Belle Poule*. A huge crowd had gathered on the quayside to welcome him. To everyone's surprise, Decaen first set foot on the soil of Isle de France in full military uniform, and was surrounded by his troops in arms. It goes without saying that this demonstration of power was not to the taste of all the settlers! But if the future governor had sought right from the start to make a show of his authority over the inhabitants, it was because he had his own good reasons for doing so: having learnt that the Colonial Assembly took liberties and thus abused its powers, he had

decided to make a show of firmness from the very beginning. The settlers, for their part, adopted an attitude of mistrust towards this decidedly too "soldierly" general. However, when the island's worthy citizens came to appreciate the man's calibre, these misunderstandings quickly dissipated.

On 23 September 1803, Decaen was confirmed as Governor-General with the title of Captain-General of French Establishments to the east of the Cape of Good Hope. This title, which was equivalent at the time to that of Marshal of France, gave him considerable powers.

Decaen was an active and energetic man, and, as such, believed that a sound administration must rely above all on an adequate military and legal structure. Thus, his first actions included the abolition of the jurisdictions created under the Revolution, and the restoration of the island's districts. On the other hand, Decaen promulgated Code Napoléon, which he adapted to local conditions. His contribution in this respect was such that the settlers called the compendium of laws and public decrees the "Decaen Code". A special tribunal to probe into the crimes and misdeeds of slaves was also established.

Decaen displayed organisational skills in the military field. After setting up a National Guard in each area, he undertook the creation of two special units: one of them was that of the "chasseurs de Bourbon", made up of 300 Créoles from the island of Bourbon, and, the other, a reserve battalion named the "African Battalion", whose strength came up to 650 men. A powder mill was also built near the Jardin de la Compagnie, while all the fortification systems originally created by La Bourdonnais were reactivated and improved.

In 1805, Decaen decided to equip Port-Sud-Est, which had been somewhat neglected. In addition to fortifications, he also built barracks, vast warehouses, as well as many buildings for various purposes, so that the locality quickly took on the appearance of a busy little town. It was named Mahébourg in honour of Mahé de La Bourdonnais, the colony's founder. As far as education was concerned, Decaen's first concern was to provide the island with a secondary school. Completed in 1806, the Lycée Colonial received an enthusiastic welcome from the settlers. Decaen also undertook some development works, including the renovation of the mansion of the Reduit: this second home of the governors, built by Barthélemy David, was quite derelict and its gardens needed rehabilitation, having been left untended since the departure of Governor Thomas Conway. Decaen also took the initiative of adding a second storey to Government House, which provided more space for the administrative offices, while giving a more prestigious appearance to the old building. Moreover, Decaen had a bridge erected over Grande-Rivière in order to improve connections and links with Port-Louis.

While Decaen distinguished himself as an enterprising and energetic administrator, he nevertheless had his weaknesses, namely a fiery and quick-tempered disposition. We can recall his quarrels with Surcouf, who was also notorious for being quick to anger. Decaen also often criticised Rear-Admiral Linois, specially for his failure to capture the annual convoy of the English fleet which was loaded with cargoes of precious goods from China. This booty would have been welcomed in the colony, whose financial situation left much to be desired, on top of which the effects of a blockade by the English were beginning to make themselves felt. It was therefore essential for the Governor to seize some prizes so as to avoid having to impose supplementary taxes on the settlers.

Decaen was sometimes blamed for having kept the famous English navigator Matthew Flinders prisoner for six years. The latter was sent by England on a mission to explore New Holland (Australia), and was on his way back, after having been the first to accomplish a complete circumnavigation of that continent. He was forced to call at Isle de France in order to repair his ship, the *Cumberland*, which was badly damaged in a storm. He made the mistake of dropping anchor at Baie-du-Cap rather than at Port-Nord-Ouest, as he should have done. The other, more serious mistake he made was that he neglected to properly register with the authorities as soon as he arrived, even more so as he had changed ships en route, and it was the name of his first ship, the *Investigator*, which was on his passport, and not that of the *Cumberland*. Considering the state of "war" between England and France, Decaen took him for a spy from the very beginning and had him taken prisoner.

After a few months in captivity, Flinders was, however, granted some freedom of movement on the island; on parole. Although Decaen received an order to free him three years later, in 1806, he still thought it wiser to keep him captive on the island, for fear that he might divulge to his country some secret information about the defences on Isle de France. The suspicions of Decaen were not wholly unfounded, because perusal of his logbook had indeed revealed that the one of the objectives of Flinders' mission was to study conditions of access to Port-Nord-Ouest, as well as the general state of the colony. There was indeed enough reason for mistrust! Matthew Flinders was only finally freed in May 1810, six months before the capture of the island by the English.

The threat of the English was indeed General Decaen's constant preoccupation, and so he devoted his attention to improving his defence system. Decaen was fully aware of Great Britain's plans. The English unceasingly made their presence felt in India, and therefore kept trying to seize Isle de France, which had now become a real impediment to its trade, owing to the frequent attacks by its corsairs. In 1804, when the effects of the English blockade began to make themselves felt, he had dispatched his younger brother, René Decaen, to the Emperor, who was then engaged in the Austerlitz campaign, with a request for reinforcements. Although his complaints had been transmitted to Minister Decrès, they had not, alas, had the slightest effect. Later, in 1806, not knowing how to attract Bonaparte's attention to Isle de France, without irritating him too much, Decaen thought of resorting to flattery, to which, after all, the Emperor was not impervious. Thus it came about that, in 1806, on 15 August, the date of Napoléon's birthday, the island's inhabitants, assembled at the Champ de Mars for the occasion, were surprised to learn that Port-Nord-Ouest would thenceforth be called Port-Napoléon, while Port-Sud-Est, at Grand-Port, would take the name of Port-Impérial. As for the island of Réunion, it became quite simply Bonaparte Island. General Decaen did manage to derive some benefit from such flattery, as he was allowed to use his own discretion to draw "lettres de change" on the Imperial Treasury. That, at least, shows than Napoléon had taken Surcouf's suggestions seriously and seemed convinced that only the corsairs' war could weaken the English at sea. However, the often-requested reinforcements never arrived. Decaen was therefore forced to surrender when the English troops landed on the island in November 1810. In the face of such a deployment of military strength, the forces under Decaen's command were unfortunately paltry. It must be said, to Decaen's credit, that he had tried everything to keep the English at bay for as long as possible. Moreover, thanks to his skilful negotiation on the terms of surrender, the inhabitants of the island were able to preserve their customs, language and laws.

Decaen left Isle de France in January 1811 onboard the *Emma*. As soon as he reached France, he had to explain to a Commission of Enquiry the reasons for his surrender. The latter being deemed "honourable", he was acquitted. The Emperor made him a Grand Cross of the Legion of Honour and a Count of the Empire in 1812. During the Hundred Days, he accepted the command of the 15th division under the orders of Napoléon, which caused him to be arrested in 1815 at the latter's fall.

Imprisoned during more than one year at Prison de l'Abbaye, he benefited from the amnesty in 1817. Freed, largely thanks to the many interventions of Robert Surcouf in his favour, he was given extended leave until the July Revolution. He died of cholera in the hamlet of La Barre, in the township of Deuil, on 9 September 1832, and was buried at Ermont in the hamlet of Cernay, near Paris, where he had his castle.

THE BATTLE OF GRAND-PORT

While Napoléon was undoubtedly gifted with military genius and succeeded, by deploying his formidable armies, in winning splendid victories on the European continent, he never managed, on the other hand, to impose himself in the face of English naval power at sea. The overwhelming defeat of Abukir, then that of Trafalgar, confirmed the deficiencies of the French navy in comparison with its fearsome opponent, whose superiority at sea, with each passing day, became more evident, holding back Napoléon's progress in Europe. The only naval battle which ended in victory for the French during the Napoléonic wars occurred in the Indian Ocean, on the southeast coast of Isle de France.

After nearly a week of stiff fighting, the English were defeated on 26 August 1810 in the harbour of Grand-Port (Port-Impérial) and lowered the English flag two days after. The effects of the English blockade, which had begun to be implemented as early as 1794, became more and more threatening since 1809, and Governor Decaen was continually requesting reinforcements from Decrès, the Minister for the Navy. The Governor's demands were in fact very modest, as he limited them to a request for 1,600 men, a small number which surprised Napoléon. It is true that Decaen already had a contingent of 2,500 men at Port-Nord-Ouest, and an

Admiral Baron Duperré.
Engraving by Boilly from an original painting by Court, 19th century.

additional 1,500 soldiers permanently on the alert, spread out over the island in various observation posts. These posts were moreover linked to each other by a system of signals, in case the enemy were to come too close to the coasts.

Decaen was on tenterhooks, being well aware that the noose was tightening around the island. Lord Minto, Governor-General of India, had put his plan, which he had worked out in 1808, into action: his aim was to end the repeated and systematic attacks of the French corsairs. Moreover, Duperré and his small squadron had been sent as reinforcements and joined in harassing the English ships. Nearly a year had gone by since the island of Rodrigues had been captured by the English forces, under the command of Colonel Keating. The island was used as a base by the English in order to carry out their plans with their troops there under the command of Major-General John Abercromby. The island of Réunion (formerly Bourbon) had also been captured, on 9 July 1810, by the English naval forces under the command of Commodore Rowley, who had staged a landing on 7 July at the head of 16,000 men. The operation had been brilliantly conducted and the Governor of Réunion was forced to surrender. Resistance was so feeble at Réunion that the English had been encouraged to launch an attack on Isle de France as soon as possible. The French forces stationed on the coast all round the island, especially at Savanne, at the station of Jacotet, and at Black River, had already on several occasions been subjected to a series of provocative acts aimed at testing their capacity to resist. The mission of Captain Willoughby was to capture the Ile de la Passe first, then Ile Plate. Once taken, these two positions were to serve as support bases for further attacks.

Captain Willoughby, commanding the *Néréide*, left the island of Réunion on 28 July. On 13 August, he reached the coast of Grand-Port, and there, under cover of night, he overran Ile de la Passe. The 83 Frenchmen guarding the islet under the command of Captain Escussot were then taken by surprise by 140 English soldiers who had silently disembarked from their boats. They quickly tried to organise themselves to resist, but the English, having the advantage of the ambush and of superior numbers, quickly dominated the situation. Caught by surprise and the speed at which it happened, Captain Escussot, who had 18 cannons available to him, hardly had time to retaliate. After killing seven enemy soldiers and wounding eighteen others, he and his men were compelled to surrender.

Captain Willoughby had reason to be proud of his men, the operation was a complete success. Emboldened by his success, he ventured further and, the very next day, the *Néréide* entered Port-Impérial. During the seven days which followed, Willoughby carried out three sorties along the coast of Isle de France, around the region of Grand-Port. In addition, at the head of 170 men, he managed to gain control over several French military posts. At around midday on 20 August, he observed Duperré's division making its way toward the island.

Duperré, in command of the *Bellone*, was returning from a campaign on the east coast of Africa, where he had captured several English ships, including the *Ceylon* (then under Captain Moulac) and the *Wyndham* (then under Captain Darod), which reinforced his own force that was already made up of the *Minerve*, (under Captain Bouvet de Maisonneuve) and the *Victor* (under Captain Morice). Taken by surprise, Willoughby returned very quickly by boat on board the *Néréide*, which was anchored off Isle de la Passe, leaving his soldiers ashore. Duperré, mistakenly believing that he had recognised the *Charles* from afar, which had been expected to reach Port-Napoléon (Port-Louis) very shortly, continued to approach, followed by his squadron.

Willoughby then staked his all on cunning and boldness and, in order to lure Duperré towards the powerful striking force now at his command, staged a small trick of his own invention. After hoisting the French flag on Ile de la Passe as well as on his own ship in order to win his enemy's trust, he used French signalling codes from the island to send the enemy the following message: "The enemy is cruising off Coin-de-Mire."

Quite reassured, Duperré confirmed with the other ships of his squadron the order to rally round and they then sailed towards the channel situated within cannon range of Ile de la Passe and the *Néréide*. While the *Victor* was leading the way into the channel leading to Port-Impérial, Willoughby ordered that the flag of His British Majesty be raised and immediately gave the order to open fire. Thunderstruck by this sudden attack, Captain Morice, in a state of shock, lowered the French flag. The *Minerve* and the *Ceylon* continued to advance and, in turn, entered the narrow channel under full sail in order to make their way into the harbour. In spite of the sustained salvoes of the enemy lying at ambush in the fort, they headed inside at full speed. Bouvet ordered Captain Morice to follow them, an order which the latter hurried to obey.

Duperré, in turn, entered the channel on the *Bellone*, followed by the *Wyndham* which, missing the entrance as a result of a wrong manoeuvre, fired a broadside and headed for the southwest of Isle de France in order to avoid a shipwreck.

The four French ships reassembled at the far end of the harbour, at a good distance away from the *Néréide*, which remained near the islet. Then

RIGHT: Battle of Grand-Port. At the very beginning of hostilities, Duperré was seriously wounded, and Bouvet took command of the battle.
Drawing and engraving by Le Gouax, after a sketch by Mr Marçon, from J Milbert Atlas, Paris, 1812.

OPPOSITE: Map of part of Port-Impérial showing the respective positions (see legend on opposite page) of the French and English ships during the memorable battle which lasted from 23 to 26 August 1810.
Drawing by Mr Marçon, engraving by Hubert Brué, from J Milbert Atlas, Paris, 1812.

VUE DU COMBAT DE L'ÎLE DE LA PASSE.

the English troops which had been left ashore on Willoughby's sudden departure, quietly returned to the *Néréide* in rowing boats, under the very eyes of the French who, strangely enough, did not make the slightest move.

On the very next morning, while the French were busy making their prisoners disembark from the *Ceylon*, Duperré hurriedly despatched Captain Morice on horseback towards Port-Napoléon in order to warn General Decaen about the situation. Meanwhile, anticipating the worst, Duperré prepared for battle by immediately gathering his frigates in battle order. Once informed, Decaen immediately ordered Captain Hamelin and his squadron to sail towards Port-Impérial in order to give a helping hand to the Duperré division. Decaen then rode at full speed towards Grand-Port, which he reached the next day, on 22 August.

Towards evening on 22 August, the first English reinforcements appeared at sea: the *Sirius* (under Captain Pym), entered the port at Willoughby's instigation. The next day, at around one in the afternoon, the *Iphigenia* (under Captain Lambert) and the *Magicienne* (under Captain Curtis) arrived and made their way into the bay to join the *Néréide* and the *Sirius*. At around four in the afternoon of the same day, a council of war was quickly held and Commodore Pym and Captain Willoughby decided to launch their attack.

Soon it was battle stations for all. The proud English frigates immediately hastened towards the French division. With an ear-splitting crash, nearly 200 cannon mouths spewed their fire and deadly cannon balls. On the shore, General Decaen, accompanied by Major Vandermaësen and his troops, as well as by many inhabitants of Grand-Port, watched the impressive sight. But a poor knowledge of the depths in the harbour soon put the enemy at a disadvantage. Their vessels gradually drifted before coming to a standstill on the sandbanks. The battle was still raging at seven in the evening. The *Victor* was already disabled, while the seven other vessels kept on firing formidable broadsides.

Night soon fell. Fire from the cannon lit up the tropical sky with its sinister glow. With a roll of thunder, the projectiles sweeping across the decks shattered everything in their path.

Thick columns of smoke rose in the air, mingling with the smell of gunpowder. It was nearly eight in the evening. Duperré was fighting like a lion on the deck of the *Bellone* when he suddenly collapsed. He had just received a burst of grapeshot full on the face. He was carried speedily to a safer place, while Bouvet, having been informed, immediately took command of the *Bellone*. The French frigates, being close to each other, gave each other assistance. At around 10 at night, the *Néréide* fired a few more

MAP LEGEND
French squadron
a. *Bellone* (44 cannons); Captain Duperré, Squadron Commander
b. *Minerve* (48 cannons); Captain Bouvet
c. *Victor* (20 cannons, formely the *Revenant* built by Surcouf); Lieutenant Morice
d. *Ceylon* (34 cannons, English prize); Lieutenant Moulac

English squadron
e. *Sirius* (36 cannons); Captain Pym, Commodore
f. *Iphigenia* (40 cannons); Captain Lambert
g. *Néréide* (40 cannons, French prize); Captain Willoughby
h. *Magicienne* (49 cannons, French prize); Captain Curtis
k. *Iphigenia* (second position)

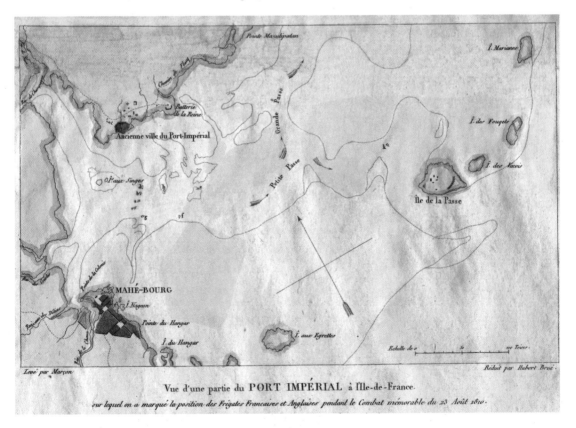

Vue d'une partie du PORT IMPÉRIAL à l'Ile-de-France.
sur lequel on a marqué la position des Frégates Françaises et Anglaises pendant le Combat mémorable du 23 Août 1810.

salvoes, then fell silent for good. The firing gradually subsided. Then, at around 11, everything went quiet. Soon, one of the French prisoners captured on Ile de La Passe managed to escape from the *Néréide* and swam ashore. He informed Bouvet that the English vessel had lowered its flag. The latter remained sceptical about this news, and waited for daybreak (24 August) to find out more. Here is the description given by Cunat of the sinister scene that morning:

"Light appeared through the clouds of smoke that floated over the bay like thick vapours. The new appearance of the battleground at first light of a dull day offered itself to my view with an indescribably sad aspect. On one side, our riddled ships, with their bloodstained decks, covered in debris, with our crews still looking menacing, but unarmed, haggard, disfigured by exhaustion and gunpowder. On the other, the English frigates which had looked so fine, so well rigged the day before, were there, but in worse shape than ours. Three of them were only fighting on to delay the moment of their utter defeat, and the fourth had submitted. To complete this gloomy scene of destruction, silence, which had fallen after the ceaseless boom of artillery, had freed the tide's ebb and flow to bring with it, around our ships, the bodies of hundreds of victims who had been struck dead while bravely defending the cause."

The sight of such horror and desolation did not reduce the fighting spirit of the opponents. In the grey light of dawn, cannon fire broke out all over again, and the battle continued raging until midday. All the survivors of the *Magicienne* were transferred onboard the *Iphigenia*, which slowly drew away from the battlefield.

The *Néréide* had been reduced to complete silence. When Lieutenant Roussin, who had replaced Bouvet on the *Minerve* went on board the *Néréide* at around three o'clock in the afternoon, a horrifying sight met his eyes: hundreds of bodies torn by bullets and wooden splinters lay in a bloodbath. Many wounded and stunned sailors were groaning among the scattered debris of the masts, sails and shrouds that lay strewn over the ship's deck. Suddenly, the lieutenant discovered, draped in the Union Jack, the apparently lifeless body of Captain Willoughby, with his face utterly bloodstained: a wooden splinter had seriously wounded him in the eye. Roussin immediately had him carried on board the *Bellone*, beside Duperré, to receive first aid. Meanwhile all the wounded were attended to and the French flag was hoisted over the *Néréide*.

That evening, the English, who had evacuated the *Magicienne*, decided to set fire to it after loading the cannons to full capacity and turning them towards the French frigates. The fire quickly spread and huge flames

OPPOSITE: Rear-Admiral Nesbit Willoughby.
Original painting by Thomas Barber.

surrounded the ship, while the cannons roared wildly. Suddenly, like an erupting volcano, the *Magicienne* exploded with a terrific crash.

The next day, 25 August, Captain-General Decaen went aboard the *Bellone* and gave instructions for transporting Duperré, together with Captain Willoughby, ashore. However, the English still had not surrendered. Commodore Pym decided to set fire to his ship too, rather than to leave it in French hands. After evacuating the *Sirius*, he set it on fire. Left to the fierce flames, the ship, which had very quickly turned into a blazing inferno, finally exploded.

On 26 August, all the English survivors assembled aboard the *Iphigenia* (under Captain Lambert), taking advantage of the chaos to attempt to escape. Protected by the Fort of Ile de la Passe, which was still in English hands, the frigate sailed slowly towards the channel in order to leave the bay. But, hampered in its advance by contrary winds, it came to a standstill. Meanwhile, Bouvet was quickly setting the *Minerve* and the *Victor* afloat again, in order to counter Captain Lambert's plan.

On the morning of 27 August, at about 11 o'clock, the Hamelin division, made up of the *Vénus*, *Manche*, *Entreprenant* and the *Astrée*, under the command of frigate captain Le Marant de Kerdaniel, appeared at last off the islet named Ile de la Passe. Delayed by unfavourable winds, they had not been able to reach the battleground in time. Decaen was then on the *Minerve* with Bouvet, who had hoisted the Admiral's flag. The *Iphigenia*, which still had not managed to get out of the port, was now in a desperate situation.

Hamelin then took up a position at the entrance of the bay, in order to block the *Iphigenia*'s exit, and bade Captain Lambert and the English troops on Ile de la Passe to surrender. Negotiations lasted up to early evening.

At dawn on 28 August, Captain Lambert received Captain-General Decaen's injunction. No longer having any choice, he lowered the British flag at about 11 o'clock. Decaen immediately sent a detachment onboard the *Iphigenia* to hoist the tricolour. The surrender was absolute. More than 1,600 sailors and soldiers were taken prisoner, together with more than 100 Navy and army officers. The four captains of the four English frigates and two ship's captains were also taken prisoner, as well as General Westerhall, a Colonel and a Lieutenant-Colonel from the Cape, from the 1st Battalion of the 24th Infantry Regiment, which were heading for the British trading posts in India. It was a splendid victory for the French navy, although unfairly minimised today by the English. The name of this battle, Grand-Port, was added to those of the many victories of Napoléon which are engraved on the Arc de Triomphe in Paris.

OPPOSITE: Sub-Lieutenant Vincent Moulac on board the *Ceylon* during the Battle of Grand-Port, 1810. Born in Lorient in 1778, this corsair was captain and second in command to the famous corsair Robert Surcouf on several ships. Moulac distinguished himself as captain of the *Ceylon* under the orders of squadron commodore Victor Duperré. Showing rare self-control and boldness, he joined in combat with exemplary courage. He was severely wounded during this naval battle and was immediately promoted to the grade of Lieutenant by General Decaen. Frigate captain, then ship's captain, he was commander of the Southern Seas squadron when he died in Lima in 1836.
Drawing by Crépin, engraving by Hulk, 1812.

THE CONQUEST OF ISLE DE FRANCE
BY THE ENGLISH

One would have thought that the splendid victory of the French naval forces at the Battle of Grand-Port might have caused the English to change their plans. The latter had just lost four ships with all their crews, at one fell swoop, which was no paltry event. But this crushing defeat, far from making an impression on the English, barely seemed to have the effect of "a mosquito bite on the back of an elephant". Its only result was actually to reinforce the conviction of the English strategists, that it was imperative to conquer Isle de France once and for all, as Lord Chatham had already advised in his time. This was the final objective sought by Lord Minto, Governor-General of India.

In the course of events, France had lost a great deal of its influence in India. The death of Tipu Sultan in 1799 had already deprived it of its most powerful ally against the English. The fall of Mysore and the defeat of the Marathi princes had, moreover, completed the process of reducing French power in the Indian peninsula. England thenceforth called the shots. In 1803, Pondicherry remained in English hands, despite the Treaty of Amiens. The Cape had also been conquered in 1806, Rodrigues in 1809, and, in July 1810, the island of Réunion was occupied. There only remained Isle de France which was included in the final phase of the plan of attack. The arrival of Captain Hamelin's fleet in the island in 1809, followed by that of Captain Duperré, had convinced Lord Minto of the necessity of

ABOVE: Sir Ralph Abercromby (1734–1801). Sir Ralph died in Egypt fighting against the French troops of General Bonaparte at Alexandria in 1801. His second son, Major-General John Abercromby (1772–1817) was Commander-in-Chief of the English forces based in Bombay. He led the English military forces that captured Isle de France in November 1810. On that occasion, a total of five French frigates and 209 canons were seized by the British. His health had suffered severely from the hard climate during his term in India and he died a few years later, in 1817, in Marseille.
Engraving by J Hoppner and JB Bird, London, 19th century.

RIGHT: In 1809, Rodrigues was overrun by English troops. Réunion surrendered in July 1810.
Map drawn by Mr Bonne, engineer-hydrographer of the French Navy.

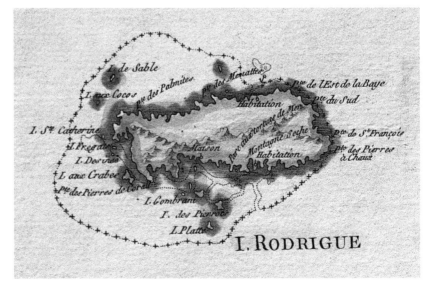

LEFT: "View from the deck of the *Upton Castle*, transport of the British army landing." A flotilla of boats poured its horde of soldiers in successive waves over the island without encountering the least resistance.
Engraving by J Temple.

acting quickly and forcefully before other reinforcements could arrive from France.

This sudden decision of the English was intended to bring to a final end the constant French attacks against the English fleet in the Indian Ocean. Between 1793 and 1797, according to the book by Robert Surcouf, grand-nephew of the famous corsair, over 2,000 enemy vessels were captured, while the French, for their part, had lost only 375 vessels over the same period. This disaster for the English, which was mainly the work of Surcouf, Perroud and their companions, put a severe strain on the English economy in that part of the world, and such a situation could not be allowed to last much longer.

Lord Minto's plan was launched in 1808, and nothing was to get in its way. Forces coming from India, the Cape, Rodrigues, Réunion and England were to join together for the final assault.

Over many months of blockade, the English had had every opportunity to observe and test the island's coastal defences, by carrying out several raids, of which the last, in the month of August 1810, had ended in the Battle of Grand-Port. The place for landing English troops was decided upon and the choice fell on the northern coast, near Cap Malheureux. The decision to attack was jointly taken by Admiral Albermarle Bertie and Major-General John Abercromby. On 29 November, all the English naval forces began to assemble off Flat Island. A formidable and threatening armada approached: 28 warships, followed by 62 supply boats, thus a total of 90 vessels under sail appeared at sea and took up their battle positions. The forces on board were impressive: the European forces from the Cape, India and Réunion, together numbered 14,850 soldiers, who, when added to the 8,740 sepoys from Bombay, Madras, Bengal and Ceylon, brought the force up to a total of 23,590 men. This was a huge attacking force, for whom

ABOVE: Sepoy, an Indian soldier in the service of the French Compagnie des Indes.

OPPOSITE: Surrender of Isle de France to the British in December 1810. An official ceremony took place when General Decaen, the last French Governor of Isle de France, surrendered to the Commander-in-Chief of the English forces, Major-General John Abercromby. The plans of Lord Minto, Governor-General of India from 1806 to 1813, were admirably executed. Commodore Josias Rowley, who commanded a frigate squadron, was close to Isle de France when Vice-Admiral Albermarle Bertie resumed the blockade of Port-Louis on 19 October 1810. They were joined on 24 October by Rear-Admiral O'Bryen Drury with the *Russell, Clorinde, Doris, Phaeton, Bucephalus, Cornelia* and the *Hesper*. On 3 November, Drury went to Rodrigues to join the troops already there under Abercromby. The fleet weighed anchor on 22 November, and on 29 November the troops landed on the coast of Isle de France at Anse Mapou, near Cap Malheureux. *From* The Illustrated London News, *4 July 1903, original painting by R Caton Woodville.*

the 2,500 men of General Decaen, based at Port-Napoléon, and the 1,500 others on guard around the island, were no match at all.

Captain Beaver was responsible for supervising the landing, which began at around two in the afternoon on 29 November at Anse Mapou, where a flotilla of boats poured its successive waves of soldiers on the shore without encountering the slightest resistance.

In fact, Decaen had hardly anticipated a landing so far from the town. The long walk through dense and thorny vegetation, and, what is more, without any watering spots, had seemed unthinkable to him. By around eight-thirty on the evening of that same day, 10,000 men had already set foot on the island. The troops, aligned in columns, then marched towards Port-Louis by following the coast. In the region of Grand Baie, they came across the first Frenchmen who, right after the very first skirmishes, blew up the Malartic gunpowder store. A few troops of the national guard and militias attempted to attack, but were far from successful in halting the enemies' advance. Major-General Abercromby then headed for Moulin-à-Poudre where he decided to camp.

The next day, at Tombeau Bay, near Moulin-à-Poudre, Decaen and his officers on horseback, accompanied by about 100 soldiers, launched an attack, but the general soon had to retreat, due to the strength of the enemy. A bullet went through his two-pointed hat, while another grazed his leg.

At around five in the afternoon, other troops joined the English forces. The next day at dawn, they pursued their relentless march to Port-Louis. The French battalions, under the command of Major Vandermaësen, tried to bar their way to Port-Louis, but the enemy's light artillery and cannon soon defeated their best intentions and Pamplemousses bridge was partially destroyed. The French, having been obliged to withdraw, reassembled at the level of Rivière-Sèche. There were 2,000 of them fighting hard, and the repeated bursts of gunfire made many victims in both camps, including Colonel Campbell and Major O'Keefe. The English then decided on a bayonet charge. Their superior numbers were overwhelming, and numerous French soldiers fell under their ruthless charge. Meanwhile, other troops had captured the fortifications along the coast of Grand Baie, Pointe aux Cannonniers, Trou-aux-Biches, then at Pointe-des-Roches, Pointe-aux-Piments, and finally at Baie du Tombeau, the last bastion before Port-Louis. At this point, lookouts observed the landing of new regiments at Petite-Rivière. It was clear by then that their objective was to surround the French troops. Decaen, judging that the situation had become desperate, and that further resistance would be useless, decided to surrender before it was too late.

Being a good lawyer, Decaen then drafted detailed terms of surrender and dispatched Captain Morice on the very morning of 2 December to Major-General Abercromby, to request a ceasefire and bring his proposal of surrender. The latter accepted the armistice but rejected certain clauses of the treaty.

Decaen then had a meeting with Captain Duperré and Major Vandermaësen at Government House to discuss the matter. After long discussions with Major Warde and Commander Rowley, both parties mutually agreed to remove certain demands from the treaty, whose terms were then finally accepted by Abercromby. The act of surrender was finally signed at around one in the morning by Captain-General Decaen and countersigned by Major-General Abercromby. Isle de France would henceforth be English. However, the inhabitants were allowed to keep their religion, their laws and their customs. At dawn on 3 December, English troops occupied Port-Napoléon and took possession of the ships in the harbour.

Thus, at the point of English swords, was the saga of French colonial rule at Isle de France ended. The fruit of nearly a century's efforts of social, economic and military construction was handed over to England, in just one day. With the signing of the Treaty of Paris in 1814, several colonies were returned to France, but the British crown kept Isle de France, which it renamed Mauritius, after its former Dutch name. Many settlers, unable to submit to the change of sovereignty, chose to return to France. On the other hand, those who remained had the wisdom to adapt to the new context. They could do so easily as the new masters of the island, with great tact and diplomacy, did all they could to make themselves accepted and respected by the inhabitants, despite a few painful episodes of tensions and frictions, which the barrister and politician Adrien d'Épinay (whose godmother, Élisabeth Broudou, was explorer Lapérouse's sister-in-law) was later to be the symbol under Sir William Nicolay's governorship. Many settlers were indeed quite satisfied with the turn of events, particularly the monarchists, for whom England was the haven of the future Louis XVIII. Indeed, anti-Republicans of all sorts were also quite satisfied with the deal.

The traders and planters, for their part, were quite happy to see the end of the English blockade, as they saw it as the end of a long period during which they had been neglected by the administration and the Emperor. But the majority of the inhabitants were aghast. Overnight, the French settlers found themselves on a land which had become British. In spite of themselves, they had to adapt to this very curious situation. At the time, it had to be said that Napoléon had other priorities than the fate of a small island in the Indian Ocean.

NOTES

1. In 1494, Spain and Portugal signed a treaty at Torsedillas, according to which these two nations shared out the world between themselves. The Spanish were to have all available territories west of the Cape Verde islands, the Portuguese, all those east of this meridian, (more precisely those situated 370 leagues west of the Cape Verde Islands).

2. *Dina* probably comes from the Sanskrit word *Dwipâ*, which means "island".

3. *Mémoire géographique sur la mer des Indes*, 1868.

4. *T'Eylandt Mauritius, Esquisses Historiques, 1598–1710.*

5. *La Découverte des îles Mascareignes*, 1948.

6. 1517, Pedro Reinel (Bayer Armeebibliothek, Munich);
1518, Pedro Reinel (British Museum);
1519, Lopo Homen (National Library, Paris);
1520, Jorge Reinel (Bayer Armeebibliothek, Munich);
1538, Anonymous (Herzog August Bibliothek, Wolfenbüttel).

7. *Une des Mascareignes*, unpublished work by Mr Durup de Balaine.

8. They were called "Les Îles Françaises Orientales", which also included the Seychelles and Chagos archipelagos. *Histoire des îles Mascareignes* by Auguste Toussaint, Paris. Berger-Levrault, 1972.

9. This was the powerful VOC (Vereenigde Oost-Indische Compagnie), created in 1602 to group all the small companies of Dutch merchants, including, among others, the "Company of Distant Lands".

10. Unlike yellow amber, which is fossilised resin, ambergris is a substance of animal origin. It is formed within whales' intestines from the remains of squid, which the cetacean feeds on. The whales regurgitate the ambergris into the sea.

11. Tortoise Bay, which was also called the "Moluccas harbour", now Port-Louis.

12. Any piece of ambergris found on the beach had to be handed over to the authorities of the VOC, which reserved exclusivity of any trade in this rare product. Offenders were liable to severe penalties.

13. From 1511, the Portuguese held a monopoly over the spices of the Moluccas Islands.

14. On 10 June 1640, the French Captain Alonz Goubert, entered the Moluccas harbour (Port-Louis), onboard the *Saint-Alexis*, with a mission to take possession of the island. Finding it already occupied by the Dutch, he went on to take possession of Mascarin island (now Réunion Island).

15. Batavia was founded in 1619.

16. The minister's instructions were dated 31 October 1714. Louis XIV having died on 1 September 1715, Captain Dufresne d'Arsel must certainly have been unaware that the reign of Louis XV had already begun when he took possession of the island for the first time.

17. Governor Denyon created the Jardin de la Compagnie at Port-Louis.

18. It was actually the ground floor of the present building.

19. This house was formerly located at the present entrance of Pamplemousses Gardens, on the left, as indicated by the eminent researcher Dr Guy Rouillard in his book, *Le Jardin des Pamplemousses*, Henry & Cie. Ltée, Mauritius-1983.

20. The 1740 Census reported 369 settlers on the island, 2,612 slaves and 150 plantations.

21. That island of 58 sq m has been Norwegian since 1930.

22. In this post, he was President of the Conseil Supérieur, Director of Public Works, Head of the police and law courts, responsible for the colony's finances, with power to levy taxes and use royal funds. As General Commissioner of the Navy, he was responsible for the arsenal, and for providing supplies to the naval forces, and also, as far as Isle of France was concerned, to the ships of the Compagnie des Indes.

23. He had bought from the Compagnie des Indes Monplaisir the former residence of the governors, built by La Bourdonnais at Pamplemousses. After spending a small fortune embellishing it, thereby creating the core of the present gardens, Poivre, on his departure, sold the property back to the Crown for exactly the same sum that he had originally paid.

24. This title had originally been bestowed by the Grand Mughal, Mahamet Shah, on the Governor of Pondicherry, Pierre Benoist Dumas (predecessor of Dupleix). At the latter's request, it had been made transmissible to all his successors. Dupleix fully adopted that role and knew how to derive benefits from it.

25. Daughter of a Parisian doctor who had settled in India, and of a Portuguese mother. Miss de Castro, whose own mother, Jeanne Albert, was Indian and whom the Indians called "Begum Jeanne" (Princess Jeanne), was the widow of Mr Vincent, councillor at Chandernagor, with whom she had had several children. Having perfect knowledge of Tamil and of Indian customs, she closely assisted Dupleix in his political planning.

26. Dupleix held this post for nine years before being made responsible for the Chandernagor trading post.

27. This memorandum was entitled: *Projet d'une Compagnie pour la découverte d'un passage aux Indes par la Russie, présenté à Sa Majesté l'Impératrice Catherine II* (Cf. *Voyage à l'Isle de France*, Vol II). The first lines of the memorandum leave no doubt as to the author's greedy ambitions: "There are only two ways of attracting men, the lure of riches and that of honour [...] The desire for honour drives some men to leave their mother country when they see an opportunity for a spectacular action, a famous siege, a bold undertaking, etc. Then, volunteers from every nation will rush to come forward."

28. He only received it on his return to France, in 1770.

29. In his thesis, *L'Esclavage à l'Isle de France*, published by Two Cities, Karl Noël declares that the condition of the slaves at Isle of France was not comparable to that of the West Indian colonies: "On the whole, they had generous masters, to whom they were for the most part very attached."

30. He was in command of the division despatched urgently by Decaen to support Duperré's division in the battle of Grand-Port. But, having been hampered by contrary winds, his fleet only got there at the end of the battle.

31. From June 1789 to September 1791; from June 1793 to May 1796; from

Translations of de Bry's illustrations on page 33

ENGRAVING I (DE BRY, 1601)
Landing on the island of Cirné (Mauritius)

A. Entrance to the port.

B. Tree trunk planted on a small island to act as a marker.

C. Rocks and shallows.

D. The island which the Dutch named Heemskerck Island.

E. Place where the sailors went fishing.

F. Many fish-eating birds are to be found here.

G. Valley in which seeds were sown.

H. The islands which protect the harbour.

ENGRAVING II (DE BRY, 1601)
Account of what the Dutch saw in Mauritius and what they did there:

1. They saw large tortoises which always remain on land because they do not know how to swim. They feed on crayfish which they manage to catch, and which are sometimes as big as a human foot.

2. This is a bird which the Dutch call *walgh voguel* [Dodo], as tall as a swan, with a large head, but, instead of wings, it only has three or four feathers. They (the Dutch) cooked these birds, but they were not good to eat.

3. This is a palm tree. Its leaves are so large that a man may shelter from the rain under a single leaf. If one pierces a hole into the trunk, wine flows abundantly. It tastes almost like Spanish wine, but goes sour if kept for more than two days. They call it "palm wine".

4. That is a bird called *rabos forcados*. Its tail is like a pair of scissors, it is black with a white chest and a long beak. It feeds on small flying birds. After having removed the entrails, it throws them into the sea to the fish, which eat them.

5. A bird called the Indian crow, twice the size of a parrot, it has two or three different colours.

6. That is a wild tree on which they have fixed the coat of arms of the Netherlands, Zeeland and Amsterdam as a memorial.

7. This is another species of palm tree. They have cut down many of these. They pick the fruit, indicated by the letter A, which they have eaten and enjoyed.

8. A bat which has a head almost like a monkey's. They hang together from the trees in a great crowd.

9. The blacksmith has set up his forge.

10. The huts which they built with small branches and leaves, and in which they slept at night.

11. They preached here. Half the people came to listen in the morning, and the other half in the afternoon. Pastor Philips Petersen from Delft gave the sermon. A certain Laurent, a native of Madagascar, was baptised there, with two or three other sailors.

12. Here, the sailors caught three and a half tons of fish at one go.

ENGRAVING III (DE BRY, 1601)
How the Dutch brought giant tortoises from Mauritius.

On their way to India in 1598, the Dutch took possession of that island and named it Mauritius. There, giant tortoises carried such enormous shells that they were able to carry on their backs, for a long time and without any trouble, two seated Dutchmen, and by no means the thinnest. Some of them were so huge that when the shell of one of them was removed, ten people could sit down comfortably and have a party inside the shell. They found in this island a great number of parrots and doves, which were so tame that they could kill them with sticks. But other birds were seen there, which the Dutch named *walch voghel*, and which they also brought with them.

December 1798 to January 1801; from June 1807 to November 1808. Over a total period of a little more than nineteen years of his life, Surcouf was in fact based on Isle of France for nine years.

32. Actually "Port-Nord-Ouest" as from 1793, then "Port-Napoléon" in 1806.

33. Although the Convention had abolished slavery in 1794, that hateful practice was, however, still tolerated on Isle of France for economic reasons.

34. "Navigation leave" only gave the right to defend oneself against the enemy in case of attack, but not the right to attack.

35. During his administration (1755–1759), he brought over some salt workers from Saintonge and was thus the first to create salt pans on Isle of France. He returned to the island in 1768 and settled on his sugar estate of La Villebague, where he died in 1778. His tomb is at the Pamplemousses cemetery.

BIBLIOGRAPHY

Austen, HCM, *Sea Fights and Corsairs of the Indian Ocean, being the naval history of Mauritius from 1715 to 1810*, Port-Louis, Government printer, 1935.

Balonet, Jean-Christophe and Alibert, Eric, *Le Grand Livre des espèces disparues*, Paris, Editions Ouest-France, 1989.

Barquissau, Raphaël, *Les Isles*, Paris, Grasset, 1935.

Bayly, CA, editor, *The Raj, India & the British, 1600–1947*, London, National Portrait Gallery Publications, 1991.

Bellec, François, Admiral, *Les Esprits de Vanikoro, le mystère Lapérouse*, Paris, Gallimard, 2006.

Bernardin de Saint-Pierre, *Oeuvres complètes*, Paris, Méquignon-Marvis, 1806.

Bertrand, *M. Suffren de Saint-Tropez aux Indes*, Paris, Perrin, 1991.

Bionne, Henry, *Dupleix*. Paris, Éditions Maurice Dreyfus, 1881.

Boisanger, Béatrice de, *Mémoires des Isles*, Paris, Olivier Orban, 1986.

Boissel, Thierry, *Bougainville, un homme de l'univers*. Paris, Olivier Orban, 1991.

Bonaparte, Prince Roland, *Le Premier établissement des Néerlandais à Maurice*, Paris, 1890.

Boorstin, Daniel, *Les Découvreurs*, Paris, Robert Laffont, coll. Bouquins, 1983.

Bougainville, Antoine de, *Voyages autour du Monde*, Paris, La Découverte, 1992.

Branda Pierre & Lentz Thierry, *Napoléon, l'esclavage et les colonies*, Fayard, 2006.

Brosse, Jacques, *Les Tours du Monde des explorateurs*, Paris, Bordas, 1983.

Chelin, Antoine, *Une île et son passé*, Port-Louis, Mauritius Printing & Co Ltd, 1972.

Crépin, Pierre, *Les Îles de France et de Bourbon, Histoire des colonies françaises*, vol. VI, Paris, Plon, 1933.

Crépin, Pierrre, *Mahé de La Bourdonnais*, Paris, Éditions Leroux, 1922.

Dance, SP, *Les Oiseaux*, Paris, Studio Édition, 1990.

Diderot, Denis, *Supplément au voyage de Bougainville*, Paris, 1796.

Ducray, Charles Giblot, *Île Maurice, ancienne Isle de France*. Port-Louis, 1973.

Dumas, Jacques, *Fortune de mer*, Paris, Atlas Film, 1981.

Dunmore, John, *Lapérouse*, Paris, Payot, 1986.

Épinay, Adrien d', *Renseignements pour servir à l'histoire de l'Isle de France*, Port-Louis, Nouvelle Imprimerie, 1890.

Épinay, Prosper d', *Le Poignard de Tippoo Saïb*, end 19th Century.

Épinay, Prosper d', *Souvenirs d'Adrien d'Épinay*, Fontainebleau, imp. Mr Bourges, 1901.

Ferloni, Julia, *De Lapérouse à Dumont d'Urville*, Édition de Conti, Paris, 2006.

Froberville, Léon Huet de, *Le Combat du Grand-Port*, 1910.

Garneray, Louis, *Corsaires de la République*, Paris, Imprimerie du Standard, 1991.

Garneray, Louis, *Marin de Surcouf*, Paris, Les Éditions de la Nouvelle France, 1944.

Girard, Just, *Une famille créole des îles Maurice et de la Réunion*, Tours, 1862.

Glachant, Roger, *Histoire de l'Inde des Français*, Paris, Plon, 1965.

Hamont, Tibulle, *Dupleix*, Paris, Plon. 1881.

Haudrère, Philippe, *La Bourdonnais, marin et aventurier*, Paris, Éditions Desjonquières, l992.

Haudrère Philippe, *Les Compagnies des Indes*, Éditions Ouest-France, Paris, 2001.

Hein, Raymond, *Le Naufrage du Saint-Géran*, Paris, Éditions Océan-Indien et Nathan, 1981.

Herpin, E, *Mahé de La Bourdonnais et la Compagnie des Indes*, Saint-Brieux, Éditions René Prud'homme, 1905.

Herubel, Michel, *Surcouf, Titan des mers*, Paris, Perrin, 1989.

Hollingworth, Derek, *They came to Mauritius*, Oxford University Press, 1965.

Hulot, Baron, "D'Entrecasteaux, 1737–1793", Paris, extract from *Bulletin de la Société de Géographie*, 3e trimestre 1894.

La Bourdonnais, Bertrand François Mahé de, and Gennes, Pierre de, *Mémoire pour le Sieur La Bourdonnais et pièces justificatives*, Paris, 1750.

La Bourdonnais, Louis Charles Mahé de, *Mémoires historiques*, Paris, Pelicier et Chatet, 1827.

La Caille, Abbot Nicolas de, *Journal historique du voyage fait au cap de Bonne-Espérance*, Paris, Nyon aîné, 1776.

Lagesse, Marcelle, *L'Isle de France avant La Bourdonnais (1721–1735)*. Port-Louis, Imprimerie Commerciale, 1978.

Lecomte, Georges, *Les Prouesses du bailli de Suffren*, Paris, La Renaissance du Livre, 1929.

Leguat, François, *Aventures aux Mascareignes, Voyages et aventures de François Leguat et de ses compagnons en deux îles désertes des Indes Orientales*, Amsterdam, Jean-Louis de Lorme, 1708.

Lenoir, Philippe, *Île Maurice, ancienne Isle de France*, Éditions du Cygne, 1979.

Magon de Saint-Élier, Ferdinand, *Tableaux historiques, politique et pittoresque de l'Isle de France*, Port-Louis, 1839.

Mahé, Patrick & Zulli Guillaume, *Pondichéry*, Éditions du Chêne, Hachette Livre, Paris, 2003.

Malleret, Louis, *Pierre Poivre*, Paris, École française d'Extrême-Orient, 1974.

Martin, L Aimé, *Essai sur la vie et les ouvrages de Bernardin de Saint-Pierre, Voyage à l'Isle de France*, vol I, Paris, Méquignon-Marvis, 1806.

Milbert, Jacques, *Voyage Pittoresque à l'Isle de France, au cap de Bonne-Espérance et à l'île de Ténérife*, Paris, N Neveu, 1812.

Noël, Karl, *L'Esclavage à l'Isle de France*, Éditions Two Cities, 1991.

North-Coombes Alfred, *The island of Rodrigues*, Printed by Book Printing Services Ltd, Mauritius, 1971.

Piat Denis, *Pirates & Corsairs in Mauritius*, Éditions Christian le Comte, Mauritius, 2007.

Pitot, Albert, *T'Eylandt Mauritius: Esquisses historiques, 1598–1710*, Port-Louis, 1905.

Pitot, Albert, *L'Isle de France 1715–1810*, Port-Louis, E Pezzani, editor, 1899.

Poivre, Pierre, *Mémoires d'un Botaniste & Explorateur*, complete with a biography and notes by Denis Piat & Dr Jean-

Claude Rey, La Découvrance Éditions, La Rochelle, 2006.

Poivre, Pierre, *Oeuvres Complètes*, Paris, Fuchs, 1797.

Poivre d'Arvor, Olivier and Patrick, *Coureurs des Mers*, Paris, Mengès, 2003.

Poivre d'Arvor, Patrick, *Le Roman de Virginie*, Paris, Balland, 1985.

Rauville, Count Hervé de, *L'Isle de France Légendaire*, Challamel et Cie Editor, 1889.

Raynal, Abbot, *Histoire philosophique et politique des établissements et du commerce des Européens dans les deux Indes*, Paris, Jean Edmé Dufour, 1775.

Ribaut, JC and Nantel, B, *Le Jardin des Épices*, Paris, Éditions Du May, 1992.

Rogers, Stanley, *The Indian Ocean*, London, George G Harrap & Co Ltd, 1932.

Rouillard, Guy, *Le Jardin des Pamplemousses*, Port-Louis, General Printing, 1985.

Rouillard Guy & Guého Joseph, *Les Plantes et leur histoire à l'Ile Maurice*, Printed by MSM Ltd, Mauritius, 1999.

Ryckebush, Jackie, *Mahé de La Bourdonnais entre les Indes et les Mascareignes*. La Réunion, 1989.

Sandeau Jacques, *Le général Decaen à l'Ile de France*, Éditions Amalthée, Paris, 2006.

Surcouf, Robert, *Un Capitaine corsaire: Robert Surcouf*, Paris, Plon, 1925.

Taillemite, Etienne, *Sur des Mers inconnues, Bougainville, Cook, Lapérouse*, Paris, Gallimard, coll. Découvertes, 1987.

Toussaint, Auguste, *Avant Surcouf*, Université de Provence, 1989.

Toussaint, Auguste, *Histoire des îles Mascareignes*, Paris, Berger-Levrault, 1972.

Toussaint, Auguste, *Les Frères Surcouf*, Paris, Flammarion, 1979.

Toussaint, Auguste, *Port-Louis, deux siècles d'histoire*, Port-Louis, Typographie Moderne, 1936.

Tuloup, François, *Bertrand François Mahé de Labourdonnais et la Compagnie des Indes*, l'Amitié par le Livre, 1967.

Unienville, Noël d', *L'Île Maurice et sa Civilisation* (collective publication), Port-Louis, G Durassié, 1949.

Unienville, Raymond d', *Hier Suffren*, Port-Louis, Mauritius Printing, 1979.

Vaissière, Philippe de, *Dupleix*, Paris, Plon, 1931.

Varende, Jean de, *Surcouf corsaire*, Paris, Marcus, 1946.

Vaxelaire, Daniel, *Les Chasseurs d'épices*, Paris, Jean-Claude Lattès, 1990.

Vox, Maximilien, *Correspondance de Napoléon, six cents lettres de travail*, Gallimard, Paris, 1943.

Verin, Pierre, *Maurice avant l'Isle de France*, Paris, Fernand Nathan, 1983.

Vigié, Marc, *Dupleix*, Paris, Fayard, 1993.

Visdelou Guimbeau, Georges de, *La Découverte des Mascareignes*, Port-Louis, General Printing, 1958.

VARIOUS PUBLICATIONS AND MAGAZINES

Citadelle de Port-Louis, Lorient, Museum of the Compagnie des Indes, 1990.

Combat du Grand-Port, Association des Amis de Mahé de La Bourdonnais, special anniversary bulletin, Dispatches of Captain-General Decaen with the Ministry of the Navy, sld Pr Ph. Haudrère, Paris, 2010.

Dictionnaire de biographies mauriciennes, Dr Auguste Toussaint, S Pelte, N Régnard, O Béchet, L Halais. Société de l'Histoire de l'île Maurice, Port-Louis. [Most of the biographies consulted have been written by the great historian Dr Auguste Toussaint, to whom we owe the basis of the information contained in the biographies in this book.]

Du Tage à la Mer de Chine, Musée Guimet, Paris, RMN, 1992.

La France de l'océan Indien, Société d'Éditions Géographiques, Maritimes et Coloniales, Paris, 1952.

Les Grands Voiliers, directed by Joseph Jobe, Paris, Éditions Lazarus, 1967.

Les Habitants de l'île Maurice ont été Français, Berthelot, Lilian, Lausanne, Îles, 1993.

Notes inédites sur Mahé de La Bourdonnais, Dr. Georges Baschet, Paris, 1940.

Notice et annotations à Paul et Virginie, de Bernardin de Saint-Pierre. Dupouy, A. Paris, Bibliothèque Larousse.

"Notice historique sur Bernardin de Saint-Pierre", preface for *Paul et Virginie*, Sainte-Beuve, Paris, Furne et Cie, 1863.

Pierre Poivre en son temps, Ly-Tio-Fane, Port-Louis, Précigraph Ltd, 1993.

Preface for *Paul et Virginie*, de Bernardin de Saint-Pierre. Clarette, J Paris, 1878.

Le rêve des Indes, Documentation of the Association des Amis de Mahé de La Bourdonnais. Written by Patrick Mahé O'Chinal with the collaboration of Denis Piat, Paris, 2007.

Silk Roads and China Ships, JE Vollmer, EJ Keal, E Nagay Berthrong, Royal Ontario Museum).

Terre, Air, Mer, La Géographie, SÉGMC, Vol. LX, 1933.

Vaisseau de ligne et Frégate anglais, venant de mouiller.

INDEX

Principal personalities and names of ships.

Corvette française, appareillant.

Vaisseau marchand anglais, venant de mettre a la voile.

Printed in 2010
by Star Standard, Singapore